Customer Service and Support

Implementing Effective Strategies

Customer Service and Support

Implementing Effective Strategies

COLIN G ARMISTEAD

GRAHAM CLARK

FINANCIAL TIMES
PITMAN PUBLISHING

Pitman Publishing
128 Long Acre, London WC2E 9AN

A Division of Longman Group UK Limited

First published in 1992

© Longman Group UK Limited, 1992

British Library Cataloguing in Publication Data
A CIP catalogue record for this book
can be obtained from the British Library

ISBN 0 273 032739

Phototypeset in Linotron Times Roman
by Northern Phototypesetting Co. Ltd., Bolton
Printed and bound in Great Britain
by Biddles Ltd., Guildford

This book is dedicated to our wives, children and pets, who were deprived of our attention during the time we were writing, and to all the customer service and support managers who have contributed either directly or indirectly to our research.

CONTENTS

Foreword   ix

1   WHAT IS CUSTOMER SERVICE AND SUPPORT?   1

2   FORMULATING SERVICE AND SUPPORT STRATEGIES   15

3   STRUCTURE FOR CUSTOMER SERVICE AND SUPPORT   42

4   ELEMENTS OF CUSTOMER SERVICE AND SUPPORT   60

5   MARKETING AND MARKET RESEARCH   77

6   MANAGING THE CONTACT WITH CUSTOMERS   97

7   MANAGING THE PEOPLE   117

8   CAPACITY MANAGEMENT   136

9   QUALITY MANAGEMENT   151

10 IMPROVING PRODUCTIVITY   179

11 INFORMATION SYSTEMS AND CONTROL   196

12 MATERIALS MANAGEMENT   208

13 MANAGING THROUGH INTERMEDIARIES   229

14 RECOVERY STRATEGIES   243

15 INTERNATIONALISM – MANAGING THE NETWORK   256

16 MANAGING CHANGE   270

Index   285

FOREWORD

The search for service excellence for those concerned with providing customer service and support for a product and installed equipment is being driven by a number of factors. Not least is the reducing level of differentiation between competing products, which has led to customers making their choice on the basis of service and support rather than on product performance. Adding fuel to this fire is the realisation that customer service and support can be profitable if quality of delivery is consistent and risk free for the customer and that costs can be controlled. Rather than customer service and support being a 'necessary evil', as an after sales service, it must take on a whole new dimension and become the *inspiration* of other parts of the business.

We have been working with customer service and support organisations and researching in the area for a number of years. Our conclusion is that this field of service endeavour aspires to the same features of world class service provision that we see in other service sectors. We recognise world class service organisations by the extent to which they fulfill the following criteria:

- World class services give a high level of customer satisfaction judged on value for money
- World class services have a high level of customer retention over a period of years
- World class services have a very good 'service image'. People talk about their experiences with them
- World class services have their costs under control
- World class services find people want to work for them
- World class services display a high level of innovation in the services offered and the way they deliver them
- World class services give clear and often unconditional guarantees
- World class services cope with change

We see a number of organisations in the customer service and support area who are well along the path to being world class. Caterpillar, Hewlett Packard, Rank Xerox, Hitachi, and Otis are all companies we would put in this category of able aspirants to the title.

In this book we have attempted to give an approach for customer service and support managers to take them along the road to service excellence. We do not claim it as a prescription for success but rather our intention is to highlight approaches that we have found of help to service and support managers. The main thrust of the book is the formulation and implementation of service strategy that takes into account the changing environment for customer service and support in which many organisations find themselves.

The structure of the book follows the workshop process, which we have used with service and support organisations to develop their capabilities. We wish to thank those service and support people who have contributed to the process by their participation or by their contribution to our knowledge as part of our research programme.

COLIN ARMISTEAD and GRAHAM CLARK
September 1991

2 FORMULATING SERVICE AND SUPPORT STRATEGIES

Introduction

In this chapter we will look at what we mean by a service strategy and how we can develop a service strategy for customer support. We will consider how we can spread an understanding of the strategy to all parts of the customer service and support organisation so that everyone is clear on what it means for the company and for them as individuals.

Where are we going?

We have heard this from a manager of a customer support branch, 'My company never seems to know what it's doing. We have had a succession of new managers and managing directors over the last few years. Most of them have seemed interested in what we are doing but none of them have been able to tell us what is happening. I know we are losing orders to our competitors and that our customers complain about our service but the company never seems to do anything'. We don't think this statement is uncommon and it indicates either a lack of clear thinking on the part of the directors and senior managers about the direction of the company or an unwillingness to share their thoughts with all the service and support personnel. In our own investigations we have found that few customer support operations have a clear idea of where they are going. Even when there is a direction for the company as a whole the customer support function is excluded or overlooked.

What do we mean by a service strategy?

'What is strategy?' is a question which is posed in every book on strategy and business policy. The words strategy and policy seem to be used synonymously and there is no clear consensus on a definition for strategy.

However what is clear is that there are a number of ways of looking at *strategy*, all of them seeking to give a clear direction to the organisation.

First we need to understand that there is more than one type of strategy for any organisation. We recognise the following aspects of strategy:

Strategic Scope. Strategies can be broad in scope or concerned with more narrow areas. For example we can have a strategy which deals only with the UK or we can have a strategy for Europe or the world.

Strategic Level. Strategies can be for the business as a whole or for a business unit or for a function within the business. A manufacturing company making a range of different products in different divisions will have a *corporate strategy* for the company, a *divisional strategy* for each of the divisions, and perhaps a *functional strategy* in each of the divisions for marketing, personnel, manufacture and customer support.

Strategies of Purpose. Strategies can be classified according to their purpose, for example *competitive*, *defensive*, or *expansive*.

Personal Strategies. Managers have *personal strategies* which capture the manager's values, motivations, ways of getting things done and methods for effective change.

Clearly these different types of strategies can overlap and at times form subsets of one another. They illustrate the complexity of the word when it comes to describing strategy. We need to appreciate this complexity when we are trying to decide *'What is the "best" strategy'*.

We will be concentrating on strategies which relate to level and purpose, although we recognise the importance of personal strategies on our ability to implement other corporate strategies. In looking for our strategic direction, one of the most powerful models is Bowman's *strategy compass* (Fig. 2.1). The strategy compass allows us to set the direction for our customer service and support based on the way our customers perceive the value of our customer service and support and the price which is charged. We will give a more detailed explanation of how the strategy compass fits into the formulation of strategy later; for the moment let us recognise the direction it gives us.

What's the difference between strategy and tactics?

The difference between strategy and tactics can be described as: *'Strategy is the *direction* of power whereas *tactics* is the *immediate application* of

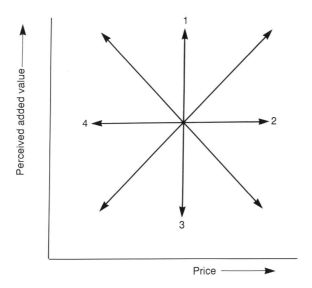

Figure 2.1 The strategy compass

power'. This can be seen in the quote of the Chinese emperor Sun Tzu, 'All men can see the tactics whereby I conquer, but what few can see is the strategy out of which victory is evolved'. This statement encapsulates some of the general differences between tactics and strategy.

1 *Level of conduct*: Strategy is developed at the highest level . . . tactics are employed at and relate to the lower levels of management.

2 *Regularity*: Formulation of strategy is both continuous and irregular . . . tactics are usually governed by the timing of budgets.

3 *Subjective values*: Strategy is more influenced by subjective values of those developing the strategy than tactics.

4 *Range of alternatives*: The total possible range of alternatives is far greater in strategy than tactical decision making.

5 *Uncertainty*: Uncertainty is usually much greater in both the formulation and implementation of strategy than in deciding upon and knowing the results of tactical decisions.

6 *Nature of problems*: Strategic problems are generally unstructured . . . tactical problems are structured and often repetitive in nature.

7 *Information needs*: Formulating strategy often relies heavily on information generated outside of the organisation while tactical information needs, in contrast, rely more on internally generated data.

8 *Time Horizons*: Strategies are intended to last for long periods of time. Tactics cover a shorter duration and are more uniform for all parts of the operating programme.

9 *Reference*: Strategy is original in the sense that it is the source of origin for the development of tactics, tactics are formulated within and in the pursuit of strategies.

10 *Detail*: Strategies are usually broad and have many fewer details than tactics.

11 *Type of personnel involved in formulation*: Strategies for the most part are formulated by top management and their staff. The numbers of people involved are comparatively few as contrasted with the formulation of tactics where large numbers of managers and employees participate in the process.

12 *Ease of evaluation*: It is considerably easier to measure the effectiveness and efficiency of tactics than of strategies.

13 *Importance*: Strategies, by definition, are of the highest importance to an organisation. Tactics are of considerably less significance.

It is easy to appreciate the underlying meaning of the complaint from our support manager which we gave earlier. She was concerned with tactics of her day-to-day work and the lack of a clear strategy meant she had no context or direction in which to work.

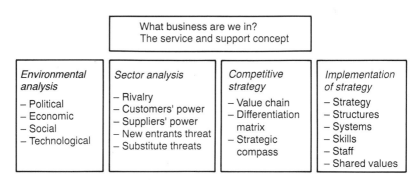

Figure 2.2 Service and support strategy formulation

How do we set about getting a service strategy?

Whichever approach is taken to develop a strategy there are a range of decisions which will need to be addressed in the course of the process (Fig. 2.2). These can be described as:

- Decisions about the *scope* of the organisation's activities. What business are we in? What is the nature of customer service and support?
- Questions about *matching* of the organisation's activities to its *environment*. Here we need to take account of social, political, economic and technological changes.
- Decisions on the *direction* the organisation will move in the long term. How can we gain competitive advantage? How is the competition likely to react? How might the industry we are in change in the future?
- Questions about the *matching* of the activities of an organisation to its *resource capability*. Here we will assess whether any changes we make in our strategy have implications for the way we deliver customer support and the allocation or re-allocation of resources.
- Questions relating to the *values, expectations* and *goals* of those influencing strategy.
- Assessment of the implications for *change* throughout the organisation.

We can easily see from this list that in developing and implementing strategy we are concerned with *assessing and managing change.*

To be able to arrive at a strategy for customer support we have an understanding of a number of stages in the process:

1   The *environment* for businesses generally influenced by political, economic, social and technological influences (the *PEST* effects).

2   The *industry sector* influenced by competitors, suppliers and customers for our firm, newcomers into the industry, and substitute products and services.

3   Our *competitive position* broadly based either on price and/or a uniqueness, which differentiates our products and services such that customers perceive a higher value for which they are willing to pay.

We will look at each of these areas in turn.

Is our business an island?

If our island was completely self sufficient we would still be affected by changes in the environment; weather, coastal erosion and disease could all dramatically change what happened to us. Likewise the normal environment for all businesses is influenced by the four effects of changes in the political scene, economic cycles, social changes, and the advent of new technology; these are known as the PESTs of the business environment.

Political

The government has an influence on all types of organisation whether they are profit seeking or non-profit seeking, private or within the public domain. Influences are through:

- Laws controlling the way in which businesses should conduct themselves, including safety regulations and ecological controls
- Financial policy, subsidies and loans
- Trade agreements
- Competitive environment, brought about, for example, through regulation as against deregulation.

The development of the trading areas controlled by bodies like the European Commission and General Agreements on Tariffs and Trade (GATT) are increasing the complexity of the political influences.

Economy

Economic forces have a significant and wide reaching effect on companies. The following are some of the more important factors which can have a major impact on strategy:

- The state of the economic cycle (recession or growth)
- Monetary policy (money supply, interest rates, inflation rates etc)
- The income and spending of consumers

Socio-cultural

The socio-cultural factor concentrates on the values and attitudes of the population from which the employees, customers of the service organisation, other stakeholders and interest groups are drawn. The factors which make up the socio-cultural factor are wide ranging but include:

- Family size
- Age distribution
- Working population mix, men/women, age distribution
- Lifestyles
- Leisure time

- Work attitudes
- Environmental attitudes
- Business attitudes
- Disposable income
- Ethics.

All of these social factors will influence both our customers for service and support and also the service and support personnel. They will change attitudes and expectations to which the customer support organisation has to respond.

Technology

New technologies open up new possibilities for existing businesses, create new businesses and lead to the demise of existing businesses. The technology impacts on both the means of production and delivering services, for example through information technology (IT) and the use of robotics. Technology also influences the lifestyles of consumers so changing the expectations of customers for the availability of information, speed of response and remote monitoring of equipment.

Therefore any business needs to have an understanding of the environment in which it operates if it is to try to make *proactive* strategic decisions rather than only being *reactive* to external changes. It is through an understanding of the external environment that a firm can appreciate threats and opportunities, and gauge the rate of change.

What's happening in our business sector?

While our PEST assessment gives us a picture of the general business environment it does not go far enough in understanding what is happening in our own industrial sector. It is in this area we now need to focus our attention. A model for this purpose was suggested by Michael Porter and is known as the 'Porter Five Competitive Forces'. These are the competitive forces caused by the intensity of competition between the players in the industry; the bargaining power of the customers; the bargaining power of suppliers; the entry of newcomers into the market; the threat of substitute products and services from firms in other industries. We will look at the factors which make up the five forces.

Intensity of competition

Intensity of competition between the players in an industry is increased where:

- There are a large number of equally balanced competitors
- Industry growth is slow so markets are maturing
- There are high fixed costs in facilities, people, materials, or systems
- There is very little difference in the customer support offered by the different players
- The costs of changing between competitors (i.e. switching costs) are low for customers. Emphasis on service would be a case in point whereas support with more involvement in the customer's business increases switching costs
- The risk perceived by the customer of switching to another competitor is low. As with the cost factor, customers perceive the risk to be higher in switching for support rather than service, as it is harder to evaluate beforehand.

Customers' power

The main factors which increase the power of customers are:
- The number of possible alternative suppliers for customer service and support
- Only a few customers who control the purchase of a large volume of services. We can see this effect in the computer and office equipment sector within large companies
- The cost to the customer of changing the supplier is low. The presence of strong third party providers of customer service and support in an industry would lower these switching costs
- Price sensitivity of the market is high when there is little difference between the customer service and support offered by the different players in the sector.

Suppliers' power

The power of the suppliers to the organisation is high when:

- There are few alternative suppliers
- There are no substitutes

- It costs us as a firm a great deal to change to other suppliers (i.e. our switching costs are high)
- Suppliers pose the threat of carrying out the customer service and support themselves. This could be the threat to dealers who carry out customer service and support for manufacturers. The manufacturers may choose to integrate forward to offer customer service and support directly to the end customers.

Barriers to entry

Barriers to entry for newcomers into the market sector are highest when:
- There are economies of scale, for example due to large information systems controlling customer service and support
- Geographic coverage is important to the customer and this takes time and resources to establish
- There is strong loyalty to existing firms perhaps gained by the quality of the customer service and support
- The switching costs for customers to change to the newcomers is high
- Knowledge of the business sector, the needs of the customers, and how to deliver customer service and support is detailed and takes considerable time to develop
- Government policy favours only selected suppliers
- The existing firms are able to extend the range of service and support products offered to enhance the existing offering
- There are strong ties to the customer through the specialist nature of the product being serviced or through the nature of the contracts
- The capital required to set up the customer service and support operation is high.

Substitution threat

The threat from alternative offerings from outside of the industry sector is high when:

- Alternatives exist which are cost effective for the customers. The rise of third party customer support operations in a number of sectors has followed this path
- The main competitors are seen to be earning high profits which encourages others to enter the market

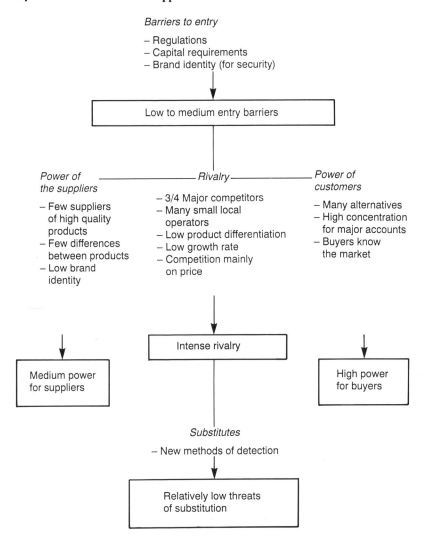

Barriers to entry

   – Regulations
   – Capital requirements
   – Brand identity (for security)

Low to medium entry barriers

Power of
the suppliers

   – Few suppliers
     of high quality
     products
   – Few differences
     between products
   – Low brand
     identity

Rivalry

   – 3/4 Major competitors
   – Many small local
     operators
   – Low product differentiation
   – Low growth rate
   – Competition mainly
     on price

Power of
customers

   – Many alternatives
   – High concentration
     for major accounts
   – Buyers know
     the market

Intense rivalry

Medium power
for suppliers

High power
for buyers

Substitutes

   – New methods of detection

Relatively low threats
of substitution

Figure 2.3 Porter's Five Forces for an Intruder Alarm Company

A structural analysis of our industry sector gives a snapshot of our customer service and support relative to other companies in the sector. The Five Forces Analysis for an Intruder Alarm company is given in Fig. 2.3; it shows an industry in which there is currently intense competition between a small number of major national players and many small local operators. There is very little difference between the equipment offered, and service and support is perceived as being equally indifferent by the majority of customers. While there are few barriers to entry for small operations, the image, the need both to meet regulations administered by the police and for capital to build a network, are barriers to national coverage. It is important for us to remember that such an analysis is only a picture at one point in time, and a useful extension of the model is to consider the effect of changes in the PEST environment on the five forces.

What is our competitive position?

We now come to the final part of developing a service strategy, that of looking at the way in which we are going to compete in the general business environment and in the competitive conditions within our industrial sectors. We have an understanding of these from an examination of the PEST model and the Five Forces of Competition.

There are, according to Michael Porter, three basic ways in which organisations can gain competitive advantages: *cost leadership*, *differentiation* and *focus*. The cost leadership and differentiation strategies can be pursued either on a broad front or concentrated on a narrow, focussed or niche market which leads to Porter's third generic strategy of *cost focus* and *differentiation focus*. Porter says that an organisation can only survive in the long term if it is successful in implementing one of these two basic approaches. He tells firms of the danger of being caught in the middle between these two extremes but at the same time encourages firms which are cost leaders to look for some differentiation and for differentiated organisations to try to reduce costs.

Where a customer service and support operation does have some features which differentiate it from its competitors the provision of these features is likely to lead to some additional costs which must be recouped through customers recognising their value and being willing to pay a higher price. It is likely that in any market sector only one firm can have the lowest cost and in consequence sustain a low price as the main means of competition. It follows that for most companies we need to look at some form of differentiation so that the firm stands out from its competitors in some way, perhaps by giving faster response or having more personable service staff. However as we will see, differentiation has consequences for costs which must be reflected in the prices charged for the customer service and support.

	DESIGN	INSTALLATION	TRAINING	MONITORING	SERVICE	SUPPORT
PEOPLE		Use of own staff	Specialist trainers			
EQUIPMENT						
MATERIALS	Low cost systems				Rapid supply of spares	
FACILITIES						
I.T. SYSTEMS	Customer records	Customer details		Remote monitoring		Central control
CONFIGURA- TION					Wide network	

Figure 2.4 The Value Chain for intruder alarms

There are three main models which we need to understand to get to a competitive strategy relative to the other players: the *value chain*, the *differentiation matrix* and the *strategy compass*. Let us look at them in turn and see how they can be applied.

The value chain

The value chain is in essence the sequence of activities which build to generate the mix of products and services for the whole organisation. In its simplest form for a manufacturing firm it relates the primary activities of designing the product, procuring materials, manufacture of the product, distribution, after sales customer service and support. The way in which the value is added along the chain creates both the uniqueness of what is sold to the customer and also the costs. The ability of a firm to create uniqueness and a particular cost structure is influenced by the arrangement of resources including people, equipment, facilities, information systems and materials.

When looking at the sequence of activities which make up a value chain we want to try to identify *drivers for uniqueness* and *cost drivers*. An example for an intruder alarm company is shown in Fig. 2.4. We have identified the factors which contribute to uniqueness like the use of their own staff for installation, and the customer training package. Factors that also cost drivers are the control of spares inventories, and the information systems allowing access to customer records and remote monitoring.

When considering ways to increase uniqueness and hence differentiation there are a number of areas where we might look:

Policy choices relating to:

- product features and product performance
- intensity of the activity, for example the intensity of advertising or the design activity
- technology employed in performing the activity
- skill and experience of the personnel employed in the activity
- information systems employed in controlling the activity.

Linkages and *Interrelationships*: Uniqueness can come from the way the value chain activities are linked together. Better handover of installed equipment from the installation engineers to service and support engineers may reduce the incident of failure and give a perceived improvement in service quality. Likewise relationships with suppliers may improve the availability of spares so reducing average time to fix and downtime of equipment. Information systems play a crucial role in making an integrated value chain.

Scale and *location*: Uniqueness may result from the geographical location of a company and the scale of the operations. For the customer service and support organisation this corresponds to aspects of availability. A national or international customer service and support organisation is able to offer a wider range of options than a local business confined to a limited small area.

As well as these features which lead to differentiation there are associated costs or *cost drivers*. The main cost drivers are:

- Economies of scale which reduce costs
- Economies from learning which reduce costs by things being carried out more efficiently
- Capacity utilisation through good capacity management which reduces costs
- Integration of the value chain which reduces time and waste. It may lead to reduction in the material costs through more effective just-in-time management of spares.

We need to understand what the main cost drivers are for each of the activities in our value chain. We are then in a position to try ways to gain a cost advantage either by controlling the main most important cost driver better or changing or re-configuring the value chain to reduce the cost drivers. Ways in which we can re-configure the value chain are:

- Developing different ways of making the product or delivering customer service and support
- Changing the level of technology used in the delivery process
- Using different materials or components in the manufacturing or installation process
- Changing the structure for the customer service and support operation through the use of the 'military model' (Chapter 3)
- Moving facilities relative to the customers, for example by re-configuring the location of service depots
- Changing the mix of activities which are carried out in-house or bought from other suppliers of goods or services.

So we can use the value chain analysis to identify where potential competitive advantage is gained by building in uniqueness or lowering costs.

The differentiation matrix

How do we gain competitive advantage through competition on factors of differentiation or price? The differentiation matrix was suggested by Shiv Mathur as a route to understanding where we are positioned better. Our starting point is the distinction between *merchandise* and *support.*

Merchandise consists of items which are available to the customer within the product package. An important aspect in the definition of merchandise is that the features can be both tangible and intangible and so would include customer service dimensions like availability, and ease of use of documentation.

Support consists of those features which could be seen as constituting personalisation, including the giving of advice, and information. In Mathur's terms it may include know-how and professional expertise.

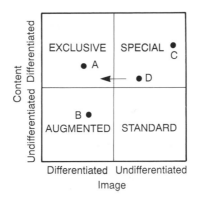

Figure 2.5 Differentiation matrix

An organisation may choose to differentiate itself either by merchandise or support or by a combination of the two. Alternatively there may be no differentiation except for the price charged. Mathur has terms for each of the positions by which the product is delivered to the customers which form the matrix (Fig. 2.5). The different states are illustrated by reference to industrial capital equipment.

A *system*: the business analyses customer requirements and designs, builds and installs a tailor made package. So the firm is differentiated on support and merchandise.

A *product*: here the product is differentiated by way of superior designs or construction but the support offered is not differentiated.

A *service*: the business offers advice to the customer on identifying needs and possible solutions but equipment is supplied from a standard range. So the support is differentiated but the merchandise is not.

A *commodity*: the product is standard and the business does not give differentiated support. Consequently as there are no non-price aspects of differentiation, price becomes the only means of competitive distinction. .

All of the four generic strategies may be pursued to advantage by different organisations if there are sufficient customers in the target market who value the differentiation.

From the four generic strategies Mathur moves on to explore the nature of differentiation for *merchandise* and *support*. *Support* can be differentiated in two dimensions according to whether there is greater *personalisation* or *expertise*. Greater *personalisation* includes closeness to customers, knowing them, knowing their needs, and responding with individual care. Greater *expertise* means the business has more knowledge, skills and experience which differentiate it from competitors. Again Mathur creates a model for the four states of differentiated *personalisation* or *expertise*, with differentiation in both, or with neither differentiated (Fig. 2.6). The means of differentiating the support is defined in three ways with a fourth undifferentiated position. Examples from a customer service and support operation are used to illustrate the positions:

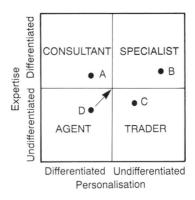

Figure 2.6 Differentiation mapping on 'support'

Consultancy: the firm works closely with the client to identify what is required for the product in operation, assesses risks of failure, trains and gives advice. Here both the personalisation and the expertise are differentiated.

Specialist: the specialist has superior knowledge of the technical content of service and support and can offer these to the client. However the firm relies on the client to identify needs. The offering consists of an undifferentiated personalisation with differentiated expertise.

Agency: here the firm has no better knowledge of service and support which are available. However it is able to work very closely with clients to deliver better advice, primarily through an intimate knowledge of the client. Consequently the firm is differentiating itself on personalisation.

Trader: here there is no differentiation through personalisation or expertise.

Differentiation of *merchandise* is dealt with in a similar fashion by identifying two main aspects of differentiation, *image* and *content*. *Image* is concerned with the bundle of attributes which surround the perception of a brand. *Content* is concerned with what the product will perform for the customer. Subsequently the four polar positions shown in Fig. 2.7 are defined as follows through the illustration of a range of trainers:

Exclusive: the manufacturer makes both a superior quality of product and also through powerful advertising links the product to celebrity designers.

Consequently the firm differentiates the product by the image as well as the content.

Augmented: here there is no difference in the basic shoe from other offerings. However the image is differentiated by way of branding through advertising.

Special: here the manufacturer may be making trainers to satisfy certain needs such as cross country running, which can differentiate the product on content.

Standard: here neither content nor image is differentiated so the firm can only sell the product on price.

The Mathur model allows us to look at the combination of product and

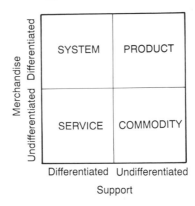

Figure 2.7 Differentiation mapping on 'merchandise'

service and support and to assess the standing of the package in relation to our competitors. It gives a map of the present position and also a pointer for where we might want to move in the future. Mapping is shown for both the support and merchandise elements in Figures 2.6 and 2.7 for our company D and three competitors.

The strategic compass

Strategy formulation is very much about direction and the strategic compass is a convenient way for us to look at the direction we are taking and the consequences for the health of the business. We can look at competition based on differentiating factors, as in the Mathur model, which lead in the eyes of our customers to a higher preceived value for the mix of product and customer service and support. If there is no perceived added value (PAV) then price is our only means of competition. However what often happens in practice is that there is a relationship between perceived added value and price. Increasing PAV may command higher prices but it is likely to bring with it higher operating costs to provide the enhancements.

The strategy compass, Fig. 2.1, shows directions of movement against axes of PAV and price. Looking at the four primary directions:

1   *North* – increasing PAV without increasing the price. Consequently, there must be a reduction in some operational costs to support the cost of increasing PAV if margins are not to fall.

2 *East* – increasing the price without increasing PAV. This is dangerous since customers will realise what is happening, sooner or later, and look for another supplier.

3 *South* – decreasing PAV while holding the price constant. Again, this is dangerous as a continuing strategy since customers will look elsewhere for other service providers.

4 *West* – holding PAV constant while decreasing the price. This strategy needs an increase in efficiency and hence lower costs to be sustained – hoping for increased volume with a decreased margin.

So any movement into the southeast quadrant brings with it the threat of long term failure. Movement into the northwest quadrant requires increases in efficiencies to deliver increased PAV while reducing the price.

If we set our company at the centre of the compass we can then position the other players in the sector relative to it and discuss the consequences for adopting strategies in different directions on PAV and price. If we choose to move from the central position care has to be taken because we may be moving into a completely different market sector. We can illustrate this with a simple example. If a pizza chain moves upmarket into the area of a cordon bleu restaurant or downmarket into the fast food business, it will have to re-assess its PAV relative to the competitors in the new sectors.

We can assess relative PAV by examining the *relative competitive advantage* for customer service and support. This will bring out those aspects of the product, customer service and support mix which give us differentiation.

Relative competitive advantage

Service and support organisations need to be clear on two aspects of customer service: the factors which give competitive advantage and which are customer catching and the factors which a customer might expect to find in an equivalent customer service and support operation. Hygiene factors are those elements of service and support which customers assume we will deliver, for example, knives and forks in a restaurant. If expected levels of service for hygiene factors are not met, it might lead to a loss of business. We use the *customer service profile*, Fig. 2.8, as a means of evaluating both the competitive factors and sensitive

Attribute	Weight (W)*	Competitive position (R)	WxR
PRODUCT	☐	☐	☐
Reliability (MTBF)	40	+1	+40
Response (MTTR)	H	0	
Warranty	10	−1	−10
Serviceability	___	___	___
Instalability	___	___	___
Price	___	___	___
SUPPORT	☐	☐	☐
Customer training	20	+1	+20
Consultancy			
Documentation	10	−1	−10
Advice	___	___	___
SERVICE	☐	☐	☐
Maintenance contract	10	−1	−10
Time to fix	H	+1	
Service price	___	___	___
Spares availability	H	0	
Flexibility of response (Standard v. Gold Star)	___	___	___
PROCESS	☐	☐	☐
Ease of contact	___	___	___
Customer feeling in control	___	___	___
Customer care	___	___	___
Service personnel	10	+1	+10
Responsiveness	___	___	___
Trust/confidence	___	___	___
Vans	___	___	___
TOTAL	100	___	+40

Relating relative to competitors

−3	−2	−1	0	+1	+2	+3
Inferior		On Par		Superior		

*Hygiene factor W = 0

Figure 2.8 Customer service profile

hygiene factors, and to establish how well they are being delivered *relative to the competition*.

The profile includes a generic list of customer service and support dimensions, although others can be added for specific organisations. The process is in four stages:

1   Decide the main dimensions from the list which give competitive advantage by differentiation and allocate 100 marks among them. We

find it is usual to have only four or five dimensions and to award not less than 10 marks to any one dimension.

2 Decide which are the most sensitive hygiene factors and mark these with an 'H'. Hygiene factors carry a mark of zero on the scoring as they do not contribute to competitive performance.

3 Assess current performance relative to the main competitors on a scale from −3 to +3 for both the competitive and hygiene factors. Establishing the weighting will often call for the use of marketing information gathered as part of marketing monitoring for a customer satisfaction index (see Chapter 5).

4 Arithmetically multiply the weighting scores by current performance to give a total score for the customer service dimension. Hygiene factors score zero since they do not lead to differentiation and perceived added value.

Fig. 2.8 shows the customer service profile for a typical customer service and support operation. Once completed in this way the points for us to look for are:

1 High positive scores for competitive factors which might be used to gain either increased market share or price increases.

2 High negative scores for competitive factors, indicating possible falling off of PAV and the potential loss of customers.

3 High performance relative to competitors on hygiene factors, indicating either the possibility of reducing service levels and taking a cost reduction or gaining increases in PAV if they are recognised by customers.

4 Low performance relative to competitors on hygiene factors, indicating the possibility of loss of customers even where, as we have found in some instances, the competitive factors are being delivered with a high relative score.

Are there dangers from trying to differentiate?

While we have perhaps tended to present differentiation as a strategy for success it is sobering to identify the traps that await the unwary strategist. Michael Porter has identified a number of pitfalls including the following:

- *Uniqueness is not perceived as adding value* as indicated by the inability of the organisation to command a price premium for the differentiated offering.

- *Too much differentiation* which is far in excess of customers needs may help competitors with a more acceptable level in that feature and who charge lower prices.

Both of these two points reinforce the need for good marketing research to understand customer needs and those factors of the product, service and support package which they perceive as being important.

- *Too high a price premium* of the differentiating feature particularly if the organisation's cost base is higher than its competitors.
- *Not knowing the cost of differentiation* and spending more on the provision of the differentiating factor than is recoverable through the price premium.

Both of these last two factors reinforce the importance of understanding our cost structures in relation to the price which is available.

- *Focus on the product, not the value chain*, thereby failing to recognise other ways of differentiating. This is especially important as price becomes more of a competitive issue. For example the ability to control inventory costs make it possible to reduce the overall cost of service and support and accept lower margins.
- *Failure to recognise buyer segments* may mean that the offering does not meet fully the needs of any market segment and the organisation is vulnerable to a focussed strategy by a competitor. Attention to the marketing function will help to reduce this danger.

Summary on competitive strategy

When we are formulating a service strategy using the various models we have presented, it is important to remember that things do not stand still. There tends to be a natural cycle which prevails. When a product is new the product's features are more likely to be the mainstay of any differentiation. As competitors introduce equivalent models it becomes more difficult to maintain the product's uniqueness and other aspects of differentiation come into play. Included in these is customer service and support. If this differentiation is lost the players in a sector can only compete on price until something new starts to happen. For instance, new technology may start movement around the cycle again.

The work of people like Tom Peters has drawn attention to the difficulty of copying aspects of customer service and support, which is why it can be a powerful way of differentiation. However, saying we have a strategy for differentiation on aspects of service and support may be no more than a wish statement. Implementation of the strategy is more complex.

What do we need to implement our service strategy?

Having a service strategy is not in itself enough to make it come about. We need a number of congruent elements to be present. One powerful way of assessing our capabilities to implement strategy is through the '7 S Framework', developed by Peters, Waterman, and Phillips at the consultants McKinsey & Co. The framework brings out the interaction between strategy, structure, systems, skills, staff, style and shared values. It reflects the many aspects that have an influence on our ability to implement strategy. So what is meant by each of the elements in the framework?

Strategy

We have spent much of this chapter talking about how to formulate a competitive strategy in terms of differentiation, leading to PAV, and price, taking into account the external environment and the competition in a particular market sector. This strategy should be accompanied by two features, clear objectives, and a means of communicating it throughout the organisation.

Objectives set the targets or mileposts for achieving the strategy. They must be capable of being understood, and measurable over time so that it is known if the mileposts are being reached.

A *mission statement* can be used to communicate strategy in broad terms to everyone in the organisation. Mission statements include some, if not all, of the following features:

- A statement of values
- The product/services to be offered
- The markets/customers
- How those markets will be reached and served
- Attitudes to growth
- The technologies to be used.

The strategy and the objectives may be presented within a company in a corporate business plan.

Structure

Structure relates to our internal organisational structure, the levels of management and lines of control. It also involves the structure for the delivery of product and customer service and support. The military model for the structure of customer service and support which is dealt with later gives some of the main choices for structure.

Systems

Systems in the 7 S framework include not only information systems but all the processes and procedures by which customer service and support is delivered. Systems reflect the way in which things should get done.

Staff

Staff concerns numbers of staff, recruitment and remuneration, training and development. The aspect of staff is of course closely linked to that of skills.

Skills

Skills of the staff can be seen from two standpoints. First is the skills and competences which are necessary to operate the systems for service and support delivery. Second is the means by which aspects of differentiation are achieved. This is especially true when differentiation involves the 'support' side of the merchandise/support mix in the Mathur model.

Style

Style addresses the way the organisation and especially managers and supervisors use their time. Organisations may be bureaucratic, auto-cratic, or laissez-faire. Managers may be distant from their staff or be close to them through MBWA – management by walking about.

Shared Values

By shared values we mean those factors which bind the culture of the organisation together. They reflect 'the way things are done around here' for an organisation. They are the history of the firm, its present management, and the type of people that come to work for the firm. In managing change with changing strategy the alteration of shared values is the most difficult. Later in this book we will look in more detail at what is involved in managing this change process.

What does a customer service and support strategy contain?

Having carried out all the analysis decided on a broad direction and reviewed the implications of our chosen strategy, we think a strategy should contain most, if not all of the following:

- A mission statement. The broad statement of the type and level of service and support to be delivered, indicating which markets are to be served;
- The business environment. An assessment of the challenges facing the organisation, attributes of major competitors, and the issues of change to be addressed;
- The segmentation of the business. For each distinct market, the question 'What do we need to do well?' must be addressed. This is likely to include
  - Customer Service Dimension
  - Productivity Targets
  - Revenue/Profit Targets;
- Service Delivery Improvements. If the strategy is to be successfully implemented, there will be some operational changes to be made:
  - Key actions to bring resources to the required standard
  - Action to reduce costs
  - Changes to organisational structure
  - Changes to network configuration
  - Targets for internal performance measures over time, with indication of key activities to be taken.
  - Linkage between internal measure and external customer satisfaction
- The future. A broader view of the long term direction of the organisation

Conclusion

In this chapter we have looked at the process of formulating a strategy for customer service and support. We have looked at the major influences in the business environment, the forces which affect the competitive environment within a market sector, and the competitiveness based on a mix of price and differentiation giving PAV. It will have become apparent that there exists a strong link between competitive strategy formulation and marketing and the two chapters should complement each other.

Implementation of strategy rests on a combination of several factors and the 7 S framework gives a way of identifying some of the main factors. The implementation of strategy is the management of change and we will deal with this in more detail in a later chapter.

Checklist

1   What are the main environmental factors which influence your customer service and support business using the PEST model?

2   What are the three most important things which you can see will change in your business environment in the next three years?

3   What are the main competitive forces for your customer service and support business from a consideration of the five competitive forces?

4   What is the value chain for your organisation? Can you identify any unique points which add value and the main cost drivers?

5   Do you know how you compete in your different market sectors for customer service and support using the differentiation matrix? (If not, you will need to seek guidance from the chapter on marketing.)

6   Where would you position your main competitors on the strategy compass with your organisation in the centre? Use a customer service profile to provide the information for the mapping.

7   In which direction do you want to move on the strategy compass with your customer service and support offering(s)? You may find there are different directions for major groupings or market sectors.

8   How would you describe your organisation according to the 7 S framework? Do you see any anomalies? You will probably want to return to this as we deal in more detail with factors which influence the different elements.

9   Do you have a mission statement for customer service and support? If

you do, are you happy it is full enough? If not, what would you want to see in a mission statement? Do not be too ambitious and remember that formulating a mission statement involves a great deal of time and effort.

3 STRUCTURES FOR CUSTOMER SERVICE AND SUPPORT

Introduction

In this chapter we will introduce the structures for customer service and support operations and explain the characteristics of each. We will describe how customer service and support operations change their structures over time and identify the main factors which cause the changes.

Are we in control of the structure?

The structure of the organisation we have for delivering customer service and support has a great influence on our ability to achieve the aims of a service and support strategy. This includes satisfying the needs of our customers and meeting our own goals for costs and quality. Getting the right structure requires a knowledge of the service and support strategy and the choices open to us for the service and support organisational structure. Just as in the formulation of service and support strategy it is important for us to make definite choices. This is more likely to happen when customer service and support is regarded as an important element of the business rather than a 'necessary evil'.

A service and support story

Let us see what often happens for a manufacturing company. Spec Pumps, making electrical pumps, was set up by a group of engineers who left one of the major pump manufacturers to develop and market a range of specialist pumps for use in the oil industry. Initially the support and service was given by the owners who had designed the product and so knew the capabilities of the product inside out. The company was successful and the pumps started to be used by all the major oil

companies. Now the original owners found they could no longer spend a lot of their time on customer service and support because they were involved in other areas of the business.

A decision was made to recruit a team of engineers who would carry out the service and support activity. Some of these were recruited from their competitors while others came from outside the industry. The company spent time and money training the new team. Also with the growth of the business they found they had to locate the team in several geographical locations. At the same time they started to get requests from their major customers for training of their own engineers to be able to carry out their own servicing.

Spec Pumps continued to be successful in the market and introduced new ranges of pumps which had a wider use in other industrial sectors. After exhibiting pumps at several trade fairs they found they were being approached by some suppliers of industrial equipment and they saw this as an opportunity to start to sell through agents. One or two of the agents already offered a service arrangement to their customers and were keen to include the servicing of Spec Pumps products in their offering. Spec Pumps were happy to go along with this arrangement as by this time their own customer service and support resources were under pressure.

Finally the customer service and support manager who had by this time taken over in Spec Pumps became aware that an increasing number of the major companies were looking for companies who could service not only the products they supplied but also pumps supplied by other manufacturers. Competition for this work also was coming from companies who were not manufacturers themselves but who offered service and support for a range of products from different manufacturers.

So now Spec Pumps were faced with their customers supported and products serviced by a mix of different types of people. There were Spec Pumps' own service engineers sometimes assisted by the experts in the company when things went wrong, by some of the customers' engineers, by their agents, and finally by outside specialist service companies. The question is 'Were Spec Pumps in control of what was happening to their customer support?'.

The showdown

Spec Pumps were surprised to find that in a survey carried out by a trade magazine they were well down in the rankings for customer service and support. They set up their own investigation internally and with their customers and agents. They found that their own engineers were aware of a growing unhappiness with their performance. Routine maintenance was not being carried out and breakdowns were becoming more frequent. Agents were complaining about the way Spec Pumps were supporting them, spares were not available when needed and delivery was unreliable. Customers spoke of the good service they had experienced from Spec Pumps in the past but now felt they could not reach the company when they were in trouble and had on many occasions turned to other third party service companies to help them out. They considered Spec Pumps' service to be expensive for what they received and were considering switching future purchases to other manufacturers. Matters came to a head when Spec Pumps launched a new range of pumps which were not well received, one of the main criticisms being that the company seemed to take no account of faults in the earlier products.

Clearly Spec Pumps had not given enough thought to the consequences of the way in which their delivery of customer support had changed over time for their own staff and for their customers. Costs of the provision of the service and support seemed high for the revenues it generated and there was no pay-off in revenues and profits from the operation. In addition measurement of performance was not good enough for them to be clear of the true position. The time had come to re-think and under-stand what had happened to them.

The Military Model

Before we are in a position to make choices about which is the best structure for delivering customer support we need to understand the different ways in which this activity can be organised. We have found it useful to use military terms to describe *five* different structures. Each of the structures has strengths and weaknesses and we will try to bring these out as we describe each in turn. The structures are based on the nature of the service delivery.

The SAS (Special Air Services)

The SAS are a group of highly specialised engineers who know the products in great detail from design to the way in which they are used. Some of the group may have been involved in the original design of the product or in using the products in the field. Also they may have worked with competitors' products. Examples of the SAS would be microprocessor specialists and CNC machine tool engineers.

Strengths of the SAS:

- Highly skilled often graduate engineers
- Motivated to learn about new products
- Able to work together in teams to solve problems, although they tend to be loners
- Committed to support of the product to maintain uptime
- Interested in improving the performance of the product
- Able to appreciate the need for design changes in the product.

Weaknesses of the SAS:

- An expensive resource
- A limited resource at times of growth in the market
- Often more interested in the product than in supporting the customer
- More focussed on solutions than on the control of costs
- Sometimes difficult to manage.

The Regulars

The Regulars are the service engineers who are able to carry out routine activities of repair and maintenance. They are often dispersed at several locations to be close to customers. Service engineers operating from a service centre and travelling to customers in a service van containing a range of equipment and spares are typical of the Regulars. Examples of Regulars are photocopier engineers, telecommunications engineers, field engineers for utilities.

Strengths of the Regulars:

- A visible sign of the company for customers
- Trained in the service and application of the company's products
- Able to train the customers in the use of the product
- May be better at customer management than the SAS
- More customer contact so they are able to identify sales leads.

Weaknesses of the Regulars:

- Costly resource because of their numbers and the facilities needed to house them and their equipment

- Consistency of service delivery may vary across the whole service network
- May be more interested in the service of the product rather than support of the customers
- May be less likely to be committed to taking ownership of problems and achieving targets like first time fix and product uptime
- Problems of motivation and career progression.

The Territorials

The Territorials are the engineers or specialists in the customers' own service and maintenance organisations who are the customers for the products. They carry out some if not all of the service activities on the product but they need support with training, availability of spares, and information and advice from the original supplier. Examples exist in large organisations like the UK Post Office and London Transport where customers' engineers service major capital equipment such as lifts.

Strengths of the Territorials:

- They know how the product is being used in their company
- Able to carry out maintenance at a time when the equipment is available which helps to minimise downtime
- They are committed to high uptime of the product in use
- They may be committed to long-term use of the supplying company's product if they are well supported
- They cost the supplying company little in the service of the products but costs may be incurred by having, for instance, a support engineer located permanently in the organisation.

Weaknesses of the Territorials:

- They may not be committed to long-term use of the products from the supplying company if they are not well supported
- They need training in the service aspects of the products by the supplying organisation both initially and as products are upgraded and engineers change
- They may not give feedback on inherent design faults in the products which affect serviceability and performance
- They may have limited capability either in skills or equipment
- They may be affected by union restrictions, for example mechanical fitters not being able to touch electrical connections.

The Mercenaries

The Mercenaries are the agents and dealers who both sell the products and offer service and support to the customers. The Mercenaries may do this just for one supplier or act for a number of suppliers depending on the nature of the products and the industry sector. The higher the price of the products the more likely they will act for only one supplier. For example the dealers for heavy earthmoving equipment are tied to one of the main manufacturers such as Caterpillar, Komatsu or JCB, whereas dealers for white and brown goods, washing machines, fridges, televisions and videos, such as Comet, Curry's and Dixons will act for a number of suppliers. In between the car dealers may or may not act for more than one supplier. Here the trend is towards single supplier agents.

Strengths of the Mercenaries:

- They can give wide geographical coverage for customer support
- They may know the needs of their own customers very well through local market knowledge
- They are tied to the supplier company by contract
- They present a lower direct cost to the supplying firm
- They allow rapid expansion of the network using someone else's money. This can be very important for international expansion.

Weaknesses of the Mercenaries:

- They may not be committed to the supplying firm's products or targets for levels of customer service and support
- They need resources to manage them from the supplying company. This may be from marketing and sales or from a separate customer service function. Problems can be caused if there is no clear responsibility for the control of dealers and agents
- They need training in the servicing of the product and in its application
- They may not give reliable feedback to the supplying firm on the performance of the product in field operation
- They are often limited in management expertise. They may be good dealers but limited at service and support.

The Enemies

The Enemies are the third party operators who provide customer support for a range of products like Granada Services in computing, local garages for automobiles, and local electrical repairers for brown and white goods. While they provide service and support for products, they are, for the most part, beyond the control of the original manufacturer. In many cases they will not be known to the original manufacturer. However their performance will impact on the customer's view of the product.

Strengths of the Enemies:

- If they have originally worked for the supplying firm or have had good experience of their products they may be committed to the products over time
- They may be able to provide support and service for products which are no longer manufactured
- They present no cost to the supplying firm for customer support and service except for the costs associated with managing the mercenaries themselves
- We may still derive some revenue from the activities of the enemies by way of the sale of spares
- They may be the only alternative in areas where service intensity if very low.

Weaknesses of the Enemies:

- They may have no commitment to the original supplier and may comment unfavourably to the customers
- They give little or no feedback to the supplying firm on the performance of the product in the field
- They may take revenue for customer support from the original supplier by direct competition
- They may be incompetent and give a poor image of the product.

Do we have a choice of structure?

We can see that Spec Pumps ended up with their products being supported by a mixture of all the military structures. Did they want this to happen? Even if they did we saw that it brought with it problems and costs and possible loss of future sales. So while there may be choices we can also see that there may be pressures which make it difficult to keep in control even when there is a commitment to customer service and support.

What then are the main factors which cause organisations to change their mix of support provision? We think that the overriding influence is the change in *service intensity* or service demand. What do we mean by service intensity? It is the number of separate service or support events per unit of time for all customers and all products which a service and support organisation has to deal with. Typically service intensity may be measured by the number of calls per day into a response centre.

As with Spec Pumps we find that customer service organisations might start off using the *SAS* structure but as the service intensity increases they have to incorporate some *Regulars* if they want to deliver the customer support themselves. If by design or default there is no customer support offered customers are left to DIY and act as *Territorials* or, if the sector is attractive enough, *Enemies* take over.

However, even when the customer service and support is kept in-house, there may be a move to the use of *Mercenaries* to do the job of customer support if the service intensity increases rapidly. These changes can occur without the organisation thinking through the consequences, as the Spec Pumps example illustrates.

If service intensity is so important we need to understand the factors which cause it to change over time.

How do we use the Military Model?

The Military Model is about change. We can probably very quickly identify where we are currently positioned. However, what will happen in the future? What changes can we see which will affect either our wish to alter our level of in-house control or the level of service intensity we need to deal with? Later we will examine some of the factors we see as being drivers for in-house control and which influence service intensity.

For the moment, however, one factor which we do recognise as being important in determining structure for customer service and support relates to the stage of a product in its life cycle. It is recognised that all products/services go through four stages in a life cycle: *launch, estab-lishment, maturity* and *decline*. We could see that in the launch and establishment stages we would wish to have the SAS/Regular structure. This would perhaps be carried on into maturity, although at this stage we might be discussing the merit of relinquishing in-house control to Mercenaries, and perhaps in decline leaving everything to the Enemies.

What influences service intensity?

If we are to be in control of our own destiny for customer support we need to understand the factors which influence changes in service intensity. We can see service intensity being affected by five main factors:

1 The product(s)
2 The type of service and support
3 The user
4 The service and support personnel
5 The internal 'support' for the customer service and support function.

Let us look at the influence of each of these in turn.

The product(s)

The nature of the products will affect the service intensity in a number of ways.

- The *initial price* of the product will determine if there is a tendency to replace the product when it fails rather than to service it. We have found there is a cut-off point at about £1000 between the two, with more expensive and probably more complex items being serviced. Increased servicing will tend to increase service intensity
- The *complexity* of the product will tend to bring with it increases in service intensity for both customer support and service requirements
- The more *reliable* a product the lower the service intensity. We have seen in some sectors a dramatic reduction in service intensity over the years. Mainframe computers and medical instruments are good examples of this trend
- The *newness* of a product in the field will tend to drive up service intensity, especially if faults are discovered which have a safety implication. An electrical supplier found a fault in a newly launched storage heater and had to repair the fault in 5000 heaters already installed in customers' premises within five days
- The *initial price* as compared to *lifetime costs* for the product has an effect in the following way. If our customers are willing to pay more for a better and more reliable system it might in the long run save them money in call-out costs and reduce the service intensity. A security company found that as it had to compete more on price it was forced to use cheaper components in its alarm systems which were more prone to

failure. Hence there was an increased service intensity for them.

- The extent to which the operation of the product is dependent on *other products not sold by the supplier* can increase service intensity. A failure reported to a computer company may be caused by other equipment in a network for which it is not responsible.

The type of customer service and support

By type of service and support we mean the nature of what is offered to the customer. Among the most important elements of service and support having an effect on service intensity are:

- The type of *warranty* which is given with the product. The more comprehensive this is the more it is likely that customers will require service and support
- The extent to which *preventive maintenance* is carried out as part of a service contract will influence the incidence of failure and hence service intensity
- The use of *remote sensing* and *diagnosis*, as well as *remote fixing*, will tend to reduce service intensity on service engineers by eliminating the need for them or by increasing the probability of first time fix. Consequently service intensity will fall
- Use of *additional support* like Helplines to give quick solutions to problems which could otherwise escalate and consume more resources.

The users

The users, as all customer support managers appreciate, have a great influence on the service intensity and some of the main aspects we need to consider are:

- The extent to which users have to be *trained* in the use of the product. The higher the probability of users not doing what they should do the higher the service intensity. Adding to this problem is when the users change over time. Whereas the original user may have been trained as part of an initial installation, commissioning or sales activity, the newcomer is a novice and things go wrong more often or more advice is needed. Also where there are many users, for example with photo-copiers, the role of the key operator becomes important, as the main link with the service and support activity

- The *cost* of a service call to the user will influence the propensity to call the support organisation
- The *location* of the product in a user's premises may lead to difficulties for the service personnel in finding the equipment. This can lead to repeat visits and hence increased service intensity.

The service and support personnel

The way in which service and support personnel approach their task and their commitment to meeting service levels affects service intensity in the following ways:

- *Competence* of personnel to perform the full range of tasks without calling for unplanned assistance is important. The service function of a major utility company found that at a time when it had a large proportion of new service engineers the service intensity rose because of a reduction in the achievement of first time fix
- The *commitment* by service personnel to first time fix may be influenced by the way in which service and support personnel are rewarded. Many service organisations we have looked at measure performance of their personnel on calls per day without any reference to whether these achieved first time fix. Poor achievement of first time fix tends to drive up service intensity and of course adds cost through overtime charges
- The *commitment* of service personnel to *ownership and resolution of problems* affects service intensity. The personnel giving support on software and hardware problems in a response centre originally worked as individuals handling a number of enquiries from customers. There was a tendency for them to keep a number of jobs on the go for many days until they were resolved. The result was many additional calls from the customers enquiring about progress. Reorganisation of the personnel into teams gained common ownership and a faster resolution of problems so reducing service intensity.

The internal 'support'

The ability of the rest of the organisation to support the service and support operation will influence service intensity because:

- Poor *supply of spares* will frustrate the achievement of first time fix and raise service intensity
- Poor supply of *information* on product use or customer records will

mean increased contact with the customers or users for each service or support incident. This has implications for the way in which the design and manufacturing, and marketing sales and accounts functions are linked to the customer support and service activity.

From this list of factors which influence service intensity we can highlight the following four points in summary:

1 Service intensity for a particular product should decrease as the product design evolves over time so that the product becomes inherently more reliable. Many customer service and support companies target and track the level of service intensity. This is especially the case for consumer products and the low value end of capital goods.

2 Service intensity would be expected to increase with the number of products in the field and the variety of products.

3 Service intensity will be expected to increase with failure to achieve first time fix.

4 Service intensity is affected for many support and service providers by the extent to which planned maintenance can be carried out to prevent subsequent failures.

Why should we want to control customer service and support?

We have seen that there are a large number of factors which change service intensity. Whatever the extent to which each factor alters service intensity, either causing increases or reductions, the overall effect for many organisations is for service intensity to increase over time. Like Spec Pumps they start to use a mixture of the military structures. One of the reasons for the problems Spec Pumps started to experience was loss of control of the customer service and support activity for their products. While they were using predominantly the SAS and Regulars structures they had relatively good control. However once they started to use the Mercenaries and then Enemies the control started to slip away from them.

So, are there good reasons why we might want to keep tight control over the customer service and support activity? We describe the control as *in-house control*. We have been able to identify a number of factors which firms talk about in relation to the level of in-house control. Essentially we are looking at those things which cause a company to look for a high level of in-house control and which cause problems as the level of control slips. Reasons for loss of in-house control may be either intentional or because the business has 'taken its eye off the ball'.

Factors driving a wish for high in-house control

Some of the most important factors which cause organisations to look for high in-house control which we have seen in practice are:

- To be able to fulfil *warranty* obligations
- The *product is complex* so a high level of skill is required to give service and support
- There is *uncertainty* about the *performance* of the product. Maybe it is in the early stages of launch so all problems of field performance have not yet been identified
- There are very real concerns about the *threat to life* in the event of product failure
- The firm has decided that its *competitive strategy* includes the delivery of strong service and support and it wants to project this as its image
- The firm wishes to maintain close contact with its customers and users of the products to gain *feedback on performance* which can be incorporated into future designs
- The firm wishes to maintain close contact with customers to *protect future sales*.

Is it to be the SAS, Regulars, Territorials, Mercenaries, or the Enemies?

How can a firm decide which is the best structure for their customer service and support activities given the demands for in-house control and the effects of service intensity? We use the framework shown in Fig. 3.1 which shows the relationship between *service intensity* and the level of *in-house control* for the military structures for customer service and support.

We have found in practice that firms which lie in the area of *high in-house control* and with relatively *low service intensity* exhibit the following characteristics:

1   The volume of products to be supported in the field is relatively low.
2   Service is carried out either by the manufacturer's own personnel,

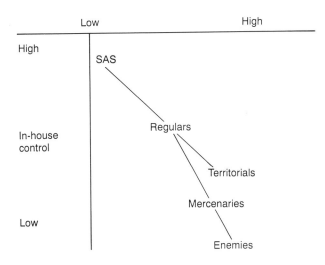

Figure 3.1 Customer support organisation

that is to say a mixture of SAS and Regulars, or by the customers' staff, Territorials, who have been trained by the manufacturer.

3 The cost of the service and support is relatively high.

4 The quality, experience and technical competence of personnel employed is higher than those required for high volume products.

5 Time factors are very important for service levels. First time fix, time to fix and rapid response are all important.

6 Additional services which add value to the service and support such as customer training, education and consultancy are commonly part of the package.

7 Marketing of the service and support where it actively takes place emphasises 'professional competence'.

In contrast we have found firms who have *low in-house control* and have *high service intensity* exhibit the following characteristics:

1 The number of products to be supported is high both in variety and in the volume of the individual products.

2 There is a shift to the use of third party service and support providers, the Mercenaries, with the emphasis placed on supporting the agents or dealers rather than the end customers or users.

3 Distribution networks for the sale of the products are highly developed.

4 High volume and low priced products are designed for replacement rather than repair. Where service is still required and economic, products are designed to simplify and speed up the service task.

5 Service in the form of 'customer care and support' is seen as the route towards competitive advantage. The emphasis is more on the way that service and support are delivered, that is the process, rather than on the content of the service and support package.

6 The total organisation is larger and the delivery of service and support to the end customer or user more complex. Consequently more effort is given to thinking through a strategy for the operation in an attempt to get better control over the activity.

As we have seen the tendency is for service intensity to increase for a particular company and consequently for them to move down the diagonal in Fig. 3.1. This results in a loss of in-house control by adding Mercenaries to the service and support provision. The trade-off for this loss is a reduction in costs of providing the level of customer service and support which is borne by the company.

We have found that the most powerful use of the framework is to consider future events which might change either the level of service intensity or the level of in-house control which might be required. We have seen instances of organisations who have made a conscious decision to increase in-house control despite a current high level of service intensity.

It is perhaps helpful to look at the experience of a number of organisations which are typical of what we have seen in the recent past.

A consumer products manufacturer

This company produces largely high volume consumer products with the addition of some more specialised products for the professional market. Their service and support function was, at best, average.

Immediate contact with consumers is limited as most products are purchased from high street retailers or discount stores. The company had a limited range of repair workshops to handle repairs, but these were mostly to be found in back street locations. Other service activities were handled by appointed agents and some repairs were carried out by the customers.

The company decided it wanted to differentiate itself on customer service and support. It put together a three-year plan. The repair shops were moved into high street locations and renamed Service Centres, staff were trained, and the facilities were given a consistent image.

By taking these actions the company was attempting to increase the level of in-house control by reducing the dependence on Mercenaries and loss of business to Enemies. At the same time the morale of the Regulars already employed was raised. It was realised that these changes could not be achieved without incurring extra costs. Higher productivity targets were set specifically for inventory.

A white goods manufacturer

Some years ago this manufacturer was under significant cost competition and saw an opportunity to cut costs, allowing service agents around the country to take responsibility for customer service and support. The customer service and support function was cut to a minimum.

It was soon discovered that this left service to be controlled by Mercenaries and Enemies which, although cheaper in the short-term, was disastrous for customer service. The long term quality costs were tending to rise. One example of this was most of the service agents no longer held the more expensive spares and so customer downtime was dramatically increased.

The company has moved to bring the support activity back to a role for Regulars and for Mercenaries, who are closely controlled.

A capital goods manufacturer

This company supplies a wide range of precision instruments to research and other professional institutions. Its products are to some extent differentiated by their performance and the customer service and support operation is recognised for its expertise. The customer service and support requires highly qualified engineers and so the structure is towards the SAS area.

The threat to this company comes from Mercenaries and Enemies, who at one stage were possibly employed and trained by the company. These groups may offer a lower cost service to a narrow range of customers. There are dangers in this for the customers as the equipment may not be fully maintained. However this may be hidden from those who make decisions about service contracts as they are not the users of the equipment. The decision makers are largely driven by cost constraints.

The company must maintain control of the service and support activities because there are safety implications if the equipment is faulty. This has required the company to concentrate on supplementing the technical expertise of the SAS group with interpersonal skills to reinforce the support aspect.

A computer manufacturer

This company's traditional business has been in the manufacture of mainframe and mini-computers with a strong customer service and support operation for after sales service and support. The company has relied on a mix of SAS and Regulars to deliver the customer service and support.

The move by the company into PCs and other peripherals increased the number of products in the field and this potentially increased service intensity. The cost of increasing the SAS/Regular organisation would have been difficult in the short term and also probably uneconomic because of the lower contract charges. Consequently the company turned to the Mercenaries structure and delivered the customer service and support through a network of agents, most of whom were responsible for the sale of the original equipment.

The change in the way in which the company delivers its total customer service and support activities has meant learning new skills in managing the Mercenaries to maintain the high standards associated with the company's original image.

Conclusion

In this chapter we have looked at the different structures for customer service and support using the military model for the mix of provision. We have looked at how the mix of provision is influenced by changes in service intensity and the wish to achieve a particular level of in-house control over the customer service and support activity. We have shown how the military model can be used to assess the effect of future changes and have given examples of how organisations have approached such changes for the successful delivery of customer support at a cost the organisation can afford.

Checklist

1 What is your current mix of service and support provision using the terms of the military model?

2 Do you experience any problems with your current mix of service and support provision?

3 What factors do you see which may significantly change the service intensity in the future?

4 What factors do you see which might cause you to want to change the degree of in-house control you exert over customer service and support to your customers or end users of your products?

5 What would you see as being the ideal structure for your own company now and in the future?

4 THE ELEMENTS OF CUSTOMER SERVICE AND SUPPORT

Introduction

In this chapter we will describe the major areas of customer service and support in more detail, recognising that not all elements will apply with equal force to every situation. Indeed, some may not apply at all – disposable products, for example, clearly do not require a repair service.

The position adopted by the organisation on the military model (Chapter 3) will influence the degree of importance placed on each element. As this position shifts in response to changes in the service and support task the emphasis placed on each element will also change. In reading this chapter you should question whether the performance of your organisation is to the standard required for your current competitive position).

In the chapter on service strategy (Chapter 2) we described the approach to developing a customer service and support profile, identifying competitive and hygiene factors. These are grouped under four main headings:

1 Product Related
2 Service and Repair Related
3 Support for the Customer to use the product
4 Process issues, describing how the customer is dealt with.

The Product Related issues are largely a matter for initial design, Mean Time Between Failure (MTBF) being determined at this stage. No classification is absolutely perfect, MTBF also being affected by the quality of service and repair. Indeed, we would encourage you to add dimensions to the original list if you believe they are critical to the performance of your organisation.

In this chapter, therefore, we will describe elements of customer service and support under the broad headings of Time, Maintaining

Uptime or availability for the customer, and Support for Customers. These descriptions should enable you to identify your competitive priorities.

The dimensions of time

To some extent all organisations are judged on their ability to respond quickly, whether it be the speed of acknowledgement of the presence of a customer need in the first instance, or the ability to deliver a completed service faster than the competition. The customer service and support manager will ignore the opportunity to improve time effectiveness at his peril.

Apart from the fact that the customer's perception of the organisation is influenced by time performance, the internal effectiveness of the organisation will obviously be improved by better time productivity.

How fast is the first response?

The first principle to be observed is surely that the customer must be able to make contact quickly and easily with the person who can deal with their request. Customers want to make one telephone call or write one letter and know that having made contact, their problem will be taken care of quickly and efficiently. In other words customers want to know that they have no longer got a problem because the organisation will deal with it.

Because we believe that managing customer contact is vital, we have devoted Chapter 6 to the subject of service delivery design, but some examples of effective approaches are given below:

- *Toll-free or 0800 telephone numbers:* These numbers are widely advertised to ensure that customers know how to contact the organisation. The person answering the telephone will be able to deal with a wide range of enquiries from invoice problems to organising response to breakdowns. It is likely that this person will be given basic product training as well as training in telephone techniques to boost customer confidence
- *Customer help-line:* This device is often employed by software suppliers who want their customers to have confidence that they will be able to use the product effectively from day one. For those who are not computer-literate it is of course important that the program will run, let

alone be used to full power, and the support employee must deal sympathetically with what may seem trivial as well as with the more interesting technical problems

- *Applications advice:* For more complex products or systems it may be a selling point to be able to offer a 'what do you need to get the required result' service prior to the sale. There is a real advantage to having this advice divorced as much as is feasible from the selling activity. There is an understandable fear that the salesman will oversell, whereas technical experts tend to be embarrassingly honest in what they say. This may result in a smaller initial order, but will probably yield long term rewards

- *Warranty claims:* Many companies are now offering genuine 'money back' guarantees. There is no doubt that a genuine, no strings attached, no quibble guarantee can build customer confidence which may tip the balance at the point of sale. For a consumer product, although we may wish they were not needed, warranties provide an excellent source of quality feedback, provided that customers are encouraged to complain

- *Call back:* Some service organisations make it routine to call back the customer as soon as possible after receiving the service request to give the estimated time of arrival of the engineer. This reassures the customers that something is happening and assists them in organising their time better. It is worth calling back relatively quickly even if nothing definite can yet be arranged, which may allow the customer to explore other options. This second approach is not recommended to be used frequently.

Two examples of initial response

During a study tour investigating service quality in the USA we visited the customer service telephone response centre of Georgia Light and Power. In order to sustain rapid response they have organised the staff into small teams each led by a supervisor who is able to monitor how well each person is doing, assess the waiting time for calls yet to be answered and is available to deal with more difficult problems as the need arises. They have utilised a powerful blend of technology in the form of a computerised call management system combined with effective human resource management in the shape of good teamwork and strong management support and example. The end result is that customers can contact Georgia Light and Power quickly and easily with high levels of problem resolution.

The organisation sometimes experiences problems as, for example, when storms bring down powerlines which leads to a surge in calls enquiring as to when power will be restored. Although response centre staff often come in voluntarily to cope with this temporary overload, the call waiting times tend to increase. To alleviate this to some extent, a recorded message indicates that Georgia Light and Power is dealing with the problem and normal service will be resumed shortly.

There is a view that customer service departments are only good because the product is bad and somebody must deal with the resulting problems. Needless to say this is not our view. All organisations must capitalise on each customer contact, knowing that there are relatively few opportunities to make a positive impression. This is particularly important for manufacturers of consumer goods, most of whom sell through intermediaries or retailers and rarely meet the final consumers.

For this sector, warranty claims must be well administered. We recently had some problems with a Britax child safety seat. Anyone who has had problems with a product knows that the thought of packaging up the goods to send them back to the factory is probably enough to deter them from complaining. It is easier to go out and buy another (competitor's) product. Britax Customer Service was easy to contact and extremely helpful, promising a replacement would be delivered by courier two days later. All we needed to do then was to put the damaged seat in the replacement box and take it to the nearest Post Office. The replacement arrived on time, and we immediately noticed that the faulty area had been redesigned to prevent the problem reoccurring. Two points emerge from this example. Britax made it clear that their warranty meant something and this was evidenced by the fact that it was very easy to deal with them. Rapid feedback from customers has enabled them to respond to problems not discovered at the prototype stage, and this tends to build rather than destroy customer confidence.

Principles of initial response

The principles that can be drawn out of these examples are:

- Make it easy for the customer to contact the right person to solve their problem quickly
- Make sure that the customer knows that the problem will be taken care of as soon as is possible

- Make sure that you acknowledge the customer's presence as soon as is possible
- Make sure that you make a meaningful response as soon as is feasible, explaining what will happen, and when.

When is the job completed?

Although the wish of all customers may be to own products that never break down, perfection is not yet within the grasp of many. Electronically based products are moving to a state where there are few if any repairs required. For products which are mechanically based and relatively complex, some breakdowns may occur during the economic lifetime, but even so, the frequency of unforeseen problems is reducing rapidly and many customer support providers would see the emphasis on pre-ventative maintenance rather than dealing with failure.

There are some products that must never break down. These will include equipment such as life support machines and computers that control critical operations. The approach to this problem is to build 'redundancy' into the products and systems. Thus, 'Never Fail' computers have a number of boards that duplicate functions enabling the computer to continue operating at virtually full power even when a board has failed. In fact, it is part of the sales demonstration to remove boards as the machine is running, showing that nothing disastrous happens. Clearly this type of product is expensive to manufacture and purchase.

Apart from relatively inexpensive consumer items, most products require some form of service, maintenance or repair at intervals in their lifetime, although this interval may well be increasing. The customer support manager must decide upon the level of service support to be provided.

The service level trade-off

Successful managers will need to understand the trade-offs that currently exist. The customer may well wish for immediate service at very low cost, though most would probably agree that this is impractical. The danger with using the term trade-off is that it can imply that the organisation is complacent, not wishing to improve. The consistently successful organi-sations are those which refuse to accept trade-offs and work hard to minimise them, while in the short term they understand how best to manage the trade-off to gain advantage.

The Service Manager must understand the customer's priorities. In setting the level of support to be provided, there are two cost dimensions to be considered:

- The cost of providing a higher level of service support to the customer
- The cost to the customer of the product not being available, which of course includes an assessment of the likelihood of there being alternatives readily available. If the electric toaster fails, toast can still be made using the oven grill or perhaps by lighting a fire.

In other words, there comes a time when improving on service response time is either too expensive or irrelevant to the customer. Response times in the computer service industry provide a good example of the change that takes place over time. Over the last 20 years 'acceptable' target response times have successively decreased from 24 hours to eight hours and finally to two hours. We visited one company that set a target of one hour 20 minutes, and measured its average achievement at one hour 18 minutes.

In general, though, there is no real pressure now to decrease response times still further, the emphasis being on the ability of the service despatcher to give an accurate time of arrival on site, with all the necessary information and spares to be able to solve the problem in that one visit. In fact there has been a distinct move towards a certain amount of response time 'tailoring' to provide for rapid response to ensure maximum uptime in critical areas of the customer's business with lower level response elsewhere. In many cases this enables the service organisation to provide very rapid support where it matters most at a lower overall price to the customer. If relatively few sites are now designated as truly critical this should allow sufficient focus to ensure key response times are maintained.

To ensure that there is no misunderstanding, we must emphasise that being able to quote an exact time of arrival does not mean that you can be as late as you like. Clearly there are still minimum response times to be achieved, but the message is that it is becoming less likely that you will gain competitive advantage beyond a given point by improving response.

Fig. 4.1a shows a typical distribution of actual response times against a target time of four hours. Although the average performance may be acceptable at four hours, the spread of response means that some customers will receive an inferior service. By providing a split level service as shown in Fig. 4.1b, the average performance is unchanged, but customer-sensitive applications will be better supported. If this better premium service can be linked to a lower level of guaranteed response for non-critical applications, say five hours in this case, customer satisfaction levels should rise at marginal cost to the service provider.

Decreasing service times

Most service providers must find ways of decreasing their Mean Time To Repair (MTTR) for reasons of improving efficiency and increasing uptime for the customer.

This is an objective shared by all service providers, but becomes a key task as overall demand on the customer support organisation increases. Those service organisations which have vast armies of Regulars (Service Engineers) or depend for their service on a network of Mercenaries (Dealers) are likely to set increasingly tight targets for MTTR and to devote significant effort to designing 'serviceability' into the product.

In our 1987 survey of after sales service in UK manufacturing we found that in the electronics sector, MTTRs averaged around two hours and that organisations were working hard to decrease this still further. For more complex products, especially those with numbers of mechanical or electro mechanical systems, MTTRs averaged over 14 hours, and some companies reported times considerably longer than these. An extreme MTTR value would be several months for something like a power station turbine or boiler overhaul.

Most manufacturers claim to consider service demands in finalising designs, but a survey carried out by Keith Goffin in 1988 suggested that the scope of areas covered at the design stage varied dramatically and was often limited to improving product reliability. Unfortunately much design for serviceability takes place at a relatively late stage in the process and since the Pareto effect applies here such that 80 per cent of the design is generally fixed after 20 per cent of the design leadtime, much so-called design for service and support is little more than a limited veto rather than a major element in the design philosophy.

The Caterpillar Tractor Company is one of the best examples of an organisation that endeavours to give design for serviceability its true importance. Caterpillar sets increasingly demanding targets for the time taken to maintain its equipment or to replace a wearing component. It is surprising what can be achieved by quick release fasteners and by standardisation when serviceability becomes a priority for the designer.

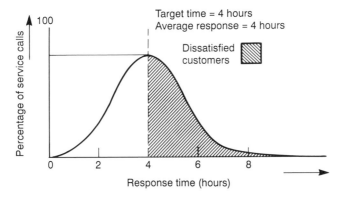

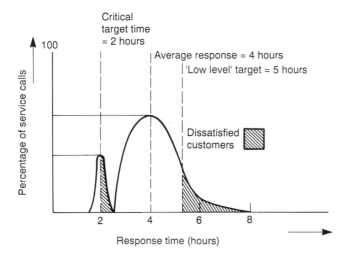

Figure 4.1(a) Response time performance: standard 4 hour response

Figure 4.2(b) Response time performance: 2 level response

There is certainly a trend to keep the product running by replacing modules or subassemblies rather than repairing on site. This allows rapid repair, which for the industrial customer is often more important than cost. It is our view that this practice will tend to increase.

Centralised service functions or 'close to customer'?

Most organisation are under cost pressure to centralise both materials and people. Many also have the problem of needing to support an ever increasing range of products as new lines are introduced but the old ones remain, having given an assurance to support them for a period of years after production has ceased.

It is unlikely that every service engineer will have the necessary expertise to carry out the full range of repairs on every piece of equipment. The trade-off to be managed here is that of cost of service provision versus a customer confidence factor of having service personnel close at hand. Some companies manage this by having regional organisations which are competent to tackle the majority of service problems but provide support from a central team of product specialists if there is the need for help to resolve more difficult problems.

As communication and distribution networks become ever more effective and products become more reliable, the continuing trend will be towards fewer regional service centres and more centralised service delivery. In this case, close attention must be paid to ensuring that customer confidence is maintained, perhaps by organising equipment check-up visits even when all is well to maintain customer contact.

Maintaining maximum uptime

Perhaps it is an obvious statement that a customer has bought equipment or a system for use rather than for it to be always under repair. A recent advertisement for Citroen cars was to the effect that they loved roads and hated garages. We think that in many industries this desire for more reliable, longer lasting products has not received the emphasis that perhaps it could. Some areas for management attention are discussed below.

Increasing reliability

Reliability is measured by MTBF. In our 1987 survey, the range of reliability was very wide indeed, ranging from as little as two months to 18 years. Alternatively MTBF may be expressed in terms of machine running time, our data indicating a range from 100 to 15,000 hours.

Where there are few mechanical parts, MTBFs may be quite high. In the Medical Electronics industry sector it is quite common for MTBFs to average four years, while the economic lifetime of such equipment is typically eight years. Thus the equipment will break down once in its life. Service becomes less of an issue in this case, though rapid repair response is still critical where a hospital may have only one piece of equipment in its intensive care ward, and the consequence of lack of availability would be serious.

The example given may not yet be typical for all industries, but there is no doubt that this trend will be followed. As customers demand more reliable equipment and cheaper service, it may become more economic to use higher specification original equipment. A burglar alarm company discovered that a small premium paid for better quality sensors used in the initial installation dramatically reduced the cost of service provided under its fixed sum service contracts. In this case the customers were happy because the system was more reliable, and the company incurred a lower cost overall. An important general point is made here that cost systems must be sensitive enough to indicate overall savings rather than merely record unit costs which often indicate the wrong course of action.

Preventative maintenance

Many customers are buying peace of mind when they take out a maintenance contract. Most companies can prove that more effective maintenance work will lead to fewer unforeseen failures, though there may still be a feeling that one shouldn't interfere with something that's working.

The reality may be that although there is a belief that maintenance is a good thing, the short term demands of delivery schedules mean that there is seldom space for it. We have known organisations that were too busy to carry out routine contracted maintenance because they were never able to get out of the vicious circle of breakdowns occurring because the service work represented an overload on the department. The end result is, in the first instance, lost service revenue through not being able to charge because contractual maintenance had not been carried out and, more seriously, deteriorating reputation with customers.

There is no substitute for making a realistic capacity plan, which allocates resources to ensuring that maintenance, particularly when it is contracted, is carried out. This may demand that some planning time is spent with customers who will only want to release equipment at times convenient to themselves.

Replace or repair?

In situations where the customer is seriously inconvenienced by the product not being available, a number of options are open to the service organisation. If the product is too complex for ultimate reliability to be possible at an economic price, the product can at least be designed for rapid service, with modules or printed circuit boards being replaced and the defective unit either disposed of or taken back for repair.

A variation on this theme may be to provide a loan machine for the duration of the repair. Obviously, it will not be economical for all organisations to have capital tied up in this way, though it could be justified as marketing expenditure in some cases. The use of courtesy cars by garages is an example of this approach.

Another alternative may be to carry out the function of the equipment under repair without providing a short term replacement as such. Toyota, for example, are investigating the possibility of providing fax facilities at some of their dealerships so that business clients can work at home when their cars are being serviced.

Remote diagnostics and predictive maintenance

For high value capital goods it may be possible to justify installing a direct line from the equipment in the customer's facility to the service organisation. A number of opportunities are now opened up for the service provider:

- It may be possible for the service organisation to detect failure before the customer is aware of it, improving the perception of service response
- In some cases, for example software, it may be possible to fix the problem through the remote line, cutting cost and response time. Again, it may be possible to solve problems before the customer is aware of them
- The ability to diagnose probable causes of failure remotely should improve the likelihood of the service engineer arriving with the correct spares to complete a 'first time fix'. Some companies despatch spares and engineers independently, increasing the utilisation of service specialists
- Using the remote link to monitor the performance of the equipment it is possible in some cases to predict that failure will occur within a given time period, allowing the service and support organisation to schedule maintenance at the most appropriate time to minimise downtime and inconvenience to the customer.

It can be seen that particularly for capital goods where the cost of downtime to the customer is prohibitive, the cost of installing and maintaining a remote link may be a small price to pay. Applications of remote monitoring are growing rapidly and already include computers, lifts and other products with microprocessor control. The problem for the service provider is how to demonstrate the value of the service given in order to justify the prices charged. If the customer doesn't see the rapid response to problems, it is a small step to thinking that nothing is being done and the service contract is now unnecessary.

Supporting customers

As products and systems become more reliable, the emphasis of the organisation moves away from the ability to fix problems (that is, reactive service), through to ensuring maximum availability, perhaps through planned maintenance. This general move in recent years to more consistent product quality and more reliable products has coincided with a new understanding that the customer doesn't just buy a product, but judges what is received on the basis of everything that the organisation does.

This shift in emphasis has meant that companies have developed broader customer support activities for the following reasons:

- Revenue earning activities are developed to replace lost service and repair income
- Actions which are more visible to the customer are emphasised in order to demonstrate the 'value' of the service and support organisation
- Close customer contact has allowed the organisation to identify broader business opportunities not necessarily directly related to the core business
- Extra service and support activities are developed to enhance or support an 'upmarket' product image.

Much of this new understanding springs from realising that the organisation may not be solely 'processing material' in the sense of turning metal and plastics into washing machines, but also 'processing customers'. In the same way that material flows through a manufacturing process, customers flow through a process as their needs are addressed. If the organisation can understand this customer process better, particularly understanding how the customer is feeling at each stage, some potential improvements may be identified.

Can the customer use the product effectively?

Most support activities are directed towards the goal of ensuring that the customer derives maximum benefit from the purchase. A customer who has paid a significant amount of money and who then uses perhaps 10 per cent of the power of the product is less likely to be satisfied with the purchase in the long run. This may be a problem generated at the selling stage where the customer was oversold a product which was not required. He was sold a computer suite when all that was required was a calculator.

It may be, of course, that some overselling is a good move as applications may be found as the customer grows in expertise. To this extent, customer support clearly starts in some cases long before the sale by providing applications advice. This has long been the practice for certain capital goods manufacturers and is spreading to the more expensive consumer goods such as sound systems and DIY equipment. Good advice, readily available, may be a powerful marketing tool.

Does the customer need training?

For all but the most basic of products some customer training is required. In fact, all products need some documentation or instruction leaflet to inform the customer as to how the product should and should not be used. Product liability legislation now puts the onus on the manufacturer to ensure safety in use, not to assume, for example, that the customer will know that electric toasters shouldn't be used in the bathroom.

Some products of course will be either so new or complex that customer training may well be offered as part of the original purchase price. There may well be continuing business here as new employees require training. We visited an engineering company who bought some manufacturing control software. Included in the purchase price was both training on how to use the software and also management education on the principles on which the package was based. After the software had been working for two years the vendor reminded the company that included in the original purchase price were some 'maintenance' days, education or training to be used as the customer decided. The customer was very impressed partly because they had forgotten about these days, but found the opportunity to revisit the basic philosophy behind the software a useful refresher which increased the effective use of the system.

Again, there is a caveat to customer training. Eventually customers will not want to pay the equivalent of the product price over again in courses to enable people to use the product effectively. Computer companies are slowly recognising that it should be easier to use their products without having a degree in computer science to enable the customer to understand their manuals. So, there is a growing trend to design the product for ease of use. In the Medical Electronics industry even the most complex products must be easy to use given the rapid turnover of nursing staff in some hospitals.

There may be a benefit to the service provider in giving effective customer training. Improper use by the customer may increase the service call-out rate which will be unwelcome particularly if the customer has a comprehensive service contract. Good customer training will also reduce damage in use and therefore warranty costs.

Is the customer happy?

For some industries at least service income is now decreasing. There may be some commercial opportunity in selling extended guarantees, giving the customer some 'peace of mind' in return for what is effectively a maintenance contract.

Organisations are increasingly seeing this area as worthy of attention for marketing product. There are a few companies that are giving broader guarantees with fewer conditions. There is nothing worse than having to employ a lawyer to go through the small print only to find that this particular circumstance is excluded. Automobile warranties are a good example of paper guarantees which often appear to be worthless for most customers because so many items are effectively excluded. This is an area which will repay attention given to it as customers become more aware of what they are getting in reality. Indeed, a guarantee or warranty which clearly limits the risk to the seller may be worse than no guarantee at all in the customer's eyes.

Also included under this heading should be the activity of customer audits, finding out whether customers are satisfied with products and service. This customer focus is fundamental for the business as a whole and is referred to in the chapters on marketing and quality. At this point it is sufficient to say that customers are often impressed that the organisation has taken the trouble to find out what they think. This dedication to quality improvement also raises customer confidence levels.

Does the customer need anything else?

As suppliers move closer to their customers it may be that further business opportunities may be identified. An example of this approach would be that of the fastener company which instead of merely supplying nuts and bolts, provides a full stock control and storage service for some of its major customers. An often quoted example is the Hartford boiler inspection service that over time built up more information about the products than the customers possessed and was able to move into a broader consultancy role as a result.

Computer companies have been quick to make a shift from selling hardware to selling 'solutions', being a mixture of hardware, software and consultancy. We know of a software supplier that now makes more money from management education. The recent move of the retailer Marks and Spencer into financial services is perhaps another example of an opportunity identified when thinking about customers' broader requirements.

Of course, it perhaps should go without saying that it is very dangerous to move into areas where you have no expertise or which will mean that management attention to the core business is diluted. The old adage that one should 'stick to the knitting' is worth remembering.

Money matters

It should be understood that adding dimensions to the service and support package has a price, and therefore enhancements must to a degree be limited by what the customer is willing to pay for. This is always difficult in that customers often want service for nothing.

There are three basic approaches to this issue:

1 Value to customer: the customer may be prepared to pay more if the inconvenience of breakdown is high.
2 Relation to product price: service is included in the original product purchase price, perhaps in the form of a warranty.
3 Cost plus: the customer is charged the cost of the service plus an acceptable margin.

Consumer goods manufacturers will tend to hide the service cost element, whereas expensive capital goods manufacturers may be able to command premium rates. If the customer is very knowledgeable as to service content and industry standards, the cost plus approach must be used.

Setting customer service and support priorities

The type of product to the supported will often determine both the structure and priorities for customer support. Fig. 4.2 illustrates the varying nature of the Customer Support task.

Product description	Customer support priorities	Customer support structure
Capital goods (high value, low volume)	Increasing MTBF Predictive maintenance Customer training Applications advice Installation & commissioning Comprehensive service support	SAS to support relatively few regulars or territorials
Industrial goods (medium value, medium volume) Consumer goods (medium value, medium volume)	Rapid response Serviceability Installation Customer documentation Ease of use Location Dealer expertise	Regulars with some mercenaries
Consumer goods (low value, high volume)	Warranties Access Customer care Spares availability Distribution network	Mercenaries (enemies)

Figure 4.2 Customer support priorities

The customer service and support organisation must be aware of current and future priorities as products move from sector to sector.

Computers, fax machines and power tools are just three examples of products which have moved from a Medium/High Value, Low Volume profile to become relatively Low Value, High Volume products. The attendant changes in customer service and support priorities have not always been so effectively managed as the product development.

Conclusion

This chapter has described the various elements of customer service and support. The objective is to enable the manager to question and review the full range of customer requirements, ensuring that no aspect is ignored. In carrying out such a review it may be that the customer service and support manager might be able to identify opportunities for the organisation to extend its operations.

A review of this kind will also allow the customer service and support manager to assess whether the organisation possesses the right mix of resources and performance measurement to deliver current customer support priorities effectively.

Checklist

1   Have you challenged the assumptions that you have made about what the customer requires in terms of service and support?

2   Have customer support priorities changed as the result of changes to product design or customer profile?

3   Are there elements of customer service and support which as yet are unexploited and may represent a source of revenue or competitive advantage?

4   Are the targets which have been set for each element now appropriate? Has the industry standard performance increased? Is there any gain to be made from increasing performance still further?

5 MARKETING AND MARKET RESEARCH

Introduction

In this chapter we will look at marketing strategy, the marketing process for customer support, pricing mechanisms, and marketing research. We will see the close link between the marketing process and the competitive strategy for the firm which we have talked about in Chapter 2 and the operational delivery of service. We will see the importance of the marketing process in creating an *image* for customer service and support.

Are we a marketing orientated organisation?

Traditionally customer service and support has been seen as a necessary evil after the sale of the product. Companies often have well developed marketing approaches to the sale of the product. Those firms selling consumer products like cars, televisions and washing machines spend large amounts on marketing. On the other hand companies making capital goods like machine tools and power generation plant have perhaps not given the same amount of effort to marketing their products. In both cases though, the marketing of the customer service and support has usually been lacking.

Why should this be? Such an approach misses an opportunity to focus on the associated needs of the customer in the use of the product and to build customer loyalty. How often in surveys of your products do you find that your customers are essentially satisfied with the product but dissatisfied with the way in which they are dealt with if they require information or during any service activity? It is easy to blame the service personnel for this failing but the fault more often lies with not really understanding the needs of the customers and users. What we are seeing is the absence of a true *marketing orientation*.

We think there are two main reasons why firms find themselves in this position. First there are those who really do see any after sales offerings as a evil which only adds costs. While many companies would deny this is their view, we see many examples of the way in which they treat their customers. Engineers do not arrive, spares are not available, contact cannot be made with the company when things go wrong. Second are those firms who do provide customer service and support and see it as being important for profits. However they make the provision on *their terms* rather than according to *what the customers want*. How many times are customers offered appointments at times which are most convenient to them rather than the service engineers? For example, most utility companies still do not offer customers evening or weekend visits, so customers who work have to take time off to get appliances repaired.

It must be clear that what needs to happen is first to understand the needs of the customers and second to make sure that those needs are satisfied. Those companies who have realised the benefits to be gained from focussing on their customers can be recognised by five obsessions:

1 customer satisfaction
2 product quality
3 listening to the customers
4 understanding the key factors for customer service
5 trying to do things better.

Can we possibly achieve these obsessions if we are only concerned with the initial sale of the product or the installation of equipment? The answer must be no. We must use *marketing* as part of the process to becoming a *customer focussed* organisation. A strong indication that an organisation has a marketing orientation is when they can say: 'We make our profits by creating opportunities to satisfy our customers' needs more effectively, within the constraints of our resources and skills limitations'. This is a very different orientation to one which focusses on the products alone. If we take a product focus we are making assumptions: either the quality of performance of the product is good enough to make the customers continue to purchase them (this may be all right for cheap products like irons and toasters which are simple to use and can be thrown away when they fail); or the costs of producing the products will always mean we can compete on price; or we only need to offer only a limited customer service and support to satisfy any safety or regulatory requirements. So if you think you are still not customer focussed and do not have a marketing orientated firm how can you make the change?

Marketing for customer focus

At its simplest level marketing is 'finding what the customer wants and providing it'. A marketing strategy is closely linked to the competitive strategy we talked about in Chapter 2. It requires an understanding of the markets and the needs of customers and what competitors are doing and of the key features which make the service offering attractive to customers. This last point is very important because if customers do not want what is on offer, no matter how good we may feel it is, the firm will fail. The steps to achieving good marketing for customer service and support are:

1   Understanding the market in relation to the customers and users and the competition. This is really the formulation of service strategy which we looked at in detail in Chapter 2.
2   Defining the critical customer service dimensions in different segments of the market.
3   Specifying the *marketing mix*, which is the way in which the whole package is delivered to the customers. The marketing mix includes six components:
(a)   The product/service/support combination or mix
(b)   The availability of the product/service/support mix in time and place
(c)   The price charged
(d)   The communication through advertising and promotion
(e)   The service people
(f)   The process of delivery
4   Monitoring performance over time to pick up changes which will inevitably lead to changes in the marketing mix.

Marketing in a customer focussed organisation is not just an isolated functional activity but one which includes everyone in the business and some outsiders. This is the concept of *relationship marketing*. There are *internal markets* concerning the people who deliver the customer service and support and there are *external markets*, including the customers, suppliers, employment markets and those who influence purchases. We must rcognise the relationship between them all and try to ensure that everyone has a shared view of what is required.

The process of marketing is closely allied to the formulation of a service strategy as can be seen from Fig. 5.1. We need to decide on the different types of customers who need to be served, whether we want to serve them and whether we have the capability. Let us start the process by first

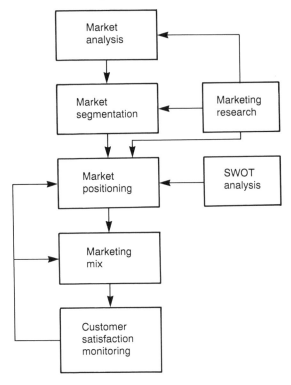

Figure 5.1   The marketing process

looking at what customers are buying and how their needs may differ
before examining the marketing mix in more detail.

What is the customer buying?

What is being offered to the customer? If we are simply selling a product
this will be the most important consideration; the product gives value.
Customer loyalty will be built on the selling process and the performance
of the product during its lifetime. However, as the amount of customer
service and support which is needed over the lifetime of the product
increases, the customer is buying a mix of tangible and intangible
elements associated with the product, the service and support. Included
in this complex mix are things associated with the product itself, the
service for the equipment, the support for customers in the use of the

product, and finally the way in which the whole process is carried out. Looking at these factors in more detail they include:

1 The product
(a) Installed price
(b) Ease of installation
(c) Reliability (MTBF)
(d) Ease of servicing
(e) Mean uptime in operation
2 Service
(a) Service price
(b) Time to fix
(c) Spares availability
(d) Maintenance contracts
(e) Flexibility of response
3 Support
(a) Customer training
(b) Documentation
(c) Consultancy
(d) Advice/problem solving
4 Process
(a) Ease of contact with the service/support people
(b) Control over the process by the individual customer
(c) Attitudes of service people
(d) Appearance of the service people and equipment
(e) Safety/trust/confidence in the service and support organisation

The customer service and support product mix will vary from firm to firm and type of product or installation. When we were considering the formulation of service strategy we saw that competitive advantage could be gained by recognising the critical parts of the product/service/support mix. We also recognised that competitiveness could be lost if we failed to deliver on the sensitive features of the hygiene factors. We can visualise this in another way which helps us in the marketing process.

The product/service/support mix can be seen as a *core* encircled by a *surround* of other features. The *core* may be the product or installation and the *surround* the service and support and the delivery process. Alternatively we may see the core as being the product and the mainten-ance service. In consequence the core is made up of the more tangible aspects of the mix and the surround less easy to define. This has impli-cations for the marketing of the surround as part of the package and for setting quality levels. Added to this is the fact that the mix between core and surround will differ for different products and customers and this leads to the *segmentation* of the market.

Are all our customers the same?

A company which installs security alarms has as customers major retailers, local authorities, corner shops and residential home owners. Would we expect them to have different needs? A first guess would be yes. Would we expect the company to deliver a different service to them all? Again we might answer yes. Do they deliver a different service to their various customers? Alas, the answer is, for the most part, no. Unfortunately what we see with this example is repeated for many service organisations. It reflects a lack of any clear attempt to understand the needs of different customers and to tailor the customer service and support to match them.

We might ask why it is necessary to recognise differences between groups of customers. Firstly, if we do not, we may provide a service which fails really to meet the needs of *any* customers in the total market. Secondly, we might be increasing our costs by offering too high service levels for what most of the market wants. Thirdly, we will probably never really understand what our customers value and hence find it difficult to retain customers over a long period of time. Finally, we may be wasting marketing resources by not concentrating on our best customers, who generate either current or potential profits.

The way forward is to *segment* the market and to *position* our offerings in different markets we have identified.

Segmenting the market

What approaches are there to help us decide which are the best ways to separate our total customers into groups? The work we have already done to formulate a service strategy is closely linked to market segmentation and positioning. We essentially have to look for answers to the following questions:

1   In what ways can we divide the total market?
2   What are the needs of the different segments?
3   Which of the groups do we want to serve?

In dividing the market into segments we are looking for characteristics which give some clear and meaningful differences. It is not an exact science, so the more we already know about the market the easier the process is likely to be. However, there are a number of factors which we might want to take into consideration as the oasis for segmentation. These fall into two categories: *customer characteristics* and *customer responses*.

By customer characteristics we mean any factors which give a clear statement about the customer which are independent of their use of the service. Customer characteristics would include:

- *Geography*: The location of customers and their coverage, urban or rural, national or regional, national or international
- *Demography*: Age and sex
- *Physchography*: life style, social class, personality.

Customer responses are dependent on how the customers buy and use the product/service/support package. They include both objective and subjective measures:

- *User type*: The type of user of the service (well informed and expert or needing hand holding)
- *Purchasing power*: The larger the user the greater may be the ability of the customer to influence the price and level of service
- *Size*: A commonly used split on size is between major accounts and smaller customers
- *Nature of the relationship*: Long standing as against new customers
- *Reasons for purchasing*: Imposed by regulation as compared with a valued offering
- *Importance of the service*: Quick response rather than tolerating an acceptable delay
- *Industry sector*: Manufacturing, retail or commercial
- *Knowledge*: The extent to which the customer recognises the benefits of the service and support
- *Growth potential*: Groups of customers or potential customers who may provide rapid growth in business
- *Price*: The sensitivity of the customer to the price of the service and the support.

Once we have the factors which seem most appropriate in our markets for grouping present and potential customers we need to identify the most important features for each of the groups by developing independent customer profiles for each segment. A simplified example of the process is given in Fig. 5.2 for a customer service and support operation for a company supplying electric motors.

	International	*National*	*Small companies*
Main requirements	Coverage/Expertise	Reputation/Price	Price
Critical factors* (5 = Important, 0 = Not important)			
Product	4	4	5
Service	5	5	3
Support	5	3	2
Process	4	4	3
Price	2	3	5

* Assessed on a scale 1–5

Figure 5.2 Market segmentation

The market for the product/service/support package has been segmented on the basis of the size and coverage of the customers as international, national or small independents. The company is also able to identify some of the factors which influence the buying behaviour for the various segments. The customer service and support profiles for each segment using our customer service and support profile has been carried out for each segment to identify the critical factors. We can see that there are clear differences in the attitudes of the three segments to the product, the service, the support, the process of delivery, and the price charged.

Having segmented the market for customer service and support we now need to decide whether we want to be involved in all segments of the market and, more importantly, whether we have the capabilities to deliver to a chosen sector. There is always the danger of coming up with 'wish statements' at this stage. It may seem attractive to be involved in the highest quality high margin market, but if our resources are not up to it we will undoubtedly fail. We may make a more rational judgement by recognising the potential of the market but realise we are not able to finance the improvement in resources to make an entry possible, at least at the present time.

Do we want to be part of a market?

Deciding whether to enter a particular market sector for customer service and support depends on a number of factors. These are linked to the sale of the original product and may in consequence limit the degree of choice we have. So in many cases the decision is linked to the overall strategy of the organisation on the products and markets it is to serve. In reaching a decision on our markets we might be addressing the following questions:

1 How important is it for us to service and support the product? There may be laws, regulations or safety requirements which make this necessary.

2 Do customers for the product expect that we will offer service and support rather than leave it to third parties? Does this influence future sales?

3 If we have a choice will the customer service and support activity give us sufficient returns for it to be profitable?

4 Can we afford to provide the resources to provide service and support in a particular segment of the market?

5 Are we good enough to operate in a particular market segment? A route to answering this question is by way of a *SWOT Analysis*, where we try to identify for each segment our *strengths* and *weaknesses* in comparison to the competition, and the *opportunities* and *threats* which result from the strengths and weaknesses.

It is clear that answering these questions must involve not only a marketing activity as it is part of the formulation of strategy we examined in Chapter 2. It is part of the marketing process, however, to establish how our products may be *positioned* in the market sectors relative to our competitors.

Positioning customer service and support

Positioning of our customer service and support in each of the market segments we have identified requires a knowledge of what is wanted by customers in that segment; what the competition is offering (here we are interested in both the composition of the customer service and support mix and also the quality levels); and our own performance (here we may use the results of our SWOT Analysis and an assessment of performance on the customer service dimensions relative to our competitors – see Chapter 2, on strategy formulation).

Our aim is to position our customer service and support in the market in a way which helps our customer recognise our position clearly. This is the idea behind the concept of *branding*. We may reinforce our positioning of our brand through advertising and we may include it in our mission statement. British Airways ('The world's favourite airline') and Avis car rental ('We try harder') are examples of this type of explicit positioning. If we do not consciously position a product the customers are likely to do it for us – 'The service company which never turns up on time', 'The most authoritarian service company'.

We need to be clear on the market positioning because it then allows us to make sure that our marketing mix of product/service/support, availability, price, communication, people and process are correct to meet the position. So if we are to position ourselves in the 'high quality' position it is going to be necessary to charge higher prices, spend more on advertising and have well trained service people well supported by equipment and systems.

Positioning maps are a useful tool for presenting our position in one market relative to other competitors. Fig. 5.3 shows a positioning map for the international company's market segments we created earlier for our customer service and support company. We have taken the two most important criteria in that market segment, servicing of the product and support for the customer, and placed ourselves on the map against the axes of high and low service, and high and low support. Our competitors in this market have been positioned in a similar way based on the research we have done. We can see that if we are to be among the best in the market we need to move more in the direction presently occupied by Elecspeed by improving or increasing our level of customer support.

We would want to make positioning maps for all of the market segments so that we can then look at the marketing mix we are using to see if it is appropriate for each segment or whether it needs changing.

Reviewing the marketing mix

The marketing mix is simply the combination of elements which enables us to reach our targeted customer with the offering they want. The elements are not independent but interact. This interaction increases the complexity of our task. Altering one may change another, for example if we reduce the price we may be unable to spend the same amount on advertising. The goal is to make the marketing mix match as closely as

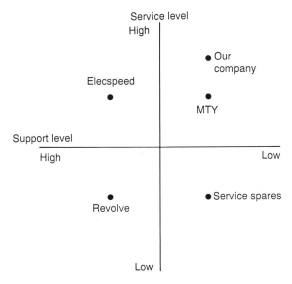

Figure 5.3 Service and support positioning map

possible the position we wish to achieve in a market. So we must look at what is included within each of the elements.

The product/service/support combination

In our earlier discussion of what the customer is buying and market segmentation we saw that for different markets we need to design the product/service/support package to match the needs of the market sector and the position we want to occupy in the sector. This is clearly a complex issue and involves not only marketing in its resolution, but also should illustrate to customer service and support managers the importance of using marketing knowledge in the design of all aspects of the product/service/support mix. For example, the importance of product design in determining ease of installation and servicing is becoming more widely recognised, even if it is not always implemented. This approach needs to be extended to consideration of the critical elements of support, for instance documentation, advice and spares provision.

Getting to the customers

The second part of the marketing mix is concerned with getting the customer service and support to the customers. Where and how is it made available? Deciding on how we achieve this requires both a strategic consideration of the choices between doing it ourselves, using agents or dealers, or leaving it to third parties. The 'military model' (Chapter 3) shows how our decision is often influenced by how much in-house control we want to keep in the face of growing service intensity. From a marketing standpoint the question is, how do we influence the distribution channels which are created by the different choices?

Let us look at a number of typical distribution channels as shown in Fig. 5.4. These show the number of intermediaries between the original manufacturers of equipment and the customer/user when the equipment/product is first bought. It also shows the typical ways in which service and support is delivered. Clearly the longer the distribution channel from the original manufacturer the lower the possibility of influencing what is happening for the end user. This has real implications for the use of marketing tools to position the service and support. It will affect advertising and promotion and with a long chain may mean that the customers of the end product are not even known to the manufacturing company. For instance, a manufacturer of electric showers, installed either by specialists who are not controlled by the company or DIY by the users, finds it very difficult to identify who the end users of their showers really are.

For our purposes it is important to see the influence of product distribution channels on our ability to market customer service and support. If we are not manufacturers the question still applies because we need to be able to influence through marketing what customers can expect from our customer service and support.

How much do we charge?

One of the most important marketing decisions is deciding what to charge for customer service and support. The price must be related in some way to the benefits which the customers perceive they gain. We have already seen this with the Strategy Compass when we set a strategic direction based on the interaction between perceived added value and price.

In considering pricing, we need to take three things into account:

1   The value of the customer service and support to the customer
2   The cost of providing the service and support
3   Actions taken by competitors to change either the price they charge or the nature of their offering.

Value of customer service and support

The value to the customer is not easy to set; it may be linked to low price, or to the quality of the service as delivered, or relieving customers of the psychological effects of worrying about failure of equipment. The last point is important for customer service and support operations where one of the benefits is customers' peace of mind. It may also be an insurance against the customer having to expend resources in the event of failure of a product in the future. We may try to bring out the critical things which make up value but ultimately we have to rely on the *net value* to the customer, being 'all the perceived benefits from customer service and support less the perceived costs of not having it or the costs for the customers of doing all or part of the process themselves'.

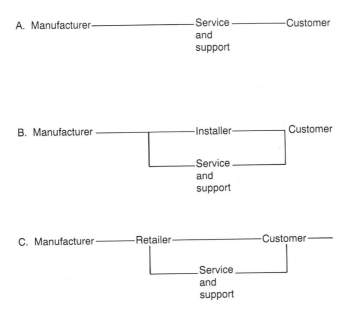

Figure 5.4 Marketing distribution channels

Costs

The prices which are charged need to be related to the costs of providing the service and support if profit margins for service and support are to be maintained. This may not apply if the cost of the service and support is taken as part of the overall cost of sales of the products. In some cases customer service and support is in effect being offered as a loss leader. We will assume that the prices charged for customer service and support determine our profit margins. So reducing prices for customer service and support without reducing costs will lead to failure in the long term. Margins will become too lean with the result that there will be insufficient contribution to cover overheads.

One of the main problems is in determining true costs for the provision of the customer service and support when there are a range of offerings. For example the cost of a two hour response is going to be higher than for a 24 hour response but by how much? If it is delivered as part of the same operation using the same response centre and engineers it may be difficult to separate accurately. It is possible to make some estimate of the volume of service and support which is needed to be covered by a *break-even analysis*, taking into account *fixed costs*, *variable costs* and *total costs*.

The *fixed costs* include the costs of equipment, transport, salaries and information systems. *Variable costs* are related to the service intensity and include fuel costs, overtime, hiring subcontractors and spares (if they are not charged separately). The *total costs* are the sum of the variable and the fixed costs. The point at which the return from charges to the customers becomes more than the total costs is the break-even point above which a profit is being generated.

The break-even analysis is useful for determining whether a particular market segment is profitable. While it may be difficult to assign the correct proportion of fixed costs to one segment, it is possible to establish the *contribution* from customers in that segment to cover fixed costs and other overheads.

Setting the price

A knowledge of the costs and the value to the customers allows prices to be set on the basis of:

- The costs plus a margin. This is a common way of charging for an isolated event where time and materials can be easily measured

- The value to the customer of the customer service and support. The implication is that the offering is highly differentiated so that price is not an issue for the customer
- The newness of what is being offered
- The prices being charged by our competitors for their services
- Linking the service price to the price of the original product. The extent to which this is possible may depend on the customers' expectation of the performance of the product. If the expectation is for high reliability it may be more difficult to charge high prices for customer service and support, unless the benefits of support can be emphasised in the selling process
- Taking into account the sensitivity to price in a particular market. If prices are openly quoted by all competitors it may reduce the flexibility for changing our prices. If the customer requires a detailed quotation of work done or to be carried out, it may have a similar effect of limiting flexibility
- The most common approach for setting the basic price charged for customer service and support is the cost plus approach. This places great reliance on the accuracy of costing systems if the contribution to fixed costs and profits from a service and support mix is to be a true representation of reality.

Communications with customers: creating the image

We are aware of the power of advertising and selling in our personal lives. For example, on a visit to the supermarket we pick goods often without really understanding why we choose one product in preference to another. Also, the actions of a salesperson in a clothes shop may mean we come out with the coat which we had not really intended to buy at that time. Both of these examples demonstrate the importance of *communication* in the marketing mix. They also show the two main methods of communication: *impersonal* and *personal*. These two make up the *communications mix* and they both inform and create the image.

Impersonal communications

Impersonal communications are essentially those concerned with advertising, sales promotions, and publicity. Advertising for customer service and support tends to be far less than for the products themselves. Any advertising which does occur is in the form of direct mail included with billing (commonly used by utilities) or in literature describing service and support contracts. Retailers may also advertise service and support within their stores rather than in media advertising.

We also see newsletters for staff and customers being used as a means of reaching existing customers. However, there are signs of change in those markets where it is becoming more difficult to differentiate products on performance. In the car industry a number of companies now promote service and support as a major component of their offering and not just the performance of the car.

Publicity is often a critical factor in the communication of customer service and support. Some publicity may be given in the media, as for the regulated companies such as telecommunications and the utilities, where their regulators publish details of their service performance. Also word of mouth between customers becomes a crucial method of publicity. Customers who have good service experiences will tell about five other people while those having a bad experience will tell ten others.

It is our feeling that customer service and support organisations could do more to communicate the benefits of their offerings through the use of the full mix of impersonal communications. It would help existing and potential customers to understand clearly what is being offered to them.

Personal communications

Personal communication concerns the use of personal selling of customer service and support. This is the most common form of communication used, and is found more for the service and support associated with the capital goods end of the capital goods – consumer products spectrum. The advantages of personal selling are clear. It is a two-way form of communication so there is the opportunity for customers to ask questions about what is being offered, for the salesperson to relate the benefits to the customer's own circumstances, and for the salesperson to ask for an order.

The selling of customer service and support is often part of the sale of the initial product and while this linking may be beneficial many organisations may be losing opportunities for maximising returns from customer service and support.

People and delivery process

The reason why we include people and delivery processes as part of the marketing mix for customer service and support is their visibility to the customers. In services generally, unlike manufacturing, the customers form part of the process so they know what is going on or they see what is happening. In consequence, what happens in the operational delivery of the customer service and support needs to match the other parts of the marketing mix. Otherwise, customers may be told to expect one thing from advertising and experience something different and worse in practice.

At one time field service operations considered it was only necessary to turn up and complete the job as though the customers were, at best, a burden to be tolerated. There is now greater recognition of the behaviour of service personnel and of their appearance. We have dealt in more detail with these and other aspects when we looked at managing the service encounter and service quality.

How well are we doing?: a customer satisfaction index

Whether or not our customers are satisfied with our delivery of customer service and support will depend on their prior expectations, based on marketing activities and our operational capabilities. Many service organisations are now trying to monitor their performance by way of a *customer satisfaction index.*

The index is determined by one of the marketing research techniques which we will look at in more detail later. Essentially we wish to gain an understanding of our customers' level of satisfaction with the main elements of the product/service/support package. We may in some cases give a weighting to different elements depending on their importance. The customer satisfaction index is the aggregation of the scores from a sample of customers into a single value. Whereas the index may have no absolute value it does provide a means of tracking trends in customer satisfaction for customer service and support.

Techniques for understanding customers

At this point we want to review the techniques which can be used to gain knowledge of present or potential customers. These techniques come under the heading of *marketing research*. We have already made extensive use of marketing information in our discussions so far of segmentation, positioning and marketing mix. The techniques which can be used to gain this information fall into two groups: information gained *externally* through approaches to customers or from publicly available information like trade surveys; and information which is available *internally* from the result of business activity or from service personnel.

The use of questionnaires

Questionnaires are a powerful method of gathering information on customer service and support from customers and from service personnel. There are three basic ways of administering questionnaires:

1   *Face to face* using an interviewer. This is costly and limits the number of people but it has the advantage that the interviewer can explain questions.
2   *By phone.* This is cheaper than face to face but does not allow detailed questions to be asked.
3   *By post.* This method has the lowest unit cost and there may be problems persuading a large enough number of people to reply. It also needs careful attention to the design of the questionnaire to avoid ambiguity in the questions.

All questionnaires require a degree of skill in their design to make the questions clear to their audience, so that the result from the analysis is reliable. A pilot study, using a small number of customers, is a way of reducing the risk of poor design.

Interviews

An extension of the questionnaire process is for us to ask customers to talk about their experiences of our service and support either individually or in groups. This allows us to ask more open-ended questions and to allow the unexpected reaction to emerge. For example, they may be asked to describe their experiences of good and bad service; this process helps to identify with whom our customers are comparing us.

Secondary information

In research terms questionnaires and interviews result in primary data which we have collected ourselves. We often want to combine these results with other secondary information which can be gained from trade associations, newspapers, consultants' reports and any other material which gives a view on the markets we are serving. Here we are often looking for changes which may affect the need for our services. For example, a security company makes use of published crime statistics and police reports to predict likely volume of demand in different market sectors.

Extending the marketing role: enhancing the image

Increasingly organisations are seeing the benefit of the role of marketing being extended to a wider audience than customers. The reasons for this are evident; the provision of good service and support requires *relations* with not only customers but also suppliers, users, public bodies and distributors. *Relationship marketing* attempts to reach all parties who have an interest in a service whether as customers or users, service personnel, or other stakeholders. Consequently a number of 'markets' can be identified:

- *Customer markets*: Clearly we know we need to keep existing customers and to gain new ones through the marketing process
- *Supplier markets*: We need to have suppliers either of materials or services who are committed over a long period to supporting our levels of quality for service and support
- *Employee markets*: Staff within a service organisation often complain they are unclear as to what is required of them. Internal marketing through training, procedures and the use of videos forms a powerful way of increasing shared values and goals
- *Influencer/referral markets*: We need to maintain contact and communication with those individuals and institutions who can either influence the purchases or refer business. For instance, being on approved lists of service and support providers can be critical in some sectors.

The most important step is to recognise those who fall into different categories and to review just how they are being included in market research and in the marketing communication processes.

Conclusion

In this chapter we have looked at the role of marketing in customer service and support. We have identified the importance of understanding the needs of different customers and of trying to group them into segments which have characteristic needs. We have looked at the methods of positioning service and support in different segments of the market and of developing a marketing mix to serve that market. Finally we have recognised the widening role of marketing to include not just customer markets but all who contribute to the provision of the service and support and those who influence purchase. The use of marketing to create an image for service and support is seen as one of the most important marketing activities.

Checklist

1   Are you able to segment your customers into different groups?

2   Do you know what your customers want in the various segments?

3   Do you use marketing research techniques to improve your understanding of your markets?

4   Do you gather information from all the relationship markets?

5   Do you consciously position where you want to be in a market segment relative to the competition?

6   Do you communicate in different ways to your various market segments?

7   Do you communicate with all of your relationship markets?

8   Do you know the products and prices and cost structures of your main competitors?

9   Do you set your prices on a rational basis or could you be more pro-active and increase contributions?

10   Do you try to match your service delivery to the needs of customers in the various segments?

11   Do you measure the results of any marketing actions through a customer satisfaction index?

6 CUSTOMER SERVICE AND SUPPORT DELIVERY – MANAGING THE CONTACT WITH CUSTOMERS

Introduction

Each customer transaction, whether it be a major training programme, routine maintenance or 'minor' telephone enquiry, is an opportunity for the organisation's reputation to be enhanced or destroyed. Richard Normann and Jan Carlzon have used the term 'Moments of Truth' to encapsulate the principle that customers judge the whole of the operation by the parts which they can see and understand.

Carlzon says that for the airline SAS there may be 50,000 'Moments of Truth' each day. A customer may wonder how the airline can maintain a complex aircraft and keep it flying safely if it cannot ensure that a passenger's luggage gets to the right place at the right time. This may seem unfair when viewed objectively in that the airline may be superb technically, but what the customers perceive to be good or bad is all that matters. Customers form their own judgement as to whether or not they have received value for money.

The 1980s saw a large number of customer care programmes which were, for the most part, unsuccessful or at best short-lived. The least effective were the 'smile' campaigns, ineffective because you can't make silk purses out of sows' ears. Some staff should never be given jobs which entail a significant degree of customer contact because their personality is such that no amount of training will make them appear friendly and sympathetic. If the service delivery design is flawed, 'smile' campaigns add insult to injury. The question 'Is every thing all right?' can be the final straw.

W. Edwards Deming along with other Quality Management gurus asserts that the people involved in the process are not the root cause of quality problems. For the most part, people prefer to do a good job rather than a poor one. He rightly states that attention must be paid to improving the systems and processes rather than exhorting people to do better.

This is a recipe for disillusionment if failure is built into the system anyway.

In this chapter we will examine the three main aspects of service delivery which make up the Service Delivery Triangle (Fig. 6.1). We will discuss the main categories of resources employed in the service system, the organisation or configuration of these resources, and the flow of people, information and material through the organisation. In this chapter we will concentrate on the direct impact these decisions have on the way that the customer views the service organisation as a whole.

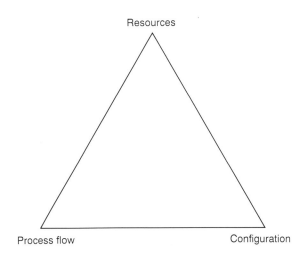

Figure 6.1 Service delivery triangle

One final word. Customers are like a well known lager, they get to places in companies they are not expected to reach. It is not sufficient to legislate that they will be dealt with only by those staff designated as 'customer service'. Customers will get everywhere and the organisation must be able to cope with this. Furthermore, those staff not in front-line roles must be conscious of the impact of their activities on how service is delivered and therefore perceived by customers.

Configuration: identifying the contact points

In this section we will introduce three broad issues:

1   The extent to which the organisation's operation is 'visible' to the

customer. Is the bulk of the resource cost and therefore value of the service vested in the customer contact area, or is it predominantly in a 'support' or backroom area?

2 The need to identify all customer contact points and to ensure that the required service is delivered effectively at these points.

3 The choice of location of service facilities and its effect on customer perception of the organisation.

The Front Office – Back Room framework

To assist in analysing the situation it will be helpful to think in terms of a simple model, where the operation is divided into two parts, Front Office and Back Room, the first being those areas which act as the interface between the organisation and its customers and the second, areas behind the scenes where 'production' often takes place. So, for a Customer Service and Support organisation, the Front Office will include telephone response centre staff and service engineers, whilst the Back Room might include repair staff and the Information Systems used to control the service activity.

An important design decision relates to the extent to which the Front Office is used mainly as a contact point rather than the place where the bulk of the work is carried out. An illustration from computer service will help. In the early years of main-frame computers much service work was carried out in the Front Office with repairs effected on the customer's premises. To a large extent, this contact was unexploited, the attention being almost exclusively focussed on repairing the equipment rather than on creating a good impression with the customer. Today, the Front Office activities are very much reduced, components and assemblies being rapidly replaced rather than repaired. Repair of modules or portable equipment takes place in a Back Room workshop and is no longer visible to the customer. The opportunities to make a good impression on the customer are proportionately diminished. Of course, the equipment itself is far more reliable and the customer is not inconvenienced which is probably more important than delivering a high quality repair service.

It may be possible to choose between carrying out work in the Front Office or the Back Room. If the customer is present when the bulk of the work is done, the potential for disruption and therefore inefficiency is greater. On the other hand, the service may be carried out predominately in the Back Room, which will be more efficient but possibly less effective in terms of enhancing the customers' perception of the quality of the service. Fig. 6.2 indicates the implications of the choice of Front Office or Back Room organisation.

	Front office dominant	Back room dominant
Front office role	Service Delivery Communication Diagnosis	Contact Communication Access to Organisation
Front office staff	Technical experts with good customer skills	Interpersonal skills with some technical knowledge
Back room role	To provide support service to front office	To carry out service delivery
Back room staff	May be perceived as inferior to front office staff	Technical experts with little customer contact
Challenge	— To maintain consistent service standards — Quality at acceptable cost — To communicate effectively with back room — To involve back room staff where possible	— To make standard service appear special to individual customers — For back room staff to understand problems of front office — To ensure timely communication with front office

Figure 6.2   Front office – back room organisation

Many high volume demand servie companies have moved towards the situation where the bulk of the work content is carried out in the Back Room. In this case they must work very hard to make sure that the very limited customer contact is effective in conveying the impression of a competent organisation which will look after the customers' requirements. The use of remote diagnostics and other call avoidance techniques have moved organisations from Front Office to Back Room dominance and the implications of this move must be fully addressed.

Some organisations have made a decision to move in the opposite direction. A good example of this approach is the car repair workshop which encourages the customer to come into the workshop, to discuss any problems directly with the technician working on the car, and, if so desired, to stay and watch the work. This may cause some delay and the technician must be able to deal with customers as well as having product skills, but there is no doubt that it presents an opportunity to create customer confidence in the organisation. Clearly there is an element of external and internal marketing in the process. Meeting customers more regularly is more effective in creating customer focus than stirring speeches.

Face to face customer contact

Most services contain an element of face to face customer contact. Even if remote diagnostics are employed and products become ever more reliable, the customer will still occasionally meet a representative of the company. Service Engineers may still carry out some repairs on site or perform routine maintenance tasks. In fact there is a case for creating such opportunities so that the customer can see that the support organisation still exists and has a valuable role to play. A reduction in breakdown calls should allow the Customer Service and Support Manager the opportunity to schedule goodwill calls to make sure that customers are satisfied with product and service.

In managing face to face customer contact, the following points should be considered:

- People who regularly deal with customers should be recruited for their interpersonal skills. The 'excellent' service organisations are spending more money on recruitment, recognising that training only enhances talent which already exists. We have all seen the face above the 'At Your Service' badge which says at a glance that too much should not be expected
- Even those who are not designated as front line contact staff meet customers sometimes. We should not expect them to know instinctively the right thing to say or to understand the impact of their actions on customer perception. Some basic customer awareness training will be worthwhile, particularly if this includes some controlled exposure to real customer demands
- A reliance on restrictive rules and procedures is unlikely to produce a 'golden moment'. Customers are aware of the attitude behind the action. Positive service attitudes are more likely to be produced by positive motivation and management example than by sets of commands
- Prolonged contact with customers can lead to deterioration in service performance or 'burn-out'. The effects of burn-out can be minimised by consciously restricting the time spent in customer contact without respite, developing the service team to provide support, and ensuring that sufficient training and resources are available to perform the task.

Telephone contact

Telephone contact is the prime customer contact for many service and support organisations. The voice at the end of the telephone line is likely to be the initial contact at a bad time (the customer's equipment has just failed at the worst possible time) and thus any perceived lack of care or professionalism will be magnified many times over. A specific problem is that neither speaker can see the reaction of the other. The service provider must put in extra words or acknowledgements to emphasise that the customer is being attended to.

As with face to face contact, some people have a rather better telephone manner than others, though even the worst can be improved to some extent. Again, the 'excellent' service providers have worked hard to ensure that their telephone response is an asset and not a barrier to service.

Some examples of the approach to managing telephone contact include:

- Monitoring the time customers wait for their call to be answered against a specified target (typically three rings)
- Provision of a single, easily remembered phone number for all customer transactions
- Effective capacity management of the telephone network to allow call switching from centre to centre to smooth load
- Thorough training of telephone contact staff in both interpersonal skills and product knowledge. The technical knowledge allows some initial advice to be given. This may be in the form of simple equipment checks to go through or safety advice as, for example, to open all windows in the event of a suspected gas leak. The fact that these people know something about the product increases customer confidence and also increases the likelihood that accurate information will be gained from the customer to initiate the appropriate service response
- Design of working environment to facilitate teamwork and to enable rapid access to information when required. We visited a medical equipment manufacturer's response centre which is designed around a central console equipped with screens for the service provider to call up prompts for each product in the range. A number of product specialists are positioned at desks behind the console ready to give advice or take over the call if necessary
- Some callers will have to wait because capacity to ensure immediate

response at all times would be extremely expensive. The software company in America, Microsoft, has recently incorporated a live disc jockey in its telephone centre. In addition to music and sales promotions, information is given as to the current average wait: 'If you have been waiting five minutes, your call is about to be answered'. Callers have been known to ask to be put back on hold to continue listening!

Many organisations undertake telephone training spasmodically. There is no doubt that training using role play and recordings of how you react on the phone can be very powerful, but the lessons learned must be regularly reinforced if regression is to be avoided. A very powerful force for good or ill is peer pressure. Once good habits are accepted as the group norm there is a reduced need for policing tactics.

Some general points about the telephone contact:

- The person answering the telephone must work very hard to communicate their interest in solving the customer's problem as the visual dimension is lacking. It must be clear that the customer is receiving their full attention. Silences appear longer when facial reactions are not visible
- The customer wants to go through as few stages as possible before the person who can deal with the request is reached. Ideally, there should be no call transfers which carry the risk of losing the customer and building a perception of delay into the response time. To achieve this requires investment in staff and systems support
- The customer expects the representative of the company to be fully informed about all customer account details and company policies. The customer expects that the person answering the phone will have all the details of the service at his or her fingertips such as whether or not the required spares have been ordered and what the promised delivery date is
- The customer should not be left in any doubt as to what will happen as a result of the conversation, and if for any reason the promised action is unlikely to take place, the customer should be informed as soon as possible to allow him to make any necessary changes in his plans.

Paper contact

Receiving a letter or an invoice is as much a 'Moment of Truth' as meeting face to face. Organisations have spent much money to ensure that the appropriate visual impact is made by logos, facilities and equipment.

The availability of word processors should facilitate the production of documents to a consistently high standard. With accurate information systems, invoices should be correct and timely. In our service quality seminars we are amazed at the frequency with which the issue of poor documentation is highlighted. There are several manufacturers with reputations for good product quality who are renowned for submitting invoices before the goods are delivered

We recently had cause for complaint with a major building society. The complaint was generally resolved to our satisfaction, but the effect was spoilt by the fact that the first reply letter was unsigned and impersonal, just saying that it came from the Customer Service Department. It is tempting to use standard letters to save time, but there are occasions when a more personal approach is required.

Locating close to customers

The siting of service facilities is a major decision for any service business. Indeed, for some it may be one of the few differentiating factors as, for example, fast food resaurants, which attract business largely by being in the right place.

Black and Decker realised that the location of their service facilities was neither close enough to their customers nor did it convey the impression of the company they wanted. Repair centres had been set up around the UK, largely on industrial estates, away from the high street. This perhaps reflected a concentration, for service at least, on the professional user of power tools. The customer base was changing as more home owners were carrying out DIY activities. As a result, Black and Decker realised that service would have to be related far more to the needs and perceptions of consumers and this resulted in a conscious switch from industrial to high street locations. The change in location reflects the need to be close to consumers and also to ensure a consistent product/service image.

The twin issues of how close to customers and the grade of the location must be addressed. For many service companies the grade of location may not matter too much because personnel visit the customer rather than the reverse. However, the fact that there is a regional service centre within 50 miles may influence the decision to purchase when the competition relies on a national service centre which is 200 miles away. The influence of customer confidence must not be underestimated, and must be carefully balanced against the cost benefits of centralisation.

Determining the resources

The resources employed by the service and support organisation can be identified under five headings:

1 People
2 Facilities
3 Information Systems
4 Equipment
5 Materials

In this section we will identify the resources to be employed in service delivery, and the impact that the choice of resource has on customer contact. The management of people, information systems and materials are covered in later chapters.

There are inter-relationships between resources: a greater investment in one area can bring cost reductions in other areas. Many organisations have found that an investment in information systems has brought about sizeable reductions in inventory costs. We have found that the value chain approach described in Chapter 2 is a useful tool to the identification of resource linkages to improve service at lower cost. An example of this approach is included later in this chapter.

People: the right service providers

Many product-related service organisations are realising that the customer service and support personnel have many opportunities to create a positive impression. Sales staff may make the initial sale, but the customer relationship is maintained by the service and support team, salesmen perhaps making occasional visits. More organisations are recognising the role of customer support in keeping customers and identifying sales opportunities. As a result, support personnel tend to be selected more for their interpersonal skills than for their technical competence. Someone can be taught relatively simple diagnostic routines, but if they do not possess the right type of personality, there is little that can be done to change it.

An issue to be addressed is when the organisation is represented by relatively junior service staff to senior customers. We visited a security system company where the engineers stated that they were much happier dealing with systems for small business premises – where they felt comfortable with the customer – than they were when fitting major systems; this made them feel uncomfortable because they had to deal with managing directors of large companies or owners of mansions.

It is very important to match the customer and service provider. In academic terms these service providers are called 'boundary spanners', forming the bridge between the organisation and its customers. The customer's perception as to how good the service is will be influenced greatly by how good the relationship is between customer and provider. A positive bond will mean that the customer may take a relaxed view when occasionally the service falls down. A negative view will often result in the customer finding fault with the most trivial details.

A possible danger in encouraging service personnel to take a customer orientated view is that in some cases they may become more loyal to their customers than they are to the organisation. Clearly, this may not be all bad, but service managers may have to be careful to reinforce company and service team loyalty if the service engineer spends the majority of working hours on customer's premises.

For many customer service and support organisations, people represent the biggest expense, representing as much as 60 per cent of the cost of service delivery. Improving service delivery may demand further investment in the service providers:

- *Recruitment Costs*: It is important to recruit people with the right service attitudes, able to cope under pressure and sufficiently flexible to deal with situations not covered by standard procedures
- *Training Costs*: Service providers will require continuing investment in training to update product knowledge and to hone personal skills
- *Support Costs*: Service providers will feel more confident in the organisation if properly supported with good equipment and effective information systems. Scheduling is a key task, service quality being maintained when the personnel are not continually overloaded.

People: managing the customers

Customers may be a valuable resource for the service organisation. By this we mean that there are functions that customers carry out in addition to purchasing the product. As Johnston has pointed out, customers have a critical role in service delivery:

- They may perform some of the service tasks themselves as, for example, carrying out oil and water checks on a car, acting as Territorials in our Support Structure model (Chapter 3)
- They provide information to start the process (my computer has broken down), during the process (the screen works but the printer doesn't), and they provide quality feedback on the performance of goods and services providing opportunity for the organisation to improve
- In some cases they also provide part of the 'scene setting' which may convince prospective customers that this is a good company to deal with because they already deal with some well known people. Customers also perform some service for other customers, with the service organisation merely facilitating this. An example in the customer support area would be the organisation of user groups which as well as providing an interface between the company and its customers also provides opportunity for exchange of experience and business development.

In a sense, then, customers must be managed in a similar way to the organisation's employees. Investment in resources and management attention will be repaid in improvements in quality and productivity.

- *Recruitment.* Many organisations use a scatter gun approach to selling, believing that by hitting as many as possible potential customers, sufficient business will be generated. This approach may generate volume of business but is unlikely to be as profitable as being more selective as to where the largest gains are to be made. Information systems should indicate the customer groups which are likely to be most profitable for the business as a whole. Selling a computer system and maintenance package may be profitable in an office environment, but not in a retail situation. Just as you would probably not recruit an accountant with convictions for fraud, it should be unlikely that some possible customers will be approached
- *Training.* Training customers may provide a range of benefits for the service organisation. The photocopier manufacturers have discovered that providing simple 'key operator' training has reduced the call-out rate for simple problems by reducing abuse caused by ignorance as well as enabling the customers to fix small problems themselves. The turnover of staff in large retailers means that security systems installers must provide ongoing training for new people to ensure the system is correctly set at closing time thus preventing call-outs or even break-ins.

Training may also be another opportunity to impress the customer as well as generate income for the organisation. Unfortunately, this opportunity may not be fully exploited. We have worked with a power equipment manufacturer who was often required to provide operator training as a part of the purchase package. There was no training facility, an area being set aside on an ad hoc basis in under utilised parts of the factory and a training programme devised largely to keep the trainees busy rather than to impart real knowledge

● *Motivation*. Most people respond to positive motivation rather than restrictions. There may be possibilities to give discounts to customers who do not abuse the product or perhaps to give recognition to those who maximise their use of their product. An example of this second approach is the software supplier who organises a seminar for present and potential customers and asks its best customer to give a presentation on the benefits of the package. Valuable publicity may be gained by both parties

● *Dismissal*. In some cases it will be necessary to withdraw service, perhaps because invoices have not been paid, or because the product is not being used as it was intended. Dismissal is never an easy task, but it must be carried out cleanly and definitely to ensure that any adverse publicity is minimised.

A final but critical point is that greater involvement of customers in the service process may well build commitment to the organisation, and also to maintaining the quality. Higher customer involvement may lead to greater customer loyalty.

Facilities: setting the scene

Our perception of the quality of an organisation is influenced by many factors. We may not be aware that we are picking up information about the company but impressions are formed by many small and not so small events. The attitude and attentiveness of service personnel clearly has a significant impact on this process, but we should not forget the influence of the facilities employed:

● The location of premises
● Size and quality of premises
● State of repair of buildings and signage
● Broken furniture in the reception area
● Cleanliness/state of service engineer's vans

- Service personnel's appearance
- The visual impact of logos and signage

This list of details is endless, and it therefore demands constant vigilance to pick up small problems which will, if unresolved, lead to larger issues later. In managing customer contact so much depends on creating customer confidence in the organisation. A customer who has doubts about the organisation will subconsciously look for evidence of incompetence. If the facilities support the view that there are problems, the customer will demand more attention, making sure that every detail is addressed before making a commitment.

Black and Decker employed a retail consultant to advise on upgrading the layout of their Service Centres to facilitate customer contact and improve the image of the company. They found that the position and style of the service counter had a significant effect on the ease with which the service staff could communicate and therefore the customers' perception of quality.

Customer-friendly information systems

The design of information systems is covered in more depth in Chapter 11. It is worth restating the point here that a good information system can add confidence to the 'Moment of Truth'. We recently visited a retailer who had invested a considerable sum in implementing a sophisticated EPOS (Electronic Point of Sale) system which, though good at tracking usage of items, was unable to answer the predictable customer enquiry of 'when do you expect the next delivery?'.

Some information systems need only to be fairly simple to be effective at least in enhancing customer contact. The insurance salesman knows the value of recording the names of spouses, children and pets in order to give the impression of personal care. Many service engineers adopt the same approach with their contacts. British Gas and British Telecom have both developed some powerful systems which allow the person who answers the customer query to be able to respond with specific information because they have full details on the screen in front of them as they speak.

The service provider represents the whole organisation to the customer and may be expected to be able to give information on the full range of activities. The employee must, at the very least, be briefed as to how to respond in general terms before ensuring that the required information is forthcoming extremely rapidly.

Equipment: The balance between technology and people

John Naisbitt, in his book *Megatrends*, coined the phrase 'Hi-Tech, Hi-Touch' to express the idea that although we want to capitalise on the increasing power of technology, we also need the contact with people rather than disappear for ever into an isolated 'electronic cottage'. The service provider must surely be aware of this need.

The service and support manager must make decisions about the quality of equipment used following the same principles outlined in the previous section on facilities. If the service engineer doesn't have the tools of the trade the customer is unlikely to be impressed and, again, an investment in a higher level of equipment, perhaps for more rapid diagnostics, may save on overall cost.

An important decision is the extent to which the service is to be delivered through equipment/technology rather than through people. Customers may require the confidence factor which comes through meeting a person rather than being treated in a totally impersonal manner. It is worth reflecting that a person may pick up sales leads and other useful feedback whereas a machine certainly will not. The service and support organisation must learn to capitalise on those moments of direct face to face contact.

Materials: first time fix

Most customer service and support organisations must develop a clear inventory policy, knowing how much stock they must hold, in what form and where it is to be held. They must also be aware of the impact on customer service arising from changes to this inventory profile. If the inventory is not available, the customer's product can not be fixed.

An organisation must realise that 100 per cent availability of everything is unlikely to be economic even if it were possible, and understand the relative impact of a stockout of each item on ultimate customer satisfaction. Many support organisations have the problem that they are dependent on the supply of components or product from external suppliers. The service from these suppliers can rarely be improved by the use of sanctions, but rather by finding ways that the two organisations can work more effectively together to improve customer satisfaction at reduced cost.

This approach is often termed *supply chain management* and is discussed in more detail in Chapter 9. It is based on developing a partnership through sharing of information, schedules and risk to attempt to become more effective as a team. A possible outcome might be for the supplier to hold more inventory at an earlier, uncommitted stage to allow the support organisation to respond more consistently.

The chain from supplier to support organisation to dealer to customer must be understood in more detail, so that each part is clear as to how customer satisfaction at the end of the chain can be maintained. Who holds which stock at which point in the chain, along with an understanding of the length of replenishment leadtimes, are fundamental questions to address if the customer contact is to be managed more effectively.

Managing the balance of resources

We started this section indicating that an approach to improving customer perception of the quality of service delivery is to identify possibilities for resource productivity, an incremental increase in resource investment in one area saving overall cost. Fig. 6.3 develops the value chain presented in Chapter 2 to indicate how the intruder alarm company might be able to improve.

For the example illustrated by Intruder Alarms, the value chain indicated a change in organisation to set resources aside for routine maintenance and better information systems to set inventory levels. Both combine to improve the effectiveness of service engineers which is the most expensive resource. Thus the customer perceives the organisation to be delivering better value, with no increase in overall cost.

Customer process flow

It is relatively easy to organise a customer support system from one's own perspective as a manager but miss how the customer might view it. It is relatively easy to think of the process employed by the organisation and to produce flow charts of materials and information flow. These flow charts can become extremely detailed and though they have value, this is not the approach we are describing here.

The customer service and support organisation must remember that it is not just following a set of procedures, it is processing customers. A customer with a need can be thought of as the input to the process, and a satisfied customer ought to be the outcome. We have found that it is worth charting or mapping the major stages in this process considering

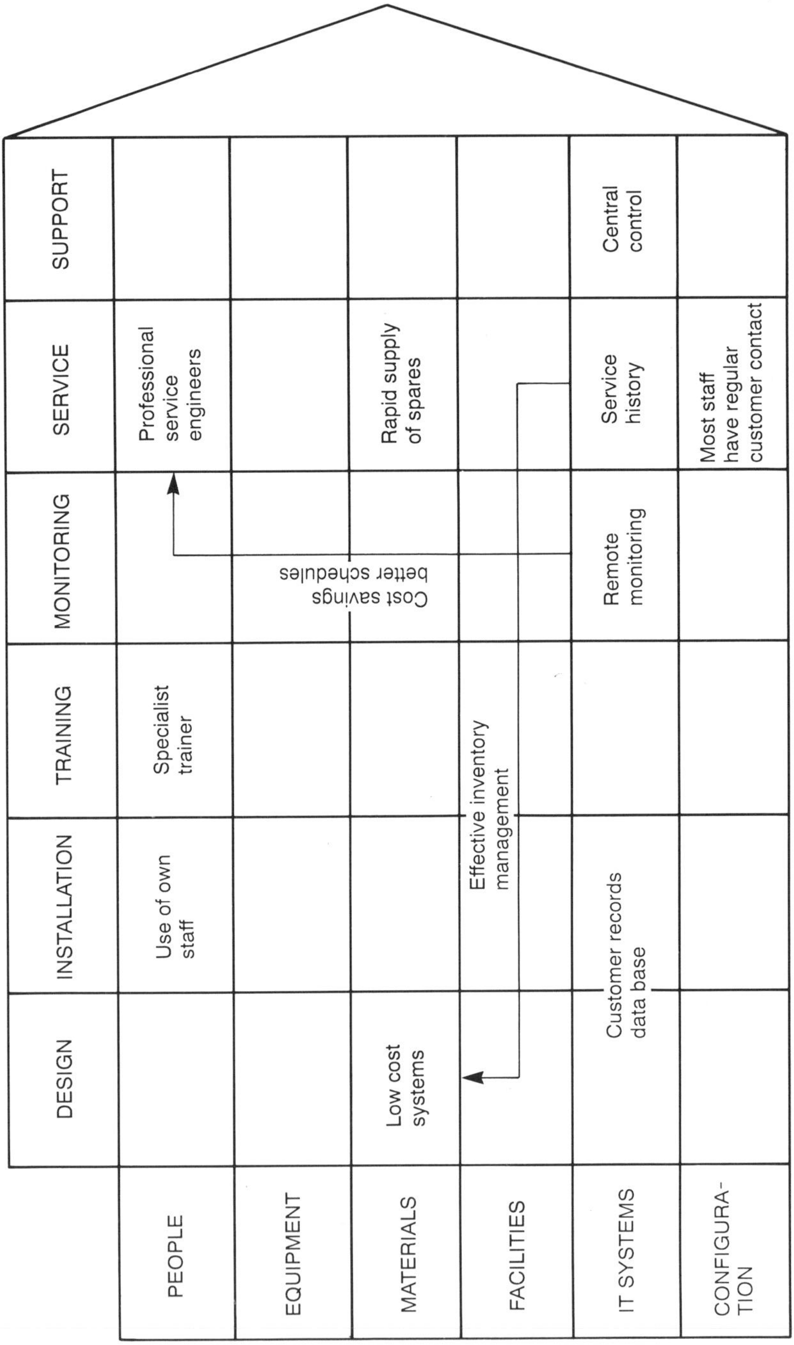

	DESIGN	INSTALLATION	TRAINING	MONITORING	SERVICE	SUPPORT
PEOPLE		Use of own staff	Specialist trainer		Professional service engineers	
EQUIPMENT						
MATERIALS	Low cost systems				Rapid supply of spares	
FACILITIES	Customer records data base	Effective inventory management				
IT SYSTEMS				Remote monitoring	Service history	Central control
CONFIGURA- TION					Most staff have regular customer contact	

Cost savings better schedules

Figure 6.3 Resource substitution in the value chain

the customer's viewpoint, particularly identifying what the customer is doing at each point.

Fig. 6.4 is an example of part of a customer process flow for the intruder alarms company. It indicates the main activities of both Front Office and Back Room. We have found it useful to identify also the critical customer service and resource dimensions to give a complete picture.

The objectives of charting process flow are:

- To identify the main stages of service delivery
- To enhance the understanding of service personnel
- To identify key customer contact points
- To identify information flows between customers, Front Office and Back Room
- To identify support requirements
- To identify failure points, their likelihood of occurrence and severity of effect on customer satisfaction.

How much does the customer see?

The customer process flow should identify how much of the total operation is visible to the customer. In general, the more the customer sees, the greater the probability that a degree of customisation will occur as the customer intervenes or interferes. By studying the process flow it may be possible to reduce the 'line of visibility', transferring more work content to the Back Room, thereby gaining some productivity benefits. Great care must be taken that the perception of customer care is not lost in this process or that the customer focus of support or Back Room staff does not deteriorate.

Where does it go wrong?

Using the process flow in a staff seminar or quality action team meeting can be a useful tool to identify problem areas. It can be used as a framework to gather data as well as a communication aid to explain how the organisation works. This is particularly valuable when the group contains staff from different departments and can gain insights into how the organisation as a whole might function more effectively.

In Fig. 6.4, an adaptation of a process flow developed during a quality workshop, the group was asked to identify the major failure points and to indicate the likely effect on the customer as well as suggesting

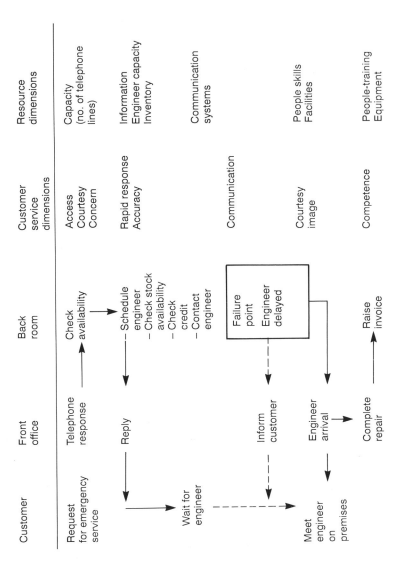

Figure 6.4 .Customer process flow for intruder alarms

improvements. Having identified the failure points a simple rating system may be applied; multiplying 'How likely' by 'How severe' will give the basis of an agenda for improvement. A refinement of this rating scheme is to add a third factor of 'How easily is a problem detected'. If a problem cannot be seen it is possible that damage to customer satisfaction will only become evident after a period of time has elapsed, making recovery impossible.

How does the customer feel?

An important issue in designing an effective customer process flow lies in gaining an understanding of the degree and type of risk that the customer feels in dealing with the organisation. The customer will probably not verbalise these anxieties, and in some cases may not be fully aware of them, but the organisations that manage to address them will improve perceived service quality.

The customer may wonder if the organisation is delivering value for money. It may be worth taking the customer through the service process to indicate where the costs lie. The provision of clear and comprehensive guarantees will build confidence, as will the professionalism of service personnel and the quality of facilities and equipment. Perversely, too low a price may have the effect of building a fear that the organisation cannot deliver to the required standard.

The customer may be concerned about risk, either to life and limb or to expensive equipment. Garages may counteract the fear of servicing and selling dangerous cars by enforcing standards through trade associations and displaying evidence of successful completion of training courses for their staff.

The customer may also question issues such as: Can I trust the service engineer to turn up? Will my business cope with the disruption of not having this machine available? Clear guarantees and accurate estimates of engineer arrival will bolster customer confidence.

Conclusion

Customer contact must be managed rather than left to happen. The best organisations manage the detail exceptionally well through careful service delivery design and quality management. A powerful tool for improvement is to consider the customer as part of the process flow, using the customer as a resource where possible.

The process of analysing the flow of materials, information, service providers and customers is extremely valuable in improving service quality and gaining ownership of the process by those involved in it.

Checklist

1   Have you thought about the way that customers come into contact with your organisation? Would you be happy with the impression they get?

2   Can you make more of the customer contacts you have to enhance the impression you make and increase customer confidence?

3   How much time do you spend with customers because they do not have confidence in the organisation to keep its promises?

4   What is the balance between the Front Office and the Back Room? Should work content be moved and how can communication between the two be improved?

5   Can resource productivity be improved by identifying the linkages between different parts of the value chain? Can investment in one area affect the customer perception of the organisation?

6   Can the Back Room support staff be more involved in the process of dealing with customers at least on an occasional basis?

7   Have the failure points in the process flow been identified? What is the effect of each on customer confidence?

7 MANAGING THE PEOPLE

Introduction

We have seen that the customer service triangle is made up of three legs, strategy, systems and people. In this chapter we will focus on the people. We will examine the role of the service and support managers and the competences they need to carry out their jobs. We will also look at ways of auditing the skills needed by the service personnel and the implications for recruitment and training. Motivation of the service team is an important issue and is also a way to increase the effectiveness of the team. We will see how teams can be managed within the organisational structure of the company. Finally we will look at 'burn-out' of service personnel and the ways of reducing its effect.

How much do you value your people?

Whenever we bring service and support managers together to talk about their work we find that issues relating to people dominate. These include the changing role of the service engineer, the search for a 'service' culture, changing demographic patterns limiting the recruitment of people, and increased responsibility for the service and support managers. All of these points indicate the need to manage change for staff and managers.

There has been a great deal mentioned in the recent past about the importance of people in the delivery of service which is not surprising, given the people-intensity of the process. There have been actions, for instance, with customer care programmes and total quality management initiatives designed to raise the awareness of service providers and to give some tools for involving service staff in the process of improvement. However, we know of many service organisations who have run one-day customer care programmes only to find that concentration on a 'smile campaign' fails when the service provider does not have the spares to do the job or they are expected to carry out tasks for which they are not trained. At least the total quality movement recognises one fundamental truth. There is no point beating people around the head if they fail to deliver or if they do not have the right skills, equipment and environment to make it possible. In short most of the problems come back to management failures.

So how well do you value your people? We have talked about perceived value for our customers when we are looking at strategy and marketing. We can apply the same concept to our own people. Look at the following list of statements and give each a score from 0 to 4 depending on how positive your answer is (0 = negative, 4 = most positive).

- I take as much trouble to find out what will help my people as I would my customers
- I know the strengths and weaknesses of all the people for whom I am responsible
- I sit down with all my people regularly to talk to them about their work
- I keep my people informed as to what the company is trying to achieve
- I ask my people about the customers they serve
- I know my people recommend our firm to their friends as a good employer
- I give my people regular feedback on what customers are saying about our service
- I know my people have a high degree of influence over the way they carry out their tasks
- I ask my people to rate their own performance
- I encourage and support my people to work together to solve problems.

Scoring:

- Over 36: You value your people and are doing most of the right things to support them
- 26–35: You recognise the need to value your people but you need to do more to support them
- 16–25: If you claim to value your people it is more of a wish than a reality
- Less than 15: You probably have difficulty in retaining staff. If you have the same attitude to customers you will probably soon be out of business if there are alternative suppliers.

Good service providers have recognised the need to treat their service people as they would their customers. We can all think of companies who are held up as examples of good providers of service and who are also companies for whom people want to work. In the retail sector Marks and Spencer have occupied this position for decades while newcomers to the service philosophy like British Airways have realised the importance of caring for their staff in achieving their goal of being 'The world's favourite airline'. We want to look at what is involved for service managers in changing their approach to people. Just how do service and support operations introduce the 'sparkle' into the customer service triangle through their service staff?

The role of the service and support manager

The service and support manager who is responsible for either front-line service and support providers or those reinforcing the front-line staff plays a crucial role. If the person sees his or her job simply in terms of allocating work or making sure spares are available he/she is missing some of the most important parts of the manager's role.

Consider the case of Kevin who is the service manager for a retail chain. As he drives to work on Friday morning he is turning over in his mind the events of the week and what the day holds in store for him. It has been a heavy week; a number of customers have rung to complain that service engineers have been late for appointments, there have been problems obtaining spares from one supplier of electrical goods, and one of his supervisors has been taken ill and is not expected to return to work for a few weeks.

Today Kevin knows he has a lunchtime meeting with a senior representative from one of his suppliers who is coming to talk to him about the results of a customer satisfaction survey they have carried out. Kevin also knows he is involved in interviewing some new service engineers. On top of these immediate tasks he knows he has to prepare over the weekend for a meeting on Monday with the regional service managers to consider changes to the structure of the service operation. Also the next budgeting round is close. Just in time he remembers it is his wife's birthday and stops at the newsagents to buy a card!

You may feel Kevin's day is less full than many experienced by someone in his position. However, the range of activities illustrates some of the different roles a manager has to perform in his/her job at different times.

One management writer, Henry Mintzberg, has identified three major managerial roles; *interpersonal*, *informational* and *decisional*, which managers perform within their position in an organisation (Fig. 7.1). These three main roles involve:

1 *An interpersonal role:* There are three activities – *leading*, *acting as a figurehead* representing the organisation, and *liaising* with others inside and outside the organistion.

2 *An informational role:* There are three informational activities – *monitoring*, *disseminating* information, and *acting as a spokesperson* for information to other parts of the organisation and outside.

3 *Decisional:* There are four activities in this category – *entrepreneurship*, when managers look for innovation; *handling disturbances* which disrupt events in the flow of the service delivery, such as shortages and breakdowns; *resolving conflicting demands* from customers, which might entail reallocating resources; and *negotiating and influencing* staff and bosses.

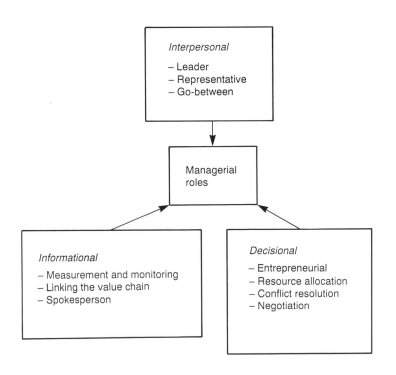

Figure 7.1 Managerial roles (after Mintzberg)

These roles are not discrete, they overlap and interact but managers are more commonly assessed on the basis of their performance in the decisional role.

While the role of the manager can be described in this way we feel we can also draw out some other critical roles which are appropriate for a customer service organisation. After all, the service and support manager is in effect the 'front-line' manager who with his staff spans the boundaries between the company and its customers and suppliers. Consequently he/she is in the best position to look critically at both the customers' needs and at the company's approaches to meeting them. How does this polarise in the make-up of the front-line manager? We see four main activities for the front-line manager: a systems architect, a role model, a psychologist, and a team builder.

The systems architect

There can be no better example of excellence through service delivery system design than that of Disney World. Each detail is thought through and planned down to the last detail, for instance, positioning the popcorn stands to ensure that the right smell greets the guests. This is only achieved by having managers who have front-line mentality. Once the service delivery system is right it becomes easier to deliver good service than to deliver bad service.

For an organisation to deliver good service consistently, there must be a service delivery system which is designed rather than just evolved. One problem we must guard against is that we often like our own design without thinking what effect it has on the customer. The maintenance scheduling which is designed to take the minimum amount of time for the engineer and give maximum utilisation of enginers looks perfect to the manager. Unfortunately the customers are never sure when the engineer is going to arrive and feel things could be better.

The design of systems requires managing the link between front-line staff and back room support. Total quality philosophy demands that everyone should have a customer or be serving someone who has. Communications from the front-line manager help to feed information on the needs of the front-line staff in the design of the internal supply chain.

The role model

There is a pub near where we work which is an illustration of how not to give good service. Going in at midday we were struck by how empty it was. It did not take long to discover where the problem lay. The landlord was on the phone explaining in none too sympathetic tones why a customer's request for sandwiches was totally unreasonable and impossible. There was no attempt to work out what could be done, just a flat refusal and inflexibility, an attitude copied by the rest of the staff.

The way front-line staff behave towards customers is strongly influenced by the behaviour they observe from their managers, who in turn are influenced by the behaviour of their bosses. The managing director who regularly calls customers to enquire about levels of service and who visits service depots is more likely to have front-line staff who are concerned about customer service and support.

The psychologist

Many types of service and support contain large sections which have prolonged contact with customers. Even with relatively simple tasks, the sheer pressure of having people demanding information or advice all the time becomes exhausting. These pressures lead eventually to 'burn-out' and a loss of the service sparkle. The reaction of most people in these circumstances is to become more defensive and less willing to put themselves out. Later we will look in more detail at the causes and effects of burn-out. It should be apparent that we think the front-line manager should spot service decline caused by burn-out and take action to limit its effect.

The front-line manager must also be a psychologist when dealing with customers, and be able to identify the unspoken needs and adapt the approach to suit. This can be a complex task when there are wide differences in the customers being dealt with, for instance corporate customers compared to domestic, rich and poor, or young and old. One group of service engineers we saw recently said they felt more at ease dealing with ordinary people than with those they saw as being rich.

The team builder

The role of the front-line manager as team builder and coach is one which we see increasingly in good service providers. The benefits are in sharing of problems, more innovation in the way things are done, support to limit burn-out, and a greater commitment from individuals to customer service. Peer group pressure can have a greater effect on the service people than admonishments from the manager or supervisor.

Team building also applies to customer partnerships. There are very strong indications that taking customers into the service team is a way of increasing loyalty and preventing customers switching to another supplier.

Recognising different roles which a service manager must perform is important because it allows us to think about the competences which are needed to do the job.

What managerial competences do you need?

In order for a service and support manager to perform any of the roles we have introduced they need to have a set of *managerial competences* which enable them to fulfil the role. By managerial competences we mean the skills, knowledge and behaviour which are appropriate to the roles.

Competences include technical, professional, and job knowledge; knowledge of the company and of its markets and customers; skills in handling interpersonal relationships, counselling, selling skills; and information gathering and problem solving. The competences set will differ in detail from organisation to organisation and it is important for each service and support team to identify the managerial competences that are important for their own circumstances. Peter Norris at the Cranfield School of Management has worked with many groups of managers, assisting them to determine the set of competences which they need. As an example, one service company identified the following managerial competences:

Business development

Commercial awareness:
Managers demonstrate the capacity to perceive the impact of decisions and activities of the organisation on customers, competitors and the future viability of the business. There is a focus on customers' needs. Business opportunities are identified and acted on.

Environmental awareness:
Managers demonstrate an awareness of changes in the political, economic, social, and technological environment that are likely to effect their jobs or the organisation. Managers show a breadth and diversity of business related knowledge about the environmental issues.

Initiative:
Managers have the ability to influence events. They do not passively accept what is happening, but are proactive.

Analysis

Problem analysis:
There is the ability effectively to identify problems, to seek relevant data and information and to identify possible causes of problems.

Numerical analysis:
Managers have the ability to analyse, to organise and to present numerical data be it financial, statistical, or operational.

Judgement:
Managers have the ability to evaluate data and information and to identify courses of action in a logical manner.

Managing

Planning and organising:
Managers have the ability to establish an appropriate course of action for themselves and for others to achieve their goals. Effective use is made of resources.

Management control:
Managers have the ability to maintain control over the service process and of the people. They appreciate the need for, and are willing to exercise, control.

Staff management

Leadership:
Managers have the ability to develop team work and to maximise the use of resources in the team to meet the goals of the team. They have the ability to motivate, to influence, and to handle people taking account of personalities, in order to carry out tasks effectively.

Team work:
Managers have the ability to make an effective contribution when the team is working on something of no direct personal interest. There is a willingness to participate fully when not necessarily the leader of the team.

Subordinate development:
The managers have the ability to develop the skills and competences of subordinates through training and development activities related to current and future jobs.

You may feel that anyone who matches up to the full list of competences is bound to be a paragon. The important point is to recognise the most important competences within your job and to rate your ability to meet the competences. Shortfalls in any areas indicate the need for training and development. We suggest that managers work in groups to identify the main competences needed for service and support managers in their own operation. It may well be that some of the competences are considered more important than others so a weighting can be given to each, as shown in Table 7.1. You can rate your own performance against each competence, on your own, and with your manager or personnel specialists.

Do you give your people a chance?

Many service and support managers would agree that the job of the front-line service providers is becoming more complex and demanding. While in the past reliance on technical skills was sufficient, now this is only one aspect of what is required. One writer on services, Christopher Lovelock, illustrates the change by talking about a 'Service Trinity' for front-line personnel. In the minds of the customer at least, the front-line person runs the organisation, sells the service, and represents what the service is worth. If this is true then the job is more complex because it involves aspects of 'production' in doing the technical bits and of 'marketing' in presenting the image of the service organisation.

Service managers must recognise the changing needs for their front-line people and take steps to enable them to fulfil their extended roles. We recognise that in a well-established organisation this can be a long and difficult process because we are managing a process of change. However,

Managerial competences	Weighting	Performance	Total	
Business development				
Commercial awareness	4	0	4	
Environmental awareness	3	−2	−6	
Initiative	4	2	8	
Analysis of problems	3	−1	−3	
Numerical analysis	4	−2	−8	
Judgement	3	0	3	Weighting
Planning and organising	4	0	4	0= Low 5=High
Management control	5	−1	−5	
Leadership	4	1	4	Rating scale
Teamwork	5	+1	5	−3 to +3
Subordinate development	3	+2	6	Low High

Table 7.1 Managerial competence

if we do nothing, or pay lip service to change, we will fail both the staff and eventually the customers.

What do our people need to do their jobs?

We have already looked at managerial competences; now we turn our attention to the mix of *knowledge*, *skills*, and *abilities* – the *KSA mix*, which the service and support personnel require. Finding out what these are requires an analysis of the service delivery process. This must be a systematic evaluation of what is needed, successfully to do the tasks at each stage so that the quality and service levels are achieved. The evaluation leads to a detailed description for each category of work in terms of the knowledge skills, and abilities required, including:

1   *Technical skills* associated with the product(s). Knowledge of the products and their use, skills associated with installation, servicing, and fault diagnosis and repair.
2   *Procedures* to be used in the job. Where the job is standardised these may include the use of scripts for communication.
3   *Information systems* used for maintaining records of customers and

equipment and for remote diagnosis.

4 *Interpersonal skills* for communicating information and for building relationships by taking account of the feelings, values and needs of others. Listening skills for active listening are necessary to reduce the chances of misunderstandings.

5 *Appearance* of service personnel and of the equipment and other materials for which they are responsible.

6 *Time management* to make the most effective use of time. This use of time becomes more important when service staff are given more responsibility for organising their own work.

7 *Selling skills* needed by technical specialists or call takers when they are encouraged to take part in the selling process either on the telephone or on visits to customers.

8 *Team working* to increase the cooperative delivery of the service and support.

9 *Self monitoring* to be able to assess their own performances and behaviour in response to customer demands.

Assessing the KSA mix for each job category has implications in the areas of *training*, *recruitment*, and *selection for promotion*. For training purposes we can carry out an audit of the training needs against the KSAs required for the job and identify any areas of weakness for a group or an individual. While it is easy to identify short falls in technical areas it is often more difficult for the less tangible parts of the KSA mix. Here there must be a great reliance on the role of the front-line manager to be close to his or her people to be able to help to identify training needs.

In selection and recruitment the KSA mix may act as a guide for those involved in the process. However, there are definite problems in making judgements about abilities in the interpersonal areas unless psychometric testing is used as a guide to behaviour. Perhaps the more important aim is to recruit those who will match the culture of the organisation and who will present the values of the organisation to the customer.

It perhaps goes without saying that having the right people with the right KSA mix for the job is not a guarantee for success. In a moment's reflection we can see that the KSA route is primarily from the organisation's view. While this may be valuable to make sure people are equipped and suitable to do the job it takes no account of what the individual's needs are from the job. Factors which give job satisfaction and motivation for a service person are largely ignored in the KSA process but are crucial to the success of the company.

How do we motivate the service people?

Industrial psychologists have long investigated the quesiton of what motivates people at work and many theories have been expounded during the course of this century. How can we best summarise these in ways which are of help to us in motivating service and support personnel?

There are three commonly used theories about motivation known as, *needs* theory, *incentives* theory, and *expectancy* theory. We also include the concept of empowerment as a fourth factor.

Needs theory

Needs theory says that behaviour of an individual is driven primarily by his or her needs. But what are needs? Maslow separated needs into five types, known as Maslow's *Hierarchy of Needs*:

1   *Physiological*, relating to warmth, light and the general conditions of the working environment.
2   *Security*, for example, job security, and freedom from physical threats.
3   *Social*, for example, acceptance into the work group.
4   *Self-esteem*, as realised by the status associated with a job title or position.
5   *Self-actualisation*, meaning job satisfaction coming, for instance, from the degree of challenge in the job.

Maslow said that the needs are in ascending order and the needs at one level need to be satisfied before the next level could be addressed. So it is no use trying to satisfy needs which give people status in a job title, of say 'service executive', if they feel their job security is threatened.

McClelland extended and refined Maslow's theory and said that needs are more influenced by social context and will vary from one culture to another. He suggests the needs which must be satisfied are:

1   *The need for achievement* to meet targets.
2   *The need for affiliation* to belong to the work group.
3   *The need for power* to control and influence others.

McClelland also suggested that the balance of a person's needs does not change over time. If this is true is has implications for the recruitment selection process and career development. It indicates to us the problems caused by changing the role of the service and support personnel in ways which may not match their individual needs.

Incentives theory

Incentives theory suggests that external factors influence motivation. Herzberg suggested that two factors are important:

1 *Hygiene* factors are the aspects of the job which a person expects to find in the job, for instance, working conditions, and wages or salary.
2 *Motivation* factors include achievement, recognition, responsibility, and money.

The idea is that hygiene factors in themselves will not motivate but if they are lacking a person will be de-motivated. The position of money is complex as it can be seen as both a hygiene and a motivating factor.

Expectancy theory

Expectancy theory concentrates on how people make choices in the way in which they behave. It suggests that individuals will look at what they are required to do and make some rational assessment of what reward they will gain from it. For instance, people will perform well if they feel they will be highly rewarded or fairly rewarded for their efforts.

Empowerment

In the service environment there is a great deal talked about the concept of empowerment for service people. This means giving the front-line service responsibility to act for themselves with the support of service managers. Service staff are allowed to take decisions on the use of resources to meet customers' needs, perhaps by spending more on the means of obtaining spares, for example, by using express courier services, or offering replacement equipment. This may seem an excellent course for some managers who see themselves as supporting rather than direct-ing activities. However moves to empowerment should also be viewed from the individual's perspective and the satisfaction of their needs. For some it could be seen as threatening and undermine their security needs, while for others, who do not feel threatened, it would be a motivator in the Herzberg sense. We need to think about empowerment in the context of the culture of the organisation. Autocratic organisations will find it difficult to move towards empowerment. Managers will resent a perceived, if not real, loss of power and staff may not wish to assume the extra responsibility.

An environment in which empowerment does seem to work is associated with a strong service team which gives support to the individual. This implies a high degree of trust between members of the team and between the team and the service managers.

The dangers of 'burn-out'

What are the messages for service and support managers from the various motivation theories? We think they are:

1   Overriding is the responsibility of the service and support manager to recognise the needs of the individual service personnel. This fits with the front-line manager's role as a psychologist.
2   Managers should try to see the relationship between the rewards and the way people are assessed. A service engineer who is paid on the basis of calls achieved per day is less likely to be motivated to spend time on achieving first time fix. In addition this behaviour is going to be reinforced if the same engineer is paid overtime for a call-out.
3   When the role of service staff is changed managers need to recognise that the new roles may be at variance with the needs set by the individual service personnel.
4   Empowerment will only be a motivator when service staff feel they are actively supported and the new role fits with their personal needs.

Failure to pay attention to these four points increases the likelihood of burn-out of front-line service providers. Burn-out has become recognised as one of the symptoms of stress for front-line service personnel. It was first recognised in the caring professions like social work and healthcare when service providers who had previously given full caring attention to their clients or patients exhibited a lack of caring, disinterest in their jobs, and signs of stress, depression, irritability, and difficulty in sleeping and relaxing. We can see outward signs of burn-out with all service people who are in continuous contact with customers. The disinterested, bored approach with robot-like service is within everyone's experience.

Certainly not everyone is as prone to stress and burn-out and will exhibit the symptoms to differing degrees. However within the context of service and support operations it may become more of an issue for service managers as the role of staff changes from one of service to supporting the customer.

The points which we drew from motivation theory have an important bearing on the limitation of burn-out. The clarity of service and support roles and the alignment of personal needs and the role of the job will all help to limit stress and burn-out. Another factor in burn-out is increased customer contact due to increased workloads. The service team approach is a powerful one of giving the support which more than anything helps to limit burn-out.

Building the service team

Why should the service team be so important? First, it gives service managers the opportunity to act as the *coach* to the team. Second, it gives individuals the chance to *learn* from others and to work towards achieving common goals. Third, it allows team members to increase their own KSAs to increase the *flexibility* of the team.

We perhaps need to remind ourselves of what we are trying to achieve from the service team; customer satisfaction and efficiencies in resource productivity. These will be our measures of the effectiveness of the team at the end of the day. Whether or not we achieve our goals will depend on three factors for teams: first, the clarity of what we are trying to achieve and who is involved in the process (that is, who is included in the service team); second, the motivation of the individual team members and the systems and process which allow the task to be done, and finally, the actions of the team leader.

The composition of service teams needs some thought. Do we just include front-line people in the team or should the team also contain Back Room people? Clearly the benefit of including Back Room people is to develop a common view of the goals and what is involved in reaching them. Sometimes Back Room people are excluded because of group size or their location. Consequently, one of the main tasks of the front-line service team is to communicate with the Back Room people.

Another area where the composition of the team becomes important is when service and support is being delivered by a mix of SAS and Regulars (see Chapter 3). There is the danger of the two groups becoming isolated, especially if there is geographical separation. Here we might want to establish mixed teams of the two groups. This idea can be extended further to build service teams around product groups so that Back Room and front-line service staff are closely associated in the same product team.

The pathway to effectiveness for teams

Teams do not simply come together and perform well. They go through four stages in their development to becoming an effective team. These are:

1 *Forming:* the team is simply a group of individuals without a clear idea of the purpose of their task and what they are trying to achieve.
2 *Storming:* the team is often in conflict about their direction and goals, the nature of leadership, and the role of the individuals within the team. We often see strong disagreement among team members or some members not being willing to take part in the activities of the group.
3 *Norming:* the team becomes clear on tasks and goals and individuals start to become strongly committed to other members of the team. There is strong peer group pressure for individuals to conform to the values of the team.
4 *Performing:* At this stage the real work is done with the team members sharing and supporting one another. It would seem that the clearer the nature of the task and the greater the degree of shared values of the service team members the more likely it is that a service team will perform well.

Some teams may never reach the performing stage, while others will reach it very quickly, especially if the outcome is very important. Developing a service team requires a very real commitment on the part of the company to devote time and effort to the process. Often firms find they need outside assistance such as that provided by the Covedale training.

The team coach

The role of the service manager as a team builder depends on his or her ability to act as a coach to the team. Tom Peters, who has studied many organisations who deliver the best customer service in their own industries, says there are five roles for the coach:

1 *Teaching* in order to:
(a) Make the goals clear

(b) Give information the team members need

(c) Help team members to increase their skills and knowledge for the tasks

(d) Give feedback on performance and what is required

(e) Introduce new members to the ways of the service team.

2 *Supporting:* Supporting or sponsoring involves aspects of empowering individuals. It means us encouraging individual team members to give their best and supporting them day to day. The support may come through giving them access to a wider range of responsibilities or skills in their work. Indications of good support are:

(a) Treating people as colleagues

(b) Looking for opportunities to assist service and support staff

(c) Discussing training needs and career opportunities at regular meetings and acting on the outcomes.

3 *Leading:* There are various leadership styles from authoritarian to *laissez-faire*. The most appropriate styles for coaching service teams include:

(a) setting a good example

(b) challenging people to do their best

(c) caring about how people are doing

(d) being accessible to staff

(e) being open and honest.

4 *Counselling:* Counselling is concerned with seeking to deal with problems which occur with the team members in a frank and open manner. For instance, there may be problems with the performance of one member or an individual may have personal problems. There are some characteristics of good counsellors. They are:

(a) *active listeners.* That is to say, they concentrate on what is being said rather than make assumptions on what is being said to them

(b) *perceptive* to the feelings of others

(c) *willingness* to spend time helping to resolve problems

(d) *trustworthy* with confidences.

5 *Confronting:* Confronting is about facing issues which need to be resolved rather than hiding from them. It may concern poor performance of a team member after counselling and training. It may concern confronting others outside the team who have an influence on the performance of the team – suppliers of spares or services, or members of other departments.

The role of the team coach is a complex one for service managers but without it we think it is unlikely that service and support operations will achieve their goals.

Conclusion

In this chapter we have looked at the role of managers and staff within the context of service and support operations. We have tried to bring out the importance of service managers having a clear understanding of the competences they need as individual managers and as members of a management team. For service staff we have stressed the need to identify the knowledge, skills and abilities to fulfil their roles.

Having the right KSA mix for service providers only gives capability and without adequate motivation these will not be used effectively. We have tried to indicate the main factors which affect motivation. The role of the front-line manager of a service team is seen as a powerful vehicle for motivating individuals and also for limiting the effects of burn-out for service and support staff.

Checklist

1 What changes have taken place in your organisation which have changed your role or the role of your staff?

2 What are the management competences which are needed in the new circumstances? What is your level of achievement in these competences? Are there deficiencies? If so, are you addressing them through training?

3 What is the KSA mix for any new roles for your service and support personnel? Can all of them be met or is there the need for new staff or training of existing staff?

4 How well do you value your service and support staff (you may wish to use the questionnaire towards the beginning of the chapter)?

5 What is the structure of your service teams? Do they bring together front-line and Back Room personnel?

6 What steps have you taken to build your service teams? What gaps do you see from what you have read in this chapter?

7 What steps do you take to motivate the service team? What gaps do you see from reading this chapter?

8 How do you match up as a team coach using the audit in Table 7.2? What actions do you intend to take to rectify any gaps? Would you be able to ask your service team to complete the audit for you?

Service team audit

The following are team coach attributes suggested by Tom Peters. Score yourself between 0 and 4 on each point depending on how well you consider you perform (0 = badly, 4 = well).

Teaching
- I make the goals clear to my service and support people.
- I give information to my service team members.
- I help my team members to increase their KSA levels.
- I give feedback on performance and what is required of my service people.
- I have a strong induction programme for new members to the service and support team.

Supporting
- I treat all my service team as colleagues.
- I constantly look for opportunities to assist my staff.
- I discuss training needs and career development with my staff and do something about them.

Leading
- I set a good example in my approach to customers.
- I challenge people to give their best.
- I care about how my service team is doing, not only in the work environment.
- I am accessible to the members of the service and support team.
- I am open and honest with the service and support staff.

Counselling
- I am an active listener.
- I am perceptive to the feelings of others.
- I am trustworthy with confidences.

Confronting
- I am not afraid to raise issues with the team members.
- I try to resolve issues rather than letting them continue to cause disruption.

Results
Low total scores overall indicate the need for action to correct your performance.
Low scores against some areas may indicate the need for training.

If you score highly overall you may wish to ask some members of your service team to give their assessment.

Table 7.2

8 CAPACITY MANAGEMENT

Introduction

In this chapter we will look at the management of capacity in service and support operations. We will consider the factors which affect both demand and our ability to change capacity to match demand. Also we will look at the techniques which are available to plan and control the operations to get the best from the use of resources while maintaining the levels of customer service we need.

Why is capacity management important?

In our studies of customer service and support we have found that one of the features which differentiates good from bad is their ability to plan and control resources to match changing levels of demand. There is a strong interaction between success in this area and quality management and resource productivity or efficiency management. Getting the balance of resource capacity and demand leads to quality and efficiency targets being achieved. However, often the main problem is dealing with changing levels of demand which can occur rapidly and with some degree of uncertainty. Managers have to try to cope with these changing levels using limited resources. Consider the following story.

Uplifts Plc is a company which manufactures, installs and services lifts. It has a number of service centres to cover the UK from where engineers carry out maintenance and attend failures. The aim of the company is to carry out preventative maintenance so that there are few call-outs for lift failures. Where lifts are installed to carry people the response to failure has to be rapid for obvious reasons. The different service stations are measured on their call-out performance. The performance of the stations varies considerably with some stations having double the call-out rate of other stations. Also the poor performers often fail to meet the published response times. The national management is concerned that the under-performing stations will bring the company a bad name especially with their large national account customers.

At a meeting of the service managers they considered the reasons for the difference in the performance between the stations. There was talk of quality control and of the mix of products in the service portfolio in different places. However one of the clearest differences which emerged in the discussion was the approach adopted by the service managers to planning and controlling resources and trying to anticipate demand.

This perhaps illustrates the problem. Some parts of the service and support are fairly predictable, like the level of preventative maintenance. Others, like call-out to breakdowns, are not. The only ways of controlling these activities are either to change the level of resources to meet demand or to make customers wait for attention. In many instances making customers wait will mean the response times specified in service contracts are not met, or customers are generally dissatisfied with the level of service. Either case may lead to loss of business.

So managing resource levels is important because it has an effect on *quality*, *resource productivity*, and *customer satisfaction*. However, before we can begin to think about controlling resource levels we need to understand what we mean by capacity and demand, or service intensity, in some detail.

What do we mean by capacity?

Sometimes explaining capacity is not easy in any service operation. What is the capacity of a supermarket, a bank, a bus? Is it the square meterage, number of cashiers, or number of seats? Whereas these measures may indicate key resources to be managed they are static measures. They do not take account of all the factors which affect capacity. We therefore prefer to say that *capacity is the ability to work off existing demand*. This is a more dynamic measure. So the capacity of the supermarket, bank and bus could be expressed in terms of customers served per day or passengers carried per day.

Once we express capacity in this way it should be clear that what we are talking about is the *level of output* from the use of resources. There are two other features about capacity:

1   Capacity measurement has a time dimension.

2   The amount of capacity may be affected by all resources, including staff, materials and equipment, and also customers.

We need to take things a bit further and consider how we view capacity for different parts of the service delivery. We can conveniently think about the capacity at various levels.

- *The business unit network*: The capacity of our network will depend on the extent of the network, and the number and size of the branches. This level may be national or regional and governed by our organisation structure for the business units. The capacity is more likely to be expressed as the output for an accounting period or calendar year. Decisions about capacity at this level will result from the planning of resources which involve capital expenditure and major shifts in the levels of manpower
- *The branch or service centre*: The capacity of our branches or service centres will depend on the size and the extent to which we can call on resources from centralised support. The service centre is the smallest unit capable of delivering most if not all of the service and support. Capacity is more likely to be expressed for time scales less than one week. Decisions about capacity will be more concerned with the deployment of existing resources although there is obviously a link with the planning at the network level for major changing in resourcing
- *The team*: The service team's capacity will depend on the numbers in the team. One team may be capable only of delivering one part of the total service and support which is available to our customers. Decisions about capacity will concern the deployment of available resources, rather than large increases in the overall potential capacity. Capacity will be expressed in periods of less than a day
- *The individual resource*: The individual resource may be a service person with special skills, or a piece of equipment. We must be aware of the capacity of individual resources which may limit capacity of the team or service centre.

How much capacity do we have?

A service manager has 50 service engineers in her establishment although at any particular time she may have only 45 available. The numbers which are actually available are what matters for getting the work done. We refer to the capacity provided by the 45 staff and other resources as the *effective capacity* assuming there is constant demand to fill their time. Effective capacity is usually what interests us most. However the service manager may also need to know the capacity which could easily be made available, at say a week's notice, by cancelling training or borrowing resources from a neighbouring service centre. The capacity provided by these additional resources, assuming demand is there, is called the *potential capacity*.

Both effective and potential capacity are affected by short-term decisions because they do not involve any major change in the resource level. Nor do they require large expenditure to increase the size of facilities or to buy equipment or hold larger inventories, or recruiting or laying-off of large numbers of staff.

When we want to assess the level of effective capacity there are three main things which have an influence:

1   Do we have *all* the resources we need available all of the time? For instance, are there the numbers of staff, spares, equipment and information about customers? Should any one of the resources not be available then our effective capacity is *zero*.

2   We need to have *access* to customers and/or their equipment for service or repairs. Without this access our output is *zero* despite having the potential to do the work.

3   The type of the service or support being offered to a particular customer will determine the capacity because the *amount of work needed* to complete the job may *vary considerably* from one service encounter to the next. So we must understand the effect on the service and support mix.

These three aspects of capacity illustrate one of the basic rules of capacity: variety in the resources and/or in the nature of the demand will tend to reduce effective capacity.

How flexible is our capacity?

The movement between effective and potential capacity is a measure of our flexibility to change capacity to cater for changes in demand or service intensity. We are interested in two things about flexibility:

1   The *response flexibility* – how quickly can we make a change in capacity.

2   The *range flexibility* – how much can we change the capacity in the response time as service intensity changes.

Consideration of the response and range flexibilities allows us to understand how easy it is for us to alter capacity and the effect on the costs of making changes.

What are our patterns of demand?

While we may have a very good understanding of the factors which influence our effective capacity at any point in time we are still likely to fail to match service intensity unless we understand our patterns of demand. The outcome of this failure is poor customer service or excessively high unit costs. The way forward, as in any planning process, is to try to be in a position to know precisely what we have to achieve. The better the knowledge, the better the planning process.

There are two main components to understanding demand: first, the main elements of the demand itself; and second, our ability to predict or forecast what is likely to happen in the future.

The elements of demand

There are three components to understanding demand itself, the *volume* or level of demand, the *variety* of service packages or products we supply, and the *variation* in demand. We will look at each in turn:

1   The volume of demand is a statement of the trends in demand over a period of time, typically between one month and a year.
2   The variety of demand is associated with the number of different services which we are offering and the number of different tasks which are involved in making it available to our customers. Segmenting customers with different offerings increases this variety.
3   The variation in demand is associated with the changes in the volume around a general trend. The nature of the demand also changes due to major differences between groups of customers. For example, we may have business and domestic customers who place demands on us at different times.

The nature of the demand, the variety of services, and the volume are factors which we should establish at the network level rather than at the day to day operational level. However, variation in the nature and volume are very much the concern of day to day operational management.

Forecasting demand

Our aim in forecasting demand is to separate out those things we can predict with a high degree of certainty and those which are less certain. In doing this we must take into account volume, variety and variation. Most forecasting methods rely on taking a mixture of information about past demand and projecting future demand. The forecast should also include known demand like service contracts for regular maintenance.

Separating the predictable and the random demand can be done by asking these questions:

- How has our overall demand changed in the past?
- Are there regular variations either throughout the day, throughout the week, throughout the month, or seasonally throughout the year? These can be found by examining past records of service intensity
- What causes these variations? The causes may be due to buying patterns, to call-out at the beginning of the week after the weekend, or longer term cycles, for instance, in the property building market
- What causes random changes in demand? These are changes which we know are going to occur but which are difficult to determine when they will occur and the extent to which they will affect service intensity. Weather can be one of the main causes of random demand changes in the short term and economic business activity in the medium term.

There are a number of forecasting techniques which can be used to predict demand fairly accurately on the basis of past service intensity. These are available on standard software packages and can be run on PCs. In all cases though the results from forecasting models should be reviewed and amended in the light of any known future events. For example, a higher level of promotional spending on advertising may be expected to lift the level of service intensity, as would the launch of a new product range. Downturns in the economy would lead to a reduction in the short-term volume of demand but not necessarily alter the short-term variations in demand, say day-to-day.

Most customer service and support operations experience cyclical variation in service intensity by time of day, day of the week, and season of the year. The demand on Mondays in winter may well be different from Mondays in summer. However the average service intensity for one particular service branch may not change to a very high degree over a period of a year. The reason for this is the variety mix. The cyclical patterns of demand are often different for the various service products and this tends to smooth the variations in service intensity.

Creating the balance

If we understand the level of service intensity as driven by customer demand and also the make-up of our capacity we are left deciding how we can create a balance between the two. There are essentially two polar opposites for managing capacity, one to hold capacity steady while influencing demand and the other of changing our capacity to stay in line with demand. In reality we find that most operations use a mixture of the two strategies, although if there is a clear capacity constraint there is a bias towards level capacity; this may be the case in customer service and support operations which have the SAS structure composed of specialists who take time to recruit and may be in short supply, so creating additional capacity takes time. However it is useful for us to appreciate what each of the approaches or capacity strategies entails.

The 'chase' capacity strategy – altering capacity

The chase strategy is appropriate where we can alter our effective capacity to include all the expected variations in service intensity. The ways open to the service management to alter capacity to achieve this continuous balance are:

Personnel and hours changes:
We may alter the number of service personnel or the hours they work. The scheduling of service personnel to correspond with the demand patterns helps to deal with daily and weekly variations in demand. Increasing the working hours of existing service people may match demand but bring with it increased costs from overtime charges. The use of flexible working hours may help us in trying to reduce the overtime burden. In one approach, we saw that an annual hours agreement for a building repair and maintenance operation gave them the flexibility to increase the working day in summer months without incurring increases in wages.

The use of part-time people to increase capacity to meet the peak demands can be useful, especially when there are peaks outside of the normal working day. An additional benefit from the use of part-timers in this way is the reduction in overtime charges.

There are dangers in using extended working hours as the means of flexing capacity in capacity-constrained service operations using the SAS structure because of the increased strain this might put on personnel. The effect of this in the long term would be service burn-out for the service personnel in the front line.

Customer participation:

We can also use the customers as part of our resources to provide capacity. As we have already seen, the role of the customer is to participate in some part of the service delivery process. This participation may mean the customer:

(a) provides part of the resources to carry out the work and service themselves.

(b) provides information which helps the service provider to decide what is needed, to receive feedback on the quality of the service, and to make suggestions on how the service can be improved or enhanced. This may save resources by preventing an unnecessary visit to a customer's premises. An example in the domestic appliance area occurs when customers are given instructions to carry out a simple diagnosis and repair for a blocked pump filter on a washing machine. This saves the customer money in call-out charges and frees resources for other activities.

When considering the contribution made by customers it is important to distinguish between the customers always doing some part of the work and customers working as part of the chase strategy to increase capacity as we run out of resources.

If the customer provides part of the existing capacity this requires our customers to be trained in the tasks which they are required to do. A problem here may be in getting customers to accept their contribution. This is easier if DIY is part of the service concept. We see it in many day to day services we encounter, self-catering holidays, car rentals and supermarkets. The role of the customers is accepted in these cases. However, where changes are made to an existing system of delivery problems may be encountered. It is interesting now to reflect that when supermarkets were first introduced in the United States a great deal of effort had to be devoted to training customers in their new role. The shops employed staff to help shoppers find their way round the new stores.

One problem for us in using customers as a resource is that they will differ in their abilities and commitment to their task. For example, setting of intruder alarms by staff in a bank tends to be more conscientious than in a small factory.

While the use of customers may make a contribution to the overall effective capacity of the service delivery system it is also important for us to consider whether customers could do more work at the times when demand is increasing. This may not be as easy as the customers providing capacity as a normal part of the service delivery. If customers are asked to participate at times when our resources are under pressure it may lead to the customers perceiving a fall in service quality. However, this may be reduced or prevented if customers can see the reasons why they are being asked to do something. Clearly this will be the case if there is a threat to lives or if the loss of use of equipment is very important.

Transferring resources:
We may be able to increase our effective capacity by transferring resources from another part of one operation. Often we may be able to transfer Back Room staff to assist in the Front Office. This is common in small telephone response centres to limit the waiting time for the calls to be answered and the number of lost calls from customers not being able to get through. Transfer of staff in this way has implications for training in multi-skills.

Alternatively equipment and people may be transferred between adjacent geographical areas to help meet peak or unexpected demand. It is important to recognise that transfers of this type may lead to a drop in the service quality of the part of the service operation from which a transfer is being made because of a decrease in their ability to respond to random short-term increases in demand. A utility repair operation providing resources to a major incident in another area may not be able to provide the desired level of all services in its own area unless it is able to increase its own capacity.

Using subcontractors:
Subcontractors may of course be used to provide capacity at all times as an alternative to maintaining that capability in-house. However where subcontractors are used as part of a chase strategy they may be seen as a special case of transferring resources where the capacity is provided by others at times of high demand.

The advantage of the use of subcontractors is clearly that the cost of the capacity is a variable rather than a fixed cost. The disadvantages with subcontractors stems from the uncertainty that they can perform to the standards of our service operation. Also there may be doubts that the resources will be available precisely at the time they are needed. Forecasting of demand helps in arranging contracts for services which can be called off from subcontractors as the demand increases and laid off as demand falls.

Sharing capacity:
If some resources are expensive to hold and not used often it may be feasible for service branches to share either discrete resources or a pool of resources. The use of specialist product teams located in one area but shared by the network may give both cost savings and increased capacity flexibility. In other cases, specialised equipment may be shared between areas.

Decrease service standards:
Dropping service standards is the final way of increasing capacity in line with demand. Unfortunately it is an all too common approach adopted by many service and support organisations. The result for the customer is at best an increased wait for the service or support. At worst there is also a fall in other parts of the service due to rushing. Jobs may not be fixed first time resulting in call backs which also exacerbate capacity problems by increasing service intensity. In some cases organisations may get away with increased waiting if the customers see it as being unavoidable; for instance, in times of bad weather demand on utilities for call-out is expected to rise.

The 'level' of capacity strategy – altering demand

Instead of attempting to change the capacity in line with demand we can try to influence demand to keep it in line with available capacity. This level strategy is more widely used in capacity-constrained service delivery systems. The methods used to influence demand are the following:

Pricing, advertising and promotion:
Pricing has always been a method of influencing demand for the sale of products. The use of advertising and promotion and pricing to stimulate non-peak demand is very important in capacity-constrained service delivery systems where there are high fixed costs in facilities, equipment and staff. A service and support operation which has high seasonal costs

may find it wants to stimulate demand in the quiet season by pricing and promotion. The utilities use this for preventative maintenance contracts sold to domestic users to increase demand in the summer months. Using pricing to suppress demand in the winter could be more difficult. What we may do is to restrict the offering of some service and support at busy times. For instance, we may limit the amount of winter maintenance we offer and concentrate on dealing with breakdowns.

Customer reservation or appointments:
Pre-booking or reserving slots in a service activity allows some smoothing of demand and transfers demand from times when the service delivery system is incapable of matching demand. The mechanism works if the customers are willing to accept a waiting period. The use of reservation systems is often combined with price inducements to help in the process.

The advantage to the service operations management is that demand is known with some certainty in advance of delivery. This assists with the planning of resources. However the downside of appointment systems can be when customers need to be involved in the process by giving access to buildings and equipment, and are not there at the time of the appointment. Some services penalise customers for this, as in the case of those restaurants which ask for a credit card number at the time of booking and charge people who do not turn up. We are not aware of this practice being employed by customer service and support organisations.

Customers being made to wait:
When capacity is constrained the most common way of dealing with the problem is to make customers wait for service. Engineers or other staff are not available to meet demand and so there is no option but for some customers to wait. In these cases a means of prioritising demand may be used. For instance, in the case of lift service operators a call for assistance with customers trapped in a lift will be attended to ahead of other calls.

Queueing is associated with a physical wait where the customer is in contact with the service organisation. In the context of customer service and support it is a feature associated with telephone response centres. In this case it is caused ultimately by the number of lines available being the limiting resource.

Reducing service intensity:
If the capacity of our operation is constrained or expensive to enlarge because of the large incremental increases in capacity an alternative is for

us to look for ways to reduce service intensity. There are a number of ways in which we might go about this:

1   Remote diagnosis and fault fixing through the increased use of technology.
2   Increasing the reliability of equipment.
3   Reducing the time taken to carry out service and support work.
4   Increasing the access to information and in-house support teams to reduce the time to complete and close down one service event.

Improving the scheduling and allocation of resources:
As we pointed out earlier most customer service and support operations employ a mix of the chase and level strategies for creating a balance between service intensity and effective capacity. The result is that the effective capacity is set less than the peaks in demand as shown in Fig. 8.1. This strategy recognises that at times there will be insufficient resources to meet demand. It also brings with it the third strategy for managing capacity. This is the *coping* strategy, by which we mean the strategy which is followed when we are unable to match capacity with the service intensity, in short-term. It is often seen in service operations in those periods when they would describe themselves as being busy or slack. In our experience not many service and support operations have a clear policy of what to do in these circumstances. Failure to think and plan a course usually has adverse effects on customer satisfaction or resource productivity.

The coping strategy:

As service managers become more clever at managing capacity and balancing it with demand it is at capacity break points where things start to go wrong (Fig. 8.1). The break points occur in four areas:

1   When a chase strategy becomes level in the short-term because our effective capacity cannot be increased to meet demand. Usually this happens because there would be an overall underutilisation of resources if we were to set resource levels to near to peak demand.
2   When a chase strategy becomes level because we are not able to reduce the level of resources any lower in the short-term. We cannot reduce the staff numbers any more in the short-term without dismissing people.

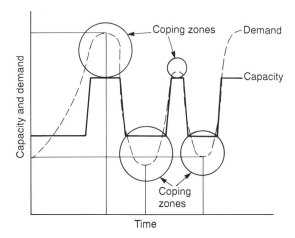

Figure 8.1 Coping capacity strategy

3 When a level strategy fails to stifle demand or overbooks appointments.

4 When a level strategy is unsuccessful in filling effective capacity because we have been unsuccessful at stimulating demand.

At these times quality of service or resource productivity will be under threat. We will look at the way to minimise the potential damage from loss of quality when we consider the important aspects of recovery strategies in a later chapter.

How do we plan and control resources?

There are a number of areas in the delivery of customer service and support where resources need to be planned and controlled. These are:

- Customer response centres
- Engineer visits for preventative maintenance
- Engineer visits for faults and breakdowns
- Support activities which take more than a few minutes to resolve
- Repair and calibration of equipment in a workshop.

To be able to plan we need to know the demand in terms of the work content for the tasks which have to be completed to deliver the service or support. The statement of work content may be in terms of minutes to deal with a telephone call, or attendance hours, or the time taken for workshop repair. When the tasks to be performed are simple and repetitive it is relatively easy to make the calculation. However for more complex tasks involving diagnosis the prediction of work content for the service or support time is more difficult to know in advance. We may deal with this by allocating some capacity knowing that further work will be required. However we also know as the work proceeds we will become clear on how much resource is required.

Customer response centres
The target for customer response centres is to answer customers' calls within a specified time, for example 20 seconds. We can approach capacity management by:

- using forecasting techniques to predict demand on a half hour daily basis allowing for weekly, monthly and seasonal variations
- estimating the work content of the average call so that we can then predict the number of receptionists we need to cover the demand
- taking account of the short-term randomness of the call rate by using what is called *queueing theory*. This enables us to predict the number of receptionists we need to limit the wait time to our target time. At one time most service managers would have been unable to take advantage of these techniques. Now there are software packages which can be used in most situations
- schedule the numbers of staff at various times during the day in line with demand and the target waiting time. The use of part-time staff and flexible working hours help in this process.

Visits for preventative maintenance
We can schedule preventative maintenance from a knowledge of the demand from customer service contracts and the work content for each task. The certainty of the work content will be highest if any additional work over and above an allocation for unplanned work is scheduled separately for completion at another time.

Scheduling of site visits needs, of course, an allocation for travelling time. The use of route planners may help the reduction in the travelling content.

Visits for breakdowns
Scheduling resources for breakdowns and faults is of course more difficult because the level and variety of demand is more uncertain. We can use

forecasting techniques to predict the service intensity so far as the number of incidents is concerned. What is less certain is the nature of the incident and the amount of resource it will consume in travelling and work content to complete the job.

Consequently we are left to schedule resources in anticipation of demand and to increase the response flexibility of our capacity. We may do this by arranging call-out transfers from other areas. In the process we will be thinking about the trade-off between having more resources than may be needed and hence the cost of this redundancy and the added call-out costs.

There is often a decision to be made as to whether or not to keep preventative maintenance and breakdown activity separated and to use teams dedicated to one or the other. The advantages and disadvantages would seem to us to be:

1   Mixed team approach: Pros
(a) higher resource productivity
(b) greater job satisfaction through increased variety
2   Mixed team approach: Cons
(a) need for multi-skilling
(b) preventative work may be reduced because of the urgency of breakdowns
3   Separate teams approach: Pros
(a) dedication brings increased learning and expertise in each activity
(b) preventative maintenance is completed which may reduce call-back rates
4   Separate teams approach: Cons
(a) higher resource productivity costs through lower utilisation of resources.

Support activities
Scheduling resources to deal with support activities requires us to have a knowledge of the expected level of demand and of the work content. Where we are dealing with standard problems it is easy to estimate the work content from past experience. In more complex cases this may not be so easy.

We have found in the support area one problem is the closing of jobs within a target time. This can happen for customers seeking help with a software package from a computer support activity. While the job may only require a few hours' work on the part of a specialist, he or she may have to consult others and request additional information, all of which takes time.

In the meantime the specialist may start other jobs and return intermittently to this one. It is rather like the juggler spinning plates. Once he has started a plate spinning he must return to it to keep it on the go. There is a limit to the number of plates which can be kept spinning and eventually one or all falls. For the customers the result of this crash is poor customer support.

A better approach is to try to progress jobs to completion once they have been started. This requires the support of people working more as a team rather than as a set of individuals. The results are that jobs are completed sooner and when there are bottlenecks they become apparent early on in the process so that some action can be taken to remove them.

Workshop repair
We can gain a lot from the new concepts of manufacturing to improve the use of resources in the workshop repair and calibration situation. The target as in the support activity above is to ensure turn-round of jobs within target times. The secret to success is to limit the number of jobs which are being worked on and to make sure they are completed once they have been started. Also we need to ensure that equipment which cannot immediately be repaired in the workshop perhaps because of the lack of spares does not remain there but is brought back to a central control point.

Availability of spares is crucial to the repair activity and again improvements in logistics through just-in-time supply of major parts can assist in the process.

The benefits of these approaches are seen in a tidier workshop where everyone can see what is happening, hence contribute to better quality of work, and a more consistent turn-round time for repairs.

Using the network?

One of the major ways in which service and support operations can flex capacity is to use the network. We have already seen how resources can be transferred from one part to another to provide extra capacity and how we might share expensive equipment between branches. When we look at managing resource productivity we will look in more detail at how the use of the network can lead to greater utilisation of resources.

Conclusion

In this chapter we have examined the meaning of capacity for customer service and support and the way in which different resources affect capacity. We have looked at how we can forecast demand for service and support to reduce the level of uncertainty. We have described three basic approaches to managing the balance between demand and effective capacity – the chase, level and coping strategies. The choice of strategy is influenced by our ability to build flexibility into the capacity from service teams in a branch to the complete network. We have described the need to understand two dimensions for flexiblity of 'How far can we change' (range), and 'How quickly can we change' (response).

Checklist

1   How do you measure your capacity?

2   How do your resources affect your capacity?

3   What is your capacity management strategy? Do you mainly try to chase demand or influence demand?

4   How much of your time do you feel you are having to adopt a coping strategy?

5   How can you flex your effective capacity?

6   How far can you flex or change your capacity and how long does it take you to make the change?

7   Are there any actions which you could take to increase either your flexibility of range or response which would help you to reduce the time you use the coping strategy?

8   What could you do to influence demand or service intensity?

9   What could you do to increase the accuracy of your forecasting of demand?

10   Are you making the best use of your network to flex capacity?

9 MANAGING SERVICE QUALITY

Introduction

In this chapter we will introduce briefly the main principles of quality management and describe how they might apply specifically to the customer service and support organisation.

Product quality and, latterly, service quality has received a great deal of attention in recent years. In the 1980s, achieving consistently good product quality levels gave some companies a strong competitive advantage. In a sense, consistently meeting specifications is only doing what customers assume we will do and the strength of advantage through consistent quality will diminish. How can you market a product by emphasising the fact that it really will work as it is intended? So in the 1990s and beyond the gap between industry leaders and the rest will close as organisations manage their processes more effectively.

The problem for quality management is that each management decision and each management action has an implication for quality. The saying that 'The management of quality is about the quality of management' is perhaps obvious, but to a large extent true. Time after time our work with service organisations brings us back to the fundamental operational issue of managing service demand and service capacity. One of the quality gurus, Philip Crosby, has said, 'There are no quality problems, there are only symptoms'. Reflecting on what is termed poor quality leads us to identify the real problem as one of the following:

- Insufficient resources were available to cope with the demand for service
- Resources were provided but they were not of sufficiently high standard for the expectations of the customer
- There were general communication problems, information not being passed to the required destination soon enough, if at all
- The people involved had received insufficient training for the task.

Fig. 9.1 illustrates the principal issues to be discussed in this chapter. The essence of service quality management lies in reaching a clear, customer-related specification of goods and services and then designing systems that consistently deliver to that specification. Both definition and delivery must be subjected to regular review in the light of the way that customers view the service and provide feedback for improvement.

Figure 9.1 Service quality improvement

It is helpful to distinguish between two activities in Quality Management. The first, *quality assurance*, relates to the need to instil customer confidence. The aim is to demonstrate that the systems and procedures of the service and support organisation are under control and will produce the required result. Activities under this heading relate to formal quality systems, audits, and the use of statistical evidence to indicate that the processes are in control or to formulate improvement priorities.

The second activity, *quality improvement*, relates more to an attitude of mind or culture within the organisation which refuses to accept that some problems are always with us. A culture that supports continuous improvement asserts that problems can be permanently fixed, often through the creativity and goodwill of employees who have been involved in the quality process rather than treated as if they had no contribution to make.

Both activities have evolved and have benefitted from the best of Total

Quality Management. Quality Assurance has moved in emphasis away from determining 'acceptable quality levels' and actions directed at preventing poor quality from being visible to the customer through to designing systems and processes that are statistically 'in control' which means that the probability of failure is often far less than one per cent. Quality improvement, likewise, has grown from 'exhortation' through stirring speeches and poster campaigns through to activities aimed at solving quality problems once and for all. This quality improvement is often linked with a structure of quality teams which serves another purpose in encouraging integration across the organisation.

This chapter addresses the following issues:

- The importance of quality management to the organisation, its customers and employees
- Defining quality: the effect of product specification on customer support and formulating service definitions
- Delivering quality: the role of management, quality systems, quality techniques and people involvement.

Why is quality management so important?

Although maintaining consistently good quality has a lot to do with systems and procedures, quality management has much to do with people. The attitude adopted by the organisation to quality will have tremendous impact on customers and employees alike.

Quality and customers

It has become fashionable to talk of customer satisfaction in terms of being 'delighted' by the goods and services received. Unfortunately, there are far too many organisations whose customers are pleasantly surprised or even amazed when things go right for a change! Organisations must know that customers have the final word. They may not be able to protest too loudly in the short-term if no alternative goods or services are available, but there will come a time when customers will find a better service and the organisation will be the loser.

It can be argued that it is always better to keep the customer happy, because dissatisfied customers tend to be more disruptive and therefore expensive to look after. There are other sound financial reasons for keeping customers happy. If a customer spends £10,000 on purchasing a car every three years, and perhaps £300 on annual service costs, it makes no sense to lose a long term annual revenue of nearly £4000 by paying insufficient attention to service quality. There are few businesses that can afford to lose a customer, and it must be remembered that if one is upset there is a strong probability that others will also be unhappy. In the same way that customers now calculate the lifetime cost of ownership, service providers must consider lifetime revenues.

The benefits of good quality are:

1 *Higher perceived quality commands high prices*. Market research and academic studies such as the PIMS (Profit Impact of Market Share) project at Harvard Business School have indicated that companies with a higher perceived quality level tend to be able to command higher prices than those with poor quality reputations. Christian Gronroos has suggested that this is a function of the relationship costs (that is, the cost of doing business with the organisation). An example of this cost is the time spent by managers and employees checking and rechecking work and, of course, correcting errors. Some people are employed by the organisation purely because things go wrong and the cost of not discovering these problems as early as possible is great. Customers have 'relationship costs' which are greater or smaller depending on the confidence they have in the organisation they are dealing with. Customers pay more for products they can depend on because they cost less in the long run.

2 *Long Term Income*. Companies should be aware of the lifetime income represented by an individual customer. A customer usually makes more than one purchase over time in addition to the service income relating to the original purchase. Good quality will secure this business and reduce the likelihood of customers switching to a competing product. It is much more expensive to generate new customers than to keep existing ones, apart from the fact that there may not be an endless supply of new business.

3 *Quality Image*. Good quality is good marketing in the sense that satisfied customers tend to tell others. The opposite is also true. On average the unhappy customer tells ten others about the poor service he has received.

Quality and employees

Quality is an important element in the morale of employees. There is nothing that disillusions people as rapidly as having to perform a substandard task. Gerald Ratner gained some publicity by suggesting that the products sold in his jewellery shops were 'rubbish' (edited version!), a pair of earrings being worth less than a prawn sandwich from Marks and Spencers. Some of his staff were not pleased to hear that they were working hard to sell poor quality goods.

The employee-related benefits of good quality are as follows:

1 *Improved morale*. Employee confidence is directly related to their view of the product they are dealing with. High morale will yield benefits in reduced employee turnover and absenteeism, and improved productivity.

2 *Positive customer contact*. For contact personnel, the benefits of good quality are multiplied. Being in regular contact with customers can be demanding at the best of times. Good quality will tend to make the job of the contact person that much easier; at times they may even receive compliments instead of complaints. Compliments tend to encourage service personnel to try harder, and so give better service, thereby building a positive spiral of improvement.

3 *Involvement*. Companies that encourage problem-solving as part of the organisation's culture have discovered a major resource in their employees. In some World Class companies, genuine suggestions are being generated at rates in excess of 100 per employee per year.

Reducing quality cost

Many organisations are aiming to be 'Right First Time'. This is because the total cost of quality may be in excess of 25 per cent of turnover. The elements of quality cost are:

1 *Failure costs*. The costs involved in repair and rework, putting in place recovery actions, warranties and guarantees. The greatest cost may be the loss of customer goodwill which will result in lost sales and ultimately business failure.

2 *Appraisal costs*. These are the costs involved in inspection procedures to ensure that specifications are met. Appraisal costs are 'policing' costs, as they add no value to the product.

3 *Prevention costs*. This is what the organisation spends in order to improve quality before the event. This cost includes quality education and process development.

Many organisations have found that their first estimate of quality cost was much too low because the full information was not available. It is not uncommon for failure costs to be the largest component of quality cost with relatively little spent initially on prevention. As more money is spent on prevention, this balance shifts and total quality cost reduces. This reduction in quality cost may be translated directly into increased profitability.

Organisations with a high degree of customer contact and involvement may assert that it is impossible to be 'Right First Time, Every Time', because it is impossible to legislate for customers. This may be true, but most would agree that it is possible to be Right First Time rather more often, and in the Back Room there is no reason why the Right First Time standard should not apply.

Defining quality

A working definition of quality is crucial if the customer is to receive a consistently high standard of goods and services. Without a clear description of what is to be produced, procedures as to how it is to be produced, and objective measurement, service standards become matters of individual opinion and service is inconsistent. The customer also has no means of judging whether the service has lived up to its promise or not, leading to potential dissatisfaction.

Various blanket definitions of quality have been developed:

- Fitness for purpose
- Quality which meets the customer's requirements
- The totality of features and characteristics of a product or service that bear on its ability to meet stated or implied needs (BS 4778).

This last definition is particularly pertinent for customer service and support. In our surveys of the manufacturing sector we have found that many companies believe that product quality levels are now consistently high. Service quality improvement is critical to support the newly enhanced quality image of the manufactured product and to differentiate the company from the competition.

We believe that quality management is about ensuring that everything the company does adds to rather than takes away from customer confidence. A wonderful product will soon be let down by poor service and support. Customer confidence can be rapidly eroded by relatively small details. Total Quality Management should mean that everything the organisation does is defined clearly and delivered consistently.

A problem arises if product quality and service quality are managed as separate entities. This means that the extent to which one impacts on the other is not understood and a major source for improvement is lost. Clearly, an upgrade in the specification of the product ought to reduce the risk of failure and should also be directed towards improvements in the ease of product maintenance. It may be difficult for product designers to balance all requirements, but they must be aware of all the implications of their designs.

Dimensions of product quality

Having said that we should consider product and service together it is useful to review a list of quality dimensions which was generated by David Garvin of the Harvard Business School, who makes an important point in looking at product quality. He says,

'Quality means pleasing consumers, not just protecting them from annoyances. Product designers should shift their attention from prices at the time of purchase to life cycle costs.'

His Eight Dimensions of Strategic Quality follow. The customer service and support manager will need to be aware of the issues here as the support task is affected to a large extent by the quality of the product and, of course, the support organisation will be a valuable source of information about product quality and customer preference.

1 *Performance*. The product's primary operating characteristics, such as maximum speed or fuel consumption for an automobile, may be intangible or subjective. Garvin quotes the noise of a product as an example. A product may appear noisy when compared to a competitor's product even though the noise is within the design specification. The customer support organisation must be able to cope with customers who are worried about their purchases, reassuring them without appearing offhand, and certainly not dismissing them as a waste of time. Quality reputations lie in the perception of the customer and are strongly related to customer confidence. The noise level of the product may not be of technical concern, but the fact that the customer is worried is all that matters.

2 *Features*. The 'extras' which, though not vital for product perform-ance, make up the value for money equation, such as the choice of

options for product or service. There will be implications for the support manager here in terms of spare parts inventory or skill requirements to service the product or to explain the range of options and facilities available. For complex products the purchase package will commonly contain a period of training which must be readily available, and therefore be carefully scheduled by the customer service and support organisation.

3 *Reliability*. Quality and Reliability are not synonymous. There will be a statistical probability that the product will last for a given period of time without problem or breakdown. This will be represented by the product's MTBF and will have a significant impact on the load on the support organisation. As products reach maturity, it is common for MTBFs to lengthen and it becomes increasingly difficult to justify expensive service contracts to customers. At this stage the emphasis may move to routine maintenance.

4 *Conformance*. Garvin here means the degree to which the organisation's processes are capable of meeting the 'ideal' or target dimensions which have been set by the organisation. If this were to be applied to a service organisation, we would need to know whether the range of service engineer response time achieved is two hours plus or minus five minutes, or plus or minus 30 minutes. If the latter is the best that can be achieved it would be wise to promise a 2½ hour response time so as not to raise customer expectations. The Japanese approach to product quality has been to steadily reduce the variability in all the organisation's processes, thereby ensuring that all performance measures are well within specifications. This reduction in variability is particularly valuable when tolerances are 'stacked up', perhaps leading to the situation where the assembled product is out of specification even though the component parts are to drawing.

This approach has general application to the support organisation in that a reduction in variability of the organisation's performance will improve the customers' view of its quality. A specific application is that if spare part manufacture is subjected to this discipline there will be few problems with interchangeability and repair times will be minimised.

5 *Durability*. Again, this dimension of product quality has significant implications for support. Is the product capable of economic repair on failure? A cheap ball point pen will be thrown away, whereas a more expensive fountain pen may be repaired. The war of ever lengthening guarantees is part of the on-going process of increasing customer expectations. Many organisations find that a significant proportion of warranty expense arises not because the basic product has failed, but because the design does not cope with all the possible uses and misuses of the product. For example, VCRs do not cope with small children posting objects in the cassette slot.

The robustness of the product in use must also be considered and the support organisation will have useful information for the designer. Computer terminals for use in a factory workshop will be 'ruggedised' to cope with adverse conditions, but can be less sturdy in an office environment.

We had a problem with a cordless iron whose design meant that it was difficult to replace on its stand. Inevitably the day came when it fell onto the floor and, being largely of plastic construction, part of it was broken. The only advice the customer service department could give was not to drop it! The product must be designed for every aspect of its purpose and environment.

6 *Serviceability*. To a large extent, the ease and speed of service is fixed at an early stage of product design. Unfortunately, most engineering departments do not address these needs until the end of the design process by which time it is too late to make a significant change. The number of stages of disassembly and the number of fixings to be removed to replace or repair a wearing part must be considered with as much importance as the primary operating characteristics of the product. The customer service and support manager must fight to ensure that these issues are fully considered as early as possible.

7 *Aesthetics*. This dimension relates to how the product looks, feels, tastes or smells. Not all will be relevant (it is not important how a machine tool tastes!), but it should look impressive.

8 *Perceived Quality*. We must recognise that a customer does not always view the product in the same light as its designers, and realise that a product's quality may be judged not by its technical merit but by image, whether someone treated the customer well or badly or by its general reputation.

The last dimension here is particularly important for the customer support manager, who can influence the perception of the customer to the extent of making or breaking the organisation's quality reputation. The Eight Dimensions of Product Quality proposed by Garvin are an extremely useful starting point to consider all aspects of product design and how they might impact on the service task. We must now consider how the service task itself can be defined more exactly.

Dimensions of service quality

Garvin's Eight Dimensions of Product Quality do not give sufficient details for the customer support manager to form a thorough definition of service quality which is necessary if the organisation is to be serious about managing quality. Schonberger proposed four more dimensions to aid this process:

1   *Quick response*. The need for the organisation and its employees to acknowledge its customers quickly, and to carry out all tasks rapidly.

2   *Quick change*. The flexibility to produce a different product from the same system in a given period of time.

3   *Humanity*. Does the organisation and its employees respond with understanding of an individual customer's needs?

4   *Value*. Does the product represent value for money in the customers' eyes?

This list adds to the Garvin Dimensions but we have found the list of service attributes generated by Berry, Parasuraman and Zeithaml to be a good starting place to generate service definition:

1   *Reliability*. Consistent performance, meeting promised dates, keeping to routine maintenance schedules. The support organisation should include here making and keeping promises to return telephone calls, confirming appointments where possible in advance and rescheduling only when absolutely necessary and on very rare occasions.

2   *Responsiveness*. Prompt service, an attitude throughout the organisation to respond to customers' needs rather than find ways of avoiding them. Most service organisations have stories about how employees have worked extraordinary hours or walked through snow drifts to ensure the customer received good service. The problem is that these stories are often very much the exception. The good service providers are those who anticipate most customer requests and who do not find reasons why these requests cannot be met.

3   *Competence*. Product knowledge and necessary skill to perform service and support tasks. Customer confidence may be boosted by employing experienced service staff with evidence of appropriate training courses completed.

4   *Access*. Easy telephone access through easily remembered telephone numbers to the right people to take and solve the customer's problem, hours of operation which fit the customers' needs, location of support personnel and facilities.

5   *Courtesy*. Politeness of service personnel, and Berry also suggests 'consideration for the customer's property'. The state in which the service engineer leaves the customer's premises may indicate the competence of the repair carried out.

6   *Communication*. Keeping customers informed about the service in terms they understand and at times which are helpful to them. Letting them know when there is a problem rather than hoping they won't find out. Giving clear and accurate cost estimates before the customer is committed.

7   *Credibility*. Reputation for honest, competent dealings, personal characteristics of customer contact personnel.

8   *Security*. Physical safety, no damage to property, confidentiality, value for money.

9   *Understanding the customer*. Distinguishing the customer's true requirements rather than what is stated, individual attention, ensuring that their needs are understood, making customers feel 'in control' rather than constrained by the system.

10   *Tangibles*. Appearance and quality of facilities and equipment, quality of invoices, tenders, letters.

This last dimension leads us back to 'perceived quality' in Garvin's list of product quality dimensions. The product itself clearly is a major ingredient in the customer's perception of the support organisation.

In a sense, it doesn't matter which set of dimensions you follow as long as the definitions you employ fully describe the breadth of product and service quality. In Chapter 2 we described an approach we have used to determine Customer Service Dimensions and the priorities within them. We have found it useful to group them under four main headings and then to develop subheadings as appropriate for the situation under review. The headings are as follows:

- *Product*. Those attributes of product design that affect customer perception and therefore also the service task. MTBF would be included here. Garvin's Dimensions might be used here.
- *Support*. The degree and extent of customer support services provided such as availability of advice and training.
- *Service*. Activities directed at ensuring that the product is maintained or repaired to give maximum availability. This would include response times and spares availability.
- *Process*. The process of dealing with customers. Is the organisation

easy to deal with, and are the employees responsive? Many of the Berry, Parasuraman and Zeithaml service determinants apply here.

How do we set the right standards?

In setting quality standards there must be an overlap with marketing because we must discover what is important to the customer in order to set the priorities for the organisation. In order to manage quality the service and support manager must be able to set clear standards, combining attributes such as those listed above, and understanding which internal standards are critical in delivering service which customers perceive to be good. Fig. 9.2 illustrates this relationship. A number of the major automobile manufacturers are working hard to establish the links between the elements of an overall customer satisfaction index for dealer network performance and the internal standards achieved at each stage of the service and supply chain. One company is considering internal customer satisfaction indices, allowing the dealer to rate the parent company's performance.

We find that many organisations pay lip service to the idea of listening to customers. The 'excellent' service providers invest significant

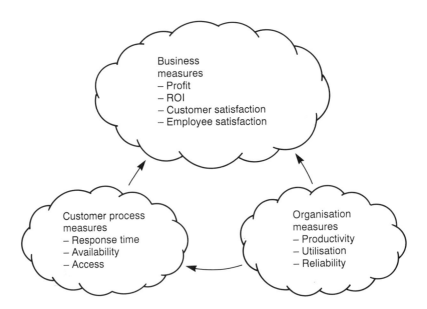

Figure 9.2 Quality relationships

resources in listening to customers, gathering objective data on customers' views of quality and spending time listening to the strength of feeling behind the hard data. Methods for customer research include:

1   *General surveys*. Customers are asked to rate their overall impression of the service as well as rating specific elements of service delivery. It is important to give space to allow the respondent to explain their rating of any of the elements as well as to give more general feedback. We have found that the questions 'What did we do well?' and 'What did we do badly?' are very valuable in indicating areas for improvement as well as opportunites to feed back praise to departments or individuals.

The warning that must be given is that simple rating scales, while easy to administer, yield 'averages' which may cover a multitude of sins. If the spread of response is consistently narrow, the average reading is a sufficient guide, but a wide spread, particularly if grouped at two extremes, indicates a problem.

2   *Transaction based surveys*. To counteract the 'average' problem, it may be valuable to design a more specific survey to investigate specific areas of the organisation. British Airways and similar organisations when surveying a particular aspect of their service now ask a number of related questions. So, if a customer says that the service was poor, they are able to link this back to operational reasons such as late flights or overloads at check-in counters.

3   *Customer focus groups*. It is often instructive to feed the results of surveys back to a cross-section of customers asking for their reaction to the figures. It may transpire that the questions and answers have subtly different meanings to organisation and customers. It is instructive for senior managers to hear the strength of feeling which may be hidden by data.

4   *Employee surveys*. The staff, and in particular those in regular contact with customers, know how well the service is delivered and they see the customers' reactions to it. Linking their view on customer satisfaction with a survey of attitudes can be very useful. A question such as 'What would help you to deliver better service?' may help direct investment plans.

Having heard what customers and employees have to say, it should be possible both to define the relevant attributes of service delivery and to set performance levels to be achieved against each of them. It is important to measure your organisation against the best in the world and many carry out 'Benchmarking' programmes, taking each aspect of the operation in turn and measuring performance against any similar organisation. Thus Rank Xerox, which has carried out extensive benchmarking, compared its logistics function against the best logistics networks of any type, not solely those in the photocopier market.

It must be said that there is no point in setting service standards if the system is not capable of delivering them or there are not definite plans to invest in improvement. Setting unrealistic targets will demotivate in the long-term if they are seen to be unobtainable and will thus become irrelevant.

It is a well-known saying 'Without measurement there can be no control'. It is also true that 'With too much measurement there is confusion'. The handful of key measures that drive the organisation must be consistent throughout service delivery. It will be no use trying to emphasise customer responsiveness if it is known that the only thing which the organisation rewards is keeping costs as low as possible. Organisations must be aware of the impact of their motivation and control systems on service quality.

How can we make sure we deliver the right quality?

Having discovered how customers view quality for the support organisation, a customer specification can be drawn up and systems and processes employed to deliver to this specification must be audited as to indicate where there are quality issues to be addressed.

The Quality Triangle (Fig. 9.3), developed by Professor John Oakland of Bradford University, provides a useful framework for a balanced approach to quality management.

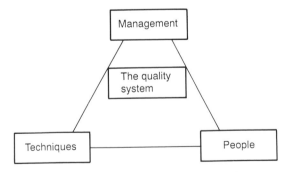

Figure 9.3 The quality triangle

The role of management

It is perhaps facile to say that quality requires senior management commitment. It is certainly too easy for senior managers to say they are committed to quality but then for their subsequent decisions to give the lie to this statement.

There is a 'tension' in quality management which must be addressed. The emphasis behind most of today's quality thinking is that continuous improvement should be a way of life, with 'zero defects' being a theoretically attainable goal. Zero defects may be possible for a manufacturing process or a routine service and support activity where each action is under the direct control of the organisation. This zero defects goal looks much more difficult when a significant part of the process, namely customer participation, is not under the support organisation's direct control. Even so, we need to press on, believing that improvement is always possible, but knowing that some imperfect short-term decisions must be made.

Having said all this, employees see the underlying attitude of their managers towards quality. They see if the fine words mean nothing at all when the crunch comes. They see and copy the example set for them. Rank Xerox claim that their organisation is driven *first and foremost* by customer satisfaction goals rather than profit goals. That is not to say that Rank Xerox are not interested in profit, rather that they believe that if customer satisfaction is managed well, profits will follow.

One of our friends was appointed as managing director of a small electronics company, which is part of a larger group. It was known that the company had quality problems and, after putting in place a quality recording system, it was soon identified that the main problem was that the company was unable to manage new products adequately from design into production and thence to support. The new managing director took the decision to delay the launch of the next product until these issues were properly addressed. This was not a popular decision either internally or with the group board who saw a decline in short-term profitability. As a consequence of his actions the company retained a major customer who was on the point of dropping them as a supplier as a result of poor quality. Signals such as these are central to quality success.

Likewise, the management team is largely responsible for what is generally termed the culture of the organisation. Is it dynamic, innovative, paternalistic or bureaucratic? We have worked with service and support organisations where employees have told us that suggestions were not encouraged and were met with the response, 'That's not your job or concern'. Clearly this will not cultivate an atmosphere for quality improvement. It takes time to wait for employees to make suggestions, when sometimes the solution is 'obvious' to managers, but the time spent will be worthwhile.

Lastly, senior management must develop and pursue a quality strategy which sets out the targets for each business area and ensures that there are sufficient resources devoted to achieving the plan. Too many quality programmes have failed because although the opening stages of announcement and increased quality awareness have gone well, there has been nothing to follow through with. Fig. 9.4 shows Caterpillar's Quality Programme, with goals and actions in each area spread over ten years. Quality improvements will not come about without a realistic allocation of resources behind it.

Using the quality techniques

A number of quality tools and techniques are available and these fall into three broad categories:

1   Presentation of statistical measurement of processes and products to gain better control and to indicate priorities for improvement.
2   Design planning techniques to ensure that customer quality priorities are given due emphasis.
3   Tools which facilitate small group discussion and effectiveness.

It is not the purpose of this book to describe each technique in detail, but rather to indicate their existence and relevance to customer service and support.

Statistics for control

Statistical Process Control (SPC) is being used increasingly to monitor performance and to identify areas for attention. SPC can range from the very simple application of the attributes of the normal distribution through to higher degree standard statistics. More organisations are now charting aspects of their processes using simple control charts such as displayed in Fig. 9.5. The **average** of a sample of repair times is plotted on a chart which portrays the performance of the process overall. This chart is sometimes known as the X chart because it is the mean of the sample, not individual readings, which is plotted.

Eight point quality program – *Milestones*

1

A quality standard setting process based on customer needs and competitive levels which incorporates product quality requirements into functional, reliability and durability terms.

	'82	'83	'84	'85	'86	'87	'88	'89	'90	'91/'92
Setting Standards	OGO/SEGO setting reliability standards	PRM 200 Hr DRF Stds set	Field follow standard reduced 50%	PRM 201-1000 hr targets set DRF lowered 20%	*Apportments developed *Response targets lowered	90% of targets set for Expansion Line Products	Reliability apportment installed in production PRM			Product & process targets represent high customer preference

2

A product design, testing/evaluation and manufacturing readiness program which results in meeting quality requirements at first production

	'82	'83	'84	'85	'86	'87	'88	'89	'90	'91/'92
New Product	Reliability Growth installed	New Product Strategy initiated	Quality Strategy reviews begun	NPI Checklist used at production readiness	Quality guide book for NPI published	Reliability apportment used for new designs	80% products meet targets			All products meet targets throughout life cycle

3

A manufacturing conformance program to plan and achieve conformance to design requirements

	'82	'83	'84	'85	'86	'87	'88	'89	'90	'91/'92
Manu-facturing	Qual indicator NOPS includes DLY loss scrap & rework	Piece part conformance at 50%, all characteristics	Conformance measure changed to Defects 1000	Worldwide plant conformance at 50%	Processes evaluated at 50% capability	CPK introduced as process improvement indicator	Internal Quality Certification established			All processes – 15 CPK major commodities certified

4

A supplier quality assurance-certification program to supply parts and components which confirm to the design requirements

	'82	'83	'84	'85	'86	'87	'88	'89	'90	'91/'92
Supplier	Certification discipline reinforced	Quality Plan guide in use	Certification video & brochure	Quality Evaluation Profile	60% of volume Certified	AQI video & brochure for suppliers	80% Certified SPC AQI required			– 5% Rejections – 15% CPK AQI Manufacturability Consolidation JIT

5

A product service to the customer from factory and dealer which maximises the return on his investment in Caterpillar product

	'82	'83	'84	'85	'86	'87	'88	'89	'90	'91/'92
Product Support				Dealer service quality survey started	Measures of CAT support to dealers defined	Dealer service surveys growing	Surveys introduced at subsidiaries			Dealers & customers acknowledge product support as superior

6

A field intelligence and response system which causes rapid and complete correction of product problems

	'82	'83	'84	'85	'86	'87	'88	'89	'90	'91/'92
Field intelligence	SIMS providing field data	Field follow feedback strengthened	Product problem system reviewed	Operations Grp reviewing past due impact problems	Problem response time improving	Dealer inquiry system in place	Apportment used to identify problems of sub impact			Field intelligence & response cause high customer satisfaction

7

An annual quality improvement program using quality education to improve the knowledge, skills and attitudes of all personnel which impacts all corporate processes

	'82	'83	'84	'85	'86	'87	'88	'89	'90	'91/'92
Education	Quality Education begun	•Juran training •SPC Course	•QUEST newsletter •Juran met w officers	•Diagnostic Tools Course •Officers met w.media on Quality	•AQI Matrix •Taguchi •QFD	Quality Institute initiated	Keynote at IMPRO 88 by CAT officer			Process improvement rate exceeds competitors

8

An accounting and evaluation system for quality improvement to help management direct resources to their most effective use by quantifying the cost of product defects and process waste

	'82	'83	'84	'85	'86	'87	'88	'89	'90	'91/'92
Non-quality costs			Product related cost elements identified	Costs estimated at $400 Mil/Yr		Corporate ADI team established				Costs reduced to < $80 Mil/Yr

Figure 9.4 Eight point quality program (reprinted from The TQM Magazine, *November, 1988. © IFS Ltd., Kempston, Bedford, UK, 1988)*

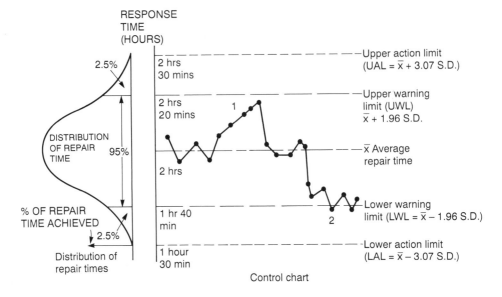

Figure 9.5 SPC charting of repair times

Warning limits are shown at ±1.96 Standard Deviations from the mean and action limit at 3.07 Standard Deviations. This means that 99.8 per cent of all outcomes should be between the action limits, unless something has changed the basic performance of the process. One in 40 readings can be expected to lie between the warning limit and the action limit. This allows the manager to review whether the process needs adjustment before disaster occurs.

A parallel chart is the range chart which charts the trend in the spread of individual readings which make up the sample. Thus it may be possible for the average plotted on the control chart to be relatively consistent, but if the range is increasing, the process variability is also increasing and this will indicate a potential problem.

Analysis of the control chart allows the customer support team to analyse performance to identify where changes have occured which must be addressed. Fig. 9.6 indicates a sustained increase in the repair times at position 1, perhaps due to the supply of out of tolerance spare parts requiring more time to fit. At position 2, the repair times are consistently shorter, perhaps as the result of more effective product training.

The procedure is to measure the current performance of the system to discover present capability in terms of mean and standard deviation, and

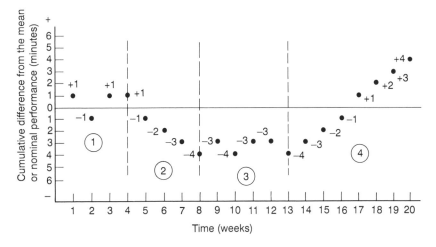

Figure 9.6 Cusum chart for service engineer response times

then to compare this to the demands of service specification. If the performance is within specification, all is well. If it is not, something must be done, either to change the system or to relax the specification.

The Cusum chart (Fig. 9.6) is an alternative way of displaying trends in performance data. This chart shows response time data. The nominal average response time is deducted from the actual time and then added to previous calculations to give a cumulative sum or Cusum. At position 1, the Cusum is distributed about the zero point and this indicates that the expected average performance is being maintained. At position 2 the Cusum is moving steadily downwards, and this indicates that the average response time is currently faster than average. At position 3 the response time returns to the original average, and at 4 the average response is slower. Trends upwards or downwards indicate that the average performance is changing, and horizontals that the response time is to the specified average. This form of presentation allows the customer service and support manager to identify trends faster than merely plotting raw data.

There are many other forms of presentation which space prevents us from describing. A final technique in this section is the use of tally charts. Fig. 9.7 shows a chart showing the reasons for equipment being returned under warranty. For 59 products returned, it can be seen that the portable TV is causing the most problems, but that scratches account for 32 per cent of all claims. This technique will quickly indicate problem areas for attention.

Product \ Cause	Loose connection	Switches	Scratches	Handles	Tubes	No fault found	
Radio	𝍸 I	I	𝍸	I		II	15 / (25)
Television 20"	I	II	𝍸 I		III	I	13 / (22)
Portable TV	II	𝍸 II	IIII	III	II	III	21 / (36)
Stereo	II	II	IIII	I		I	10 / (17)
Total	11 / (19)	12 / (20)	19 / 32	5 / (8)	5 / (8)	7 / (12)	59 / 100%

Figure 9.7 Tally chart for warranty returns

Quality by design

A design technique which is now becoming common is Quality Function Deployment (Fig. 9.8). QFD pulls together 'What' the customer requires and 'How' the designer will meet those requirements. The ticks in the matrix indicate the relationship between the two. The strength of the relationship between the Whats and Hows can be multiplied by a customer priority rating, perhaps arrived at by competitor analysis, and then summed down the column to give a score for each design parameter to indicate where the design improvement effort should be directed. This quality planning grid assists the designer to incorporate all the elements of quality in the design. Some organisations have extended this technique to include all aspects of the business, a grid then being developed by each function to indicate how business objectives will be achieved.

A further design technique which will have an impact on the customer service and support manager's task is that of Failure Mode and Effect

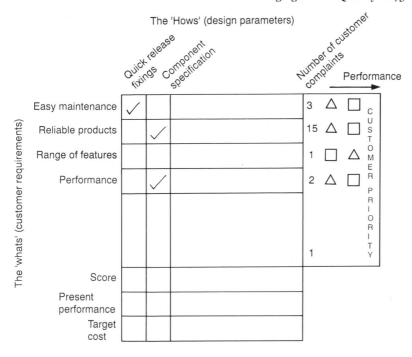

Figure 9.8 Quality function deployment

Analysis (FMEA). The questions which are being addressed here are 'What happens when it breaks?', 'How disastrous is it?' and 'How likely is it to happen?'. Some early motor cars would have benefited from this technique, particularly those which continued to accelerate even when the throttle cable had broken! Companies that use FMEA to identify possible problems or failure often then identify the processes which may contribute to failure and use SPC to ensure that they stay within control.

Techniques for involving people

There are a number of techniques which facilitate group discussion. Brainstorming is commonly used, and the results may be structured using a Fishbone or Ishikawa diagram. This allows the group to identify all possible causes of the identified problem, and can be used as a structure to collect data to indicate the relative importance of each cause.

Other techniques include SWOT (Strengths, Weaknesses, Opportunities and Threats) analysis and Force Field Analysis in which the group identifies positive and negative influences on a desired course of action. Process charting or mapping is particularly useful in identifying problem areas and has been described in more detail in Chapter 6. It is very useful for improving the understanding of the people involved in service and support both in terms of how their part of the organisation works and also how it fits with the organisation as a whole.

Involving the people

Many organisations have tried quality circles or other forms of voluntary improvement group activities and declare that they don't work. The reason for these failures often lies firmly with management who have not resourced these programmes sufficiently or thought how their efforts can be effectively coordinated.

Unguided, quality groups may solve the 'trivial many' rather than the 'critical few' problems, but this undervalues the role of such groups in communication and involvement. Organisations that have persisted with small group activity have usually evolved some sort of structure to coordinate voluntary departmental groups, groups with product focus, groups with a specific customer focus and task forces formed to solve specific problems and then disband. A critical issue for ensuring the commitment to quality from the people is that of motivation through rewards. The measures used to assess the success of customer service and support have a major contribution here. Some service organisations measure the effectiveness of their engineers on a mixture of repair time, numbers of quality failures, journey management and *customer satisfaction*. A balance of quality and productivity measures is essential to create the right motivation.

Within a service organisation there is much untapped information about quality because many people are frequently meeting customers, seeing where the organisation fails, and seeing where customer needs could be met more effectively. Management must work hard to create the right environment for quality improvement, encouraging suggestions for improvement. In some cases this will mean waiting for employees to make suggestions to gain their ownership of change rather than simply implementing management directives.

Developing the quality system

In the centre of the Quality Triangle is the Quality System. This term may bring to mind negative images of thick and boring Quality Manuals gathering dust on the shelf or Quality Auditors joyfully pointing out your shortcomings and explaining why you cannot get on with the business of making money until the correct procedure has been followed.

We think of the Quality System as giving the structure to Quality Management that it requires. It should describe the key processes employed to facilitate consistency of operation, provide the necessary checks and audits to allow review of the operation and generally act as the organisation's quality conscience.

Writing a Quality System requires some expertise, particularly where it relates to customer contact roles. Procedures must allow for some discretion where customer preferences must be acknowledged or accommodated. Flexibility is important here, while at the same time, procedures must ensure that the core of the operation is maintained.

The British Standard for Quality Systems, BS 5750, meets the requirements of European (EN 29000 etc) and International (ISO 9000 etc) Quality Standards. It gives guidelines for formulation of quality standards and the British Standards Institute audits and accredits organisations which operate systems that comply.

For many manufacturing companies BS 5750 approval may be essential if they are to be recognised as approved suppliers to certain customer organisations. At present this largely applies to the design and manufacturing functions. This trend, however, is spreading to include the service activity. A number of computer service organisations have now received BS 5750 approval. We believe that an organisation needs a Quality Structure to coordinate and audit its activities. It may be for some that BS 5750 approval will soon be a necessary qualification to operate.

Putting the Quality Triangle together

Successful Quality Management requires consideration of many things at once. Management must review its attitudes to quality, systems must be put in place and reward structures changed. Of course it is unlikely that everything can be done on day one. In putting together a quality strategy, the organisation must revist the points raised by the Quality Triangle to decide what needs to be done and which must be addressed first.

For example:

● The Ford Motor company started with an SPC programme to improve
  supplier quality before incorporating other techniques and developing

a more integrated quality strategy for the whole business. Ford's culture is such that systems govern much of the company's activities and therefore an SPC approach was not alien to its employees

- Many companies have started quality improvement campaigns with a major management announcement that they were now in a new era of excellence. Many of these programmes have failed because the necessary follow-up activities were not put in place
- Many companies have commenced a quality circle programme and have then developed broader actions as a result of lessons learned, building a structure for quality
- Some companies have sought and achieved BS 5750 recognition and have then realised that the attitude of those employed in the company has not changed for the better. They are aware that poor quality is still 'policed' rather than prevented.

The point about these scenarios is that it doesn't matter where you begin. Start somewhere, but be very clear where you have not yet been and make sure you go there!

Conclusion

A key quality principle is that systems and processes must be 'capable' of meeting the specifications laid down for them. If your system has an average customer response time of four hours, you will not achieve this every time. Sometimes you will beat it and sometimes you will be late. Let us say that 99.99 per cent of all service calls fall within a response time of four hours $\pm$ ten minutes. If response time is a key element of customer satisfaction, you must decide if this level of performance is satisfactory. If not, resources must be assigned to improving the system. 'Capable systems' in effect equate to not making promises you cannot keep.

Many quality problems boil down to having insufficient resources some or all of the time. As the organisation moves closer to full utilisation, quality problems become more frequent. The organisation copes, but at the risk of poor technical quality or poor customer care.

It is useful to address all the quality principles contained in this chapter but also to ask two final questions:

1 What happens when you run out of capacity? Which quality dimensions suffer as resource utilisation approaches 100 per cent?
2 How can you tell? What indicators or measures are in place to give you rapid feedback for recovery?

In Chapter 8 (describing capacity management) we indicated that organisations and individuals within them employ coping strategies to deal with the problems of short-term overloads. It would be better if we could address these inevitable overloads to minimise the loss of customer satisfaction by deciding what should be done rather than leaving it to people to cope in the way they think fit. The organisation's ability to recover effectively from mistakes is critical.

Measurement is one of the tools of management. We believe that three measures should be used together to balance the needs of the organisation. These measures are:

1 Customer perceived quality measures.
2 Internal productivity measures.
3 Utilisation of key resources.

Moving the organisation from 90 per cent to 95 per cent utilisation may improve productivity but may have a disastrous effect on customer satisfaction and long-term profitability.

There are many benefits for the customer support organisation in pursuing quality. Quality Management is a mixture of major strategic actions demonstrating genuine management commitment, and also many detailed actions aimed at ensuring that nothing is left to chance.

Checklist

1 Do you know what customers assume the service and support organisation will do? Can the organisation consistently meet these standards?
2 Have you carried out a quality cost audit? How much business is the total organisation losing annually through poor product and service quality?
3 Have you got a clear definition of quality for the customer service and support function? If so, when was it last revised with input from customers?
4 Are product designers aware of the way that their actions affect service and support quality? How is this quality review process controlled?
5 How is quality managed? Is there some structure for quality or do you expect it to happen? Are there any improvements to be made?
6 What is the quality strategy for the organisation? What budget has

been made available? What are the current quality improvement targets? What actions have been taken to achieve them?

7   What proportion of your time is set aside for quality improvement issues?

8   How often do you spend in face to face contact with customers, finding out what they think of your service and support?

10 IMPROVING PRODUCTIVITY

Introduction

Along with capacity and quality management the management of resource productivity is one of the trinity of operational controls which affect performance of customer service and support. In this chapter we will look at what we mean by resource productivity, the ways it can be measured, and the techniques which are available to improve resource productivity. We will examine the role of technology in both the measurement of and improvement in resource productivity.

What are your trade-offs?

Operations management in any form is concerned with managing trade-offs which affect resource productivity and quality. Common trade-offs are between capacity utilisation and customer waiting, between absolute perceived quality of the service and support and costs, and between labour costs and capital equipment costs including information systems. All the trade-offs point to there being no one system of service and support delivery able to do everything. We cannot deliver the *highest* perceived service and support in our sector, *immediately available* to all our customers, all at the *lowest* cost.

Our thinking about the trade-offs affects the quality of service and sets the parameters for resource productivity. What we are always seeking to do though is to minimise the effects of the trade-offs. For instance the Total Quality Management movement has been very successful at eliminating the traditional trade-off between consistency of service delivery and cost; an explanation for the 'quality is free' philosophy. We have also seen that the better we are at managing the match between service intensity and capacity the higher the utilisation of the resources while maintaining the minimum waiting time for customers. So we want to minimise the effects of trade-offs. Our aim always will be to look for ways in which we can get more from the resources we use while delivering the same or somewhat higher levels of service quality.

Why is managing resource productivity so difficult?

Various reasons are put forward to explain the problems of managing productivity in services; the involvement of customers, the intangible nature of part of the customer service and support mix, the complexity of the task, and the diversity of branch networks. All of these relate in the first instance to problems associated with measurement.

So if we are to get better at using resources we need to improve measurement. However, this is only part of the issue. We also need to understand how our use of resources is influenced by the demand for the service and support. This will give us clues to the best routes for understanding the barriers to productivity improvement.

Understanding productivity

At its simplest, productivity is defined as the ratio of outputs to inputs. The more we can produce from a set of resources which includes people, materials, equipment, facilities and systems, the higher will be our resource productivity. However, we soon realise that while this definition of resource productivity may seem convenient because of its simplicity when it comes to making measurement things are more difficult. As with any arithmetical ratio we need to have all the denominators in one set of common units and the numerators in another common set. Let us look at the problem this raises.

Measuring outputs

The outputs from customer service and support operations could be described as the number of service and support incidents which are dealt with. If each event were the same this would give us an acceptable measure of the output. If this is not the case and there is great variety, then things are not so easy. So the extent to which each incident is standard or customised for each customer will influence the variety.

Where incidents are standard we might get an aggregate for the service intensity simply by counting incidents. However, if each incident is highly customised it is not possible to get an aggregate number for all incidents. So when variety is high and changing we might relate the total output to a monetary value, for example the revenue generated by the total customer service and support operation over a period of time.

A second problem in measuring outputs relates to quality. It is easy to increase the number of service incidents we deal with by reducing the quality. Perhaps we spend less time resolving a problem or rush a standard maintenance, even though we run the risks of making mistakes. It is apparent that in making any measurement of the outputs we need to ensure that quality standards are being maintained. We can easily increase productivity by reducing service levels.

A third factor in measuring outputs is associated with a general characteristic of service delivery. Many types of service and support cannot be delivered until the customers request them. The service and support is then required at short notice. Also in many cases the customer takes part in the process. In setting our resource levels we usually do this on the basis of forecast demand, as we saw when discussing capacity management. If the rate at which customers want to use the service is fairly constant and we are close with our forecasts then measuring output will be realistic for that level of resource capacity. If, however, the rate at which customers use the service is erratic then the time at which measurements of output are made could affect the result. If the customer demand is lower than expected for the resources deployed the output would be low and hence the resource productivity seems low. So in measuring outputs we have to ask the question: are we working at our effective capacity? This is in line with the argument that productivity measures are only valuable when they are a true reflection of managerial skill. This happens when outputs are not constrained through lack of resources and when input resources are at the level set by the managers.

So in measuring outputs we have to be aware of:

- The mix of service offerings and their variety
- The quality service levels
- Whether output is constrained through lack of customer demand, or other resources.

Measuring inputs

If we were to make a measure of total productivity including all outputs and all inputs we would have to find a way to get these into common units. The only way to do this for the mix of resources, including people, materials and equipment, is to express them in monetary terms as the total input costs. Otherwise we must rely on what are called partial measures of productivity. Here we take one of the main inputs and use this in the productivity calculation. The commonest resource taken for the partial measure is people. In services where the labour cost is the highest proportion of total cost this is reasonable. If the labour cost is reduced considerably through the deployment of technology, then the labour cost becomes a very small proportion of the total cost; this could be a misleading measure. This is perhaps not the case in most services yet but a pointer to the future comes from the manufacturing environment where labour costs are now often less than 10 per cent of the total costs.

So in making measurement of input resources:

- Total resource input measures can only be in monetary terms
- Selecting resources for partial measures should take account of the contribution of the resource to the total costs.

Deciding on the level for measurement

When thinking about resource productivity there are a number of levels at which we need to have information. The levels correspond to:

- The business as a whole, which is usually the network of branches for the delivery of service and support
- The service branch
- A section of activity within the branch
- An individual resource.

In managing and improving productivity we need to have measurements which give information on productivity at each level. At the lower levels we will be wanting to find methods of measurement which can be used to compare the performance of different service branches, service teams, or individual resources such as people or equipment or materials.

How can we approach the complexity of measurement?

As a general comment from our work we would say that the measurement of resource productivity is not well developed. Often this results from a failure to grasp the nettle surrounding the inherent difficulties of measurement and so people give up. However there are approaches which yield valuable information which can be used for the purposes of monitoring and planning improvement. It is our contention that there can be no effective improvement in resource productivity unless there are appropriate measurements. This raises the questions:

1 What is measured?
2 Who is responsible for carrying out measurement?
3 What use is being made of the information on resource productivity which is generated?

The most general approaches to productivity measurement are ones which look for partial or surrogate measures of productivity. These can be summarised as:

- *Output/input measures:* These are true productivity measures and include revenue, generated/employee or profit/employee, both cost-based measures. Alternatively the number of service calls handled per employee which are a volume-based measure can be included.
- *Input/output measures:* These are the reciprocal of productivity and are commonly unit costs for each service incident, or costs per customers.
- *Input costs:* These are most usually expressed in terms of staff costs, rather than total resource costs.
- *Utilisation:* This is a measure of the proportion of time resources being used in the service delivery on activities which add value. The measures may apply to people as individuals or teams, or equipment, or facilities.
- *Efficiency:* Here we are making an assessment of the use of resources against a standard of performance. Standard times for the completion of activities can be established by work measurement techniques to give a target for performance. For instance, efficiency can be measured as the percentage of service calls achieved as a ratio of the target standard. Another common measurement is the service time compared to a standard, for example actual times to fix, and actual response times compared to standard times for the two tasks.
- *Effectiveness:* Here we are attempting to make an assessment of the way in which resources are used without wasting them. An example

would be the number of times we achieve first-time fix, as a percentage of the total incidents.

It is apparent that only the first two of the above measurements are in any way true productivity measures. However, the rest do help the service manager to know how well the resources are being used. Utilisation is a very useful way of monitoring the performance of an expensive resource. The linking of quality and productivity measures in effectiveness measures and achieving time targets also shows that one measurement can be used to indicate the performance on both dimensions of quality and productivity.

Which measurement at which level?

The question arises as to which measurement is appropriate for the different levels of the service and support operation? All are not suitable or applicable at all the levels: the network, the branch, the section and the individual resource.

Measurements like revenue or profit per employee which aggregates all the complexity of the customer service and support mix in monetary terms are most suitable at the level of the network and the individual branch. However care needs to be taken in making comparisons at the branch level of the performance between branches. If the revenue generated per employee in one branch is £2000/month and in another £3000/month can we draw any worthwhile conclusons about the perform- ance of the service managers of the two branches? To do so we need to know something about the mix of service and support activities each is engaged in, and also any other features of their resources which might have a strong influence on the productivity. These may be physical space or different information systems, or different levels of skills of the staff.

Efficiency measures based on work measurement or historically based estimates of times are more appropriate at the team and individual resource level. They work best when the work is standard and repetitive so that the setting up of standards is worth the cost of doing so. Pre- ventative maintenance activities lend themselves to work content and time-based efficiency measures.

Utilisation measures for a resource being used on tasks which add value are again more suitable at the team and individual resource level. They are particularly useful for separating travelling time from productive work time. However we need to know that resources are being used in similar ways if comparisons are being made. For example, measurements of the utilisation of engineers on service work in different regions are only feasible if the regions are of a similar nature.

It should be clear that if we are to gain a full understanding of resource productivity we need to be able to make measurements at all levels. At the higher levels we want to use the results to make decisions about the overall performance of the business network and the relative performance of the branches. At the branch levels we want information for the purpose of setting targets and monitoring the performance of teams and individuals. So we will now look in more detail at issues related to measurement of costs, the mix of measures to be used, and the measurement of relative performance of branches.

How accurate is our costing? Do we need Activity Based Costing?

Accuracy in costings to determine the unit costs of service and support delivery is vital if it is being used to decide the pricing of the different service and support offerings. Traditional costing systems can often distort the true costs of service delivery. This may not seem to matter if the customer service and support operation is run as a cost centre but is crucial if it is measured on profits.

So what is wrong with traditional cost? In many service companies they may not even have aggregated all of the costs that go to make up actual direct costs of providing a particular service. Even where this is the case, the overhead cost made up of all the indirect costs of service delivery, including administration costs, facility costs and energy costs, is allocated on one resource, which is often labour.

The problem with the overhead allocation is that it assumes that for each type of service and support, costs are directly related to service intensity. This is not always true; for instance, doubling the number of service calls does not necessarily double the orders for spares.

So is there a better approach, which will give us an accurate unit cost for each specific service and support product? One technique which is becoming increasingly popular is Activity Based Costing (ABC). The ABC approach has two objectives. First, it sets out to give an accurate costing for each stage in the delivery of each service and support product, by costing the use of the resources to perform the activity, i.e. *activity cost pools*. Second, it can be used to allocate overhead burden according to the features of the service and support delivery activities, which vary in a meaningful way. These are referred to as the *cost drivers*.

In setting up the costs at the stages in the delivery we may take two views. First, the total value chain from promotion through sales, installation, commissioning, to service and support, and establish costs for each product or product group on the basis of the level of activity each demands of our resources. Second, the more detailed component stage of any part of the value chain, for example, in response to a service call, call reception, engineer travelling, time on the job, and spares consumed.

Let us take another example within one cost activity pool. We might find that a large proportion of our overhead cost is associated with the handling of materials to make them available for the service activity. But what drives this process? The answer includes planning of preventative maintenance, purchasing, and stock holding. These are all ultimately proportional to the number of parts being handled, so 'the parts used in a routine preventative maintenance for a product' could be a cost driver. In using ABC we need to identify all of the main cost drivers by assessing what makes our service and support offerings different from one another.

Service	X	Y	Z	Total
Complexity	5	10	2	
Weighting	4	4	4	
Complexity factor	20	40	8	68
Serviceability	6	4	3	
Weighting	2	2	2	
Serviceability factor	12	8	6	26
Customer contact	5	3	2	
Weighting	2	2	2	
Customer factor	10	6	4	20
Spares needed	4	7	2	
Weighting	3	3	3	
Spares factor	12	21	6	39
Total	54	75	24	153
Percentage	35%	49%	16%	

Table 10.1 Activity Based Costing approach

The process to implementing ABC is to:

1   Identify the cost drivers. This is best done by teams drawn from across

the direct service and support delivery teams and those in administration and Back Room support. Some companies will make use of consultants to facilitate the process. The number of cost drivers is typically 15–20. For customer service and support possible cost drivers are serviceability of products, complexity and the extent of customer involvement.

2   Agree a relative weighting for each cost driver. This may be by giving it a weighting between 1 and 5. For example, cost drivers of spares, serviceability and complexity might be weighted 3, 2 and 4, respectively.

3   Assess how each cost driver affects each service product. This may be done simply with reference to a 10 point scale rating. For example for one product group, X, serviceability might be assessed as 6, whereas for another product group, Y, the assessment is 4.

4   Multiply the weighting factor by the rating for each cost driver for each service support product to give a *total cost driver factor*. For example, for our first product group above the cost driver factor for serviceability would be the assessment 6 multiplied by the weighting for serviceability, 2, resulting in the total serviceability cost driver for product X of 12. The process is completed for each cost driver for each product grouping (table 10.1).

5   Add the results for each product to give a total number for each product. For example for product group X the total is the sum of 20, 12, 10 and 12, that is, 54.

6   Allocate the overhead to each product group according to the relative numbers from the totals of the cost driver factors for all product groups. In our example the totals for product groups, X, Y and Z, are 54, 75 and 24 respectively. So the allocation of overheads to the service of the three product groups is 35 per cent, 49 per cent and 16 per cent respectively. This process leads to a fairer allocation of overheads in accordance with those factors which drive up the accumulation of costs and minimises the problems of allocation on the basis of a single resource.

7   If it is necessary to arrive at a unit cost allocation of overheads the previous total for a product group can be divided by the service intensity for that product.

ABC is especially useful in the context of customer service and support for standard repetitive parts of the activity. It may be in many cases more successful if the technique is introduced on a pilot scale to parts of the service and support operation.

How many measures?

The question which is often raised in considering productivity measurements is that of deciding how many different measurements are needed. A supplementary question is whether or not to try to combine measurements into a total index of performance. The answers to these questions are not easy without the context of a specific operation; however, the experience of Data General's Customer Service Group provides an example of choosing the measures and combining them into an index for total service and support profitability.

Seven productivity measures were identified as being important:

1   *Product liability:* a function of product MTBF and the mix of products for service and support.

2   *Material efficiency:* a function of changes in the costs of materials and the rates of usage of materials.

3   *Incident repair productivity:* a function of MTTR and labour costs.

4   *Off site and support productivity:* a function of the numbers and utilisation of support resources and labour rates for support staff.

5   *Logistics productivity:* a function of costs of materials as spares and the costs of distribution.

6   *Revenue yield:* a function of contract rates and the product mix being supported.

7   *Staff productivity:* a function of staff effectiveness and utilisation on service contract tasks.

Numerical quantities are calculated for each of the seven indices and these are combined into a total service productivity measurement.

How can we compare branch performance?

Making a comparison of the performance of branch units across a network has always presented problems because of the multiplicity of different inputs and outputs. Service branch units may differ in numbers of staff, costs of facilities, travelling costs and may have a different mix and volume of service and support activity. Trying to make a comparison by traditional methods of allocating cost is almost impossible. A new technique, Data Envelopment Analysis (*DEA*) takes a different approach.

DEA examines the relative efficiency of use of resources in each branch in a way which discounts the mix of service and support activities and eliminates the need to develop standard costs for each service. It can be used to identify branch units which are relatively inefficient and give indicators as to why this might be the case. However the technique will not indicate whether the performance of the best branches is an optimum performance which cannot be improved. The results are always relative within the branch network so if competitors were more efficient DEA would be no better than other techniques for identifying an optimum.

The use of DEA requires the identification of the main outputs from the operation. This could be a mix of installation of equipment, preventative service and repair and fix in response to breakdown. Similarly, the input resources needed to produce the outputs are identified as people, materials, equipment, and the facilities from which they work. The outputs and inputs are measured over a period of time for each branch. Sometimes the information is available within existing information systems, or it might have to be gathered separately.

The results from DEA can be used to identify inefficient branches as against the most efficient branches. It is up to the service management team to determine the underlying causes and to look for ways to remedy them.

Let us look at how DEA can be applied in practice by way of a simple example. If our network consists of six branches and we wish to monitor which of the branches are less efficient in their use of resources than the others. For simplicity we will take the outputs from the service and support operation to be preventative maintenance and the inputs engineer hours and the cost of spares.

The DEA 'black box' takes the data and compares each branch against all of the others to establish which are the inefficient ones. The results of the process are shown diagrammatically in Figure 10.1. The branches which on comparison are equally efficient and rated at 100% efficient are B1, B2, B4 and B6. These are joined by the solid line. The other two service branches are found to be less efficient, B3 when compared to B1 and B2 and B5 when compared to B2 and B4. Both B3 and B5 are inefficient by an amount proportional to the distance from the efficient line joining the points B1, B2, B4, B6.

DEA does not say why the service branches 3 and 5 are less efficient, but allows managers to look for the reason in the way that resources are used in the inefficient and the efficient branches.

The use of DEA requires the identification of the main outputs and inputs from each of the service units in the network and a system for

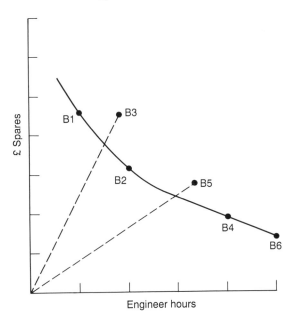

Figure 10.1 DEA curve

monitoring these for a fixed period of time. Sometimes the information will already be gathered, but in others new systems will have to be set up.

How can we improve our resource productivity?

When we consider improving productivity we mean both getting the level of costs down and using resources more effectively. Improvements in quality often in themselves lead to improvements in resource productivity though the elimination of waste.

What though is likely to frustrate our attempts to improve productivity? The answers lie in part with the nature of the service operations task. This takes us back to the elements which constitute the demand for our customer service and support, the trends in volume, the variations in volume in the shorter term and the service and support mix. Let us look at each of the demand factors and see their affect on resource productivity:

Volume

If we were just delivering one service this would give us the opportunity to:

- gain from economies of scale
- get better volume from the increased learning due to the specialisation and doing the job more frequently
- get high utilisation from the resources because they are devoted to the one activity.

Variation in demand

Variation in demand tends to take away from the high constant volume situation by:

- increasing costs from having to increase the flexibility of the effective capacity. These costs include labour charges for overtime or the use of subcontractors, and additional systems costs for planning work. Additional costs come from under utilisation of capacity through not being able to match effective capacity and demand all of the time
- the difference in the pacing of work from busy to slack times may mean that people do not work efficiently all of the time.

Variety of the service and support mix

The variety of the service and support mix tends to reduce the effects of high volume through:

- increased costs because of the need for a greater skills mix and increased costs because of the loss of any volume economies of scale
- loss of specialisation in the work tasks which decreases the tendency to get things right first. So it is more likely that leads to increases in waste
- the increased amount of managerial and supervisory effort which must be put into managing the increased complexity.

All of these factors point us towards understanding the nature of our service and support and trying to minimise the inherent effects of the demand elements. It also reinforces the benefits which can be gained from specialisation, and standardisation, and limiting the effects of growing variety.

What are the barriers to improving resource productivity?

What might we describe as the main barriers to improving resource productivity? We have seen that the demand mix can make improvement difficult. There are also the following factors which we have found from our own investigations:

1   Not having good measurements: the absence of measurements for resource productivity make it difficult to set targets and monitor progress.
2   Changes in demand: we have already seen that variation in demand tends to lower resource productivity and the effect is exacerbated if we are poor at flexing capacity.
3   Organisation of service delivery: if we do not understand and evaluate what happens in the process of delivering our service and support we will not be able to identify constraints, or where waste is occurring, and inefficient stages in the service and support delivery. We find there is often a link with lack of clear direction of what the organisation is trying to do.
4   Cost of gathering data: organisations often fail to gather data on resource productivity because of the cost of the systems and people to do the job. There is a link here with the perceived appropriateness of measures. If measurements are not seen to be useful there will be little incentive to meet the costs of gathering data and producing information on productivity.
5   Frequent changes in staff: it is not surprising that if a customer service and support operation finds itself with a high staff turnover, the need for induction and training will tend to reduce the potential productivity from resources. It takes time for new starters to 'come up to speed' in their tasks.
6   Variety of service and support: we have discussed the aspect of variety above and we can see a link with the complaint about the barrier caused by the way we do things. Increased variety will make the process more complex and difficult to understand just what is happening.

How can we break the barriers and improve resource productivity?

There are three approaches which we think are useful when we want to break the barriers to improving resource productivity:

1   Understanding the process of service and delivery

2   Measurement

3   Trade-off resources.

Understanding the process

We have discussed the importance of understanding the process flow for service and support delivery when we discussed aspects of quality and the service encounter. When the examination is taking place from the standpoint of resource productivity we are looking to identify those stages which impede the process and cause bottlenecks. If we can eliminate the effect of bottlenecks it may allow us to increase the number of service incidents we handle or to increase the utilisation of one resource which is causing the bottleneck. For example, a review of engineer activity may lead to the scheduling of a better mix of service activities which increases the proportion of time an engineer is either working on a product or interfacing with a customer.

If we are forever changing the methods by which tasks are carried out it will make the job of improving productivity more difficult. Anything which can be done to focus groups on particular tasks will increase the level of learning which will have benefits for efficiency and effectiveness including elimination of waste, for example higher levels of first time fix to reduce the number of call-backs.

The motivation of service teams with which we dealt in Chapter 7 is integral to realising productivity gains only when the service delivery system is *capable* of achieving the results.

A final part of the process of achieving capable systems for the delivery of service and support is capture of data while it is used in the *design of new products* to increase their serviceability. Any improvements in this direction will decrease the amount of resource which is need to deal with any service incident with that product.

Measurement

We have looked already at some of the options which are available for making productivity measurements at the different levels in a service and support operation. In summary we would say that measurements should be:

- Linked to the most important resources which affect productivity appropriate to the level at which measurement is made

- Taken as a series of measurements which may be combined into a productivity index
- Examined for trends in performance rather than striving for an absolute measurement. It may be time consuming and costly to gather data with great accuracy and so we decide not to make any measurement. Good indications of the use of the resources can be gained by looking for trends in measurement which in themselves may not be particularly accurate in the sense that they are only partial measures of resource productivity
- Linked to targets for improvement in productivity which are associated with the quality levels set for customer service and support
- Made visible to front-line staff as well as other service managers. The message is the same as for quality measures; make them visible to those who can make a difference.

Trade-off resources

We may be able to improve the overall productivity of resource by trading off one resource for another. For instance an increased spend on managing spares may increase the labour productivity of engineers because it increases the proportion of time they are working on value-adding tasks.

The installation of technology like remote monitoring and other information and communication systems are a similar trade-off. Expenditure on technology may increase the labour productivity while reducing what is called the capital productivity because there is now more money invested in technology. As most firms do not measure the capital productivity, expenditure on technology is often measured as a labour productivity gain if fewer people are required.

The use of remote diagnostics brings with it gains in the use of resources as well as aspects of improved customer satisfaction. We see these including:

- Reduction in warranty costs
- Maintenance increased and repair at breakdown reduced
- Reduced time on site because of improved diagnosis and accuracy of spares specification. The reduction will be increased where there is the capability for remote testing or repair
- More complete data on the performance of equipment.

Conclusion

In this chapter we have looked at the meaning of resource productivity and the ways in which it can be measured in service and support operations. We have seen the influence of demand on our ability to improve productivity. While recognising there are barriers to improving resource productivity we have presented approaches which we have seen to be successful in improving resource productivity.

Checklist

1   What are your main measurements for resource productivity?
2   Do the measurements cover aspects of costs, utilisation and effectiveness?
3   Do you see any gaps in the measures currently being used?
4   What are the barriers to productivity improvement in your delivery of customer service and support?
5   How is your ability to improve resource productivity affected by the volume, variation and variety of demand for customer service and support?
6   What could you do to remove the barriers?
7   What role is there for technology to improve overall resource productivity?
8   How are your productivity and quality improvements linked?
9   Are your front-line staff given information on productivity?

11 MANAGING THE INFORMATION

Introduction

Information is a critical asset for any service business. Not only is information necessary in order to make decisions about the future direction of the organisation and also to control its regular activities, the information possessed by the service organisation about its customers often provides a major barrier against its competitors.

In managing information systems two questions must be addressed:

1   What information is required to run the service and support organisation?
2   What impact will this information and the way that it is presented have on those involved?

Information is required for strategic decision making and for tactical control but it must be remembered that the mere fact that information exists will tend to affect actions of the members of the organisation.

A chain of restaurants marketed 'quick service with good quality food' as its main attraction. Unfortunately its management information system did not reflect this priority. Instead, the major emphasis was placed on the management of cost. Performance against cost budgets was reported weekly whereas customer service and satisfaction feedback was compiled annually. Which set of targets would you perceive to be most important? It is perhaps not surprising that the majority of actions were taken to reduce cost rather than to improve service and the reputation of the chain suffered as a result.

Do we need a new information system?

It will be critical to match the system to the state of the business. This may be best analysed by reference to the product life cycle (Fig. 11.1).

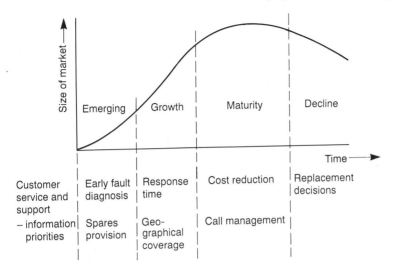

Figure 11.1 Changes in information priorities through the product life cycle

With an emerging product the demand for product and service will be uncertain, and the emphasis of the information system is therefore placed on market and customer research. For the service manager, it will be particularly important to gather a comprehensive service history, tracking fault diagnosis and reliability data for feedback into product development and to assist in scheduling resources. With a mature product, on the other hand, the emphasis is more likely to be on cost and volume, and the design of information systems will be towards cost and efficiency targets.

The service and support manager must be aware of changes in the way that product and service compete and ensure that systems are changed to reflect this. There are a number of examples of systems which are appropriate for part of the product range being 'forced' to cover the whole task and, of course, failing to do so. Given that information is central to the service manager's task, systems development must receive more than a passing interest.

Developing strategic information systems

The extent to which information can be used to create a competitive advantage can be analysed using Porter's five force model, set out here.

Combating the threat of new entrants

Service or maintenance companies are often under threat from new organisations, in some cases started by people who were previously employed by them. There are two barriers here that may be erected by the service company using information systems. Whilst ex-employees may be able to cope with those products with which they are familiar, they will no longer have access to the support required to service the full product range and of course this product knowledge will become increasingly out of date as new products are introduced.

It may be that a potential new entrant may not have sufficient data about the customers' installations to give an adequate service level. The organisation must market its own capability in this area, emphasising the full range of support available.

The second barrier will lie in those information systems that are visible to the customer. There may be a confidence factor in being able to demonstrate that the service organisation has a full service history readily available, in some cases knowing more about the customer's equipment than he does.

Good service may well depend on rapid supply and distribution channels, which again will be facilitated by the rapid interchange of information. If the organisation has control of these channels, it will be difficult for a new entrant to compete.

Quality information fed back to product designers will provide the basis for development which will ensure that the organisation stays ahead of the competition, keeping its customers satisfied.

The threat of substitute products or services

A specific threat for the service and support organisation may be the desire of the customer with a complex network of products and services to hand over service management to a single service provider, who offers the reduced administative cost of one-stop shopping. Building customer data bases which include details by customer site of related equipment which might be included in one service agreement may provide the basis of a capability to offer total system service management.

In many organisations, much information is held informally by customer contact staff. They may be able to assess how customer tastes and requirements are changing. If the products and services do not change with them, the customer may switch to new providers. An information system may be provided to 'formalise' this customer intelligence.

If substitute products or services have already come onto the market, this will probably mean that the organisation's own market will reach the mature/decline phase of its life cycle rapidly, if it is not already there. In this case, competition will be price dominated and information systems to manage this new emphasis of low cost and efficiency will be required.

The effect of industry rivalry

Fierce industry rivalry may be good for the customer in the short term if competition results in price cutting. Prolonged rivalry will be detrimental to the company's profitability, and may restrict choice in the longer term. If the service organisation is having to cut prices to compete, clear, timely information as to profitability will be one of the first priorities. This will enable the customer service and support manager to determine appropriate service levels to give value for money to the customer. This will be particularly critical if differential service levels are to be offered. Tight control is all-important.

The strategy of raising service levels may have a disastrous effect on short-term profitability, particularly if the wrong market segments are chosen for service improvement. In mature industries, there may be little that can be done to differentiate the basic product by design or price, so many companies offer extra services, many of which may be delivered at marginal cost if the information is available to make clear decisions.

The threat of strong buyers and suppliers

If the purchasing power of the organisation is relatively weak or it is supplying a dominant customer, the organisation may find that it can not manage its business as it wishes. For the service organisation this may mean not being able to purchase replacement items to meet service commitments. 'Strong arm' tactics are unlikely to work in this situation. The organisation is most likely to succeed by persuasion and clear communication of its requirements. Getting its needs into the suppliers' schedules as early as possible may not be a cast-iron guarantee, but it is surprisingly effective. If early reliable information as to requirements is followed up by regular feedback on supplier performance, the battle may be won.

The strong customer, likewise, needs to be managed. The strong customer will tend to make increasingly stringent demands if not confident that the organisation is able to deliver. Any loss of customer confidence which may arise if the customer does not feel the situation is under control will result in more demand for faster response and higher levels of service. If the service organisation can demonstrate competence, supported by good information on its own business, the strong customer's demands may be contained.

Opportunities for advantage through information

Information Systems may be used to create *time advantage*. If the service engineer can respond more quickly through better scheduling or because there are faster communications this will be reflected in higher customer satisfaction. The move to remote linkages giving early warning of failure or possible failure is a good example of this. Many service organisations are equipping their staff with hand-held terminals which allow 24-hour communication with central information systems.

Many of the systems that create time advantage also create *cost advantage*. Predictive systems which give rapid response also allow better resource management. In some cases problems may be solved over the telephone. This is known as *call avoidance*, which may also be effected by analysing service demands. For example, analysis that 40 per cent of service demands result from customer ignorance rather than product failure might justify investment in clearer documentation or free customer training. Other savings are likely to be generated through better control of the two major costs represented by inventory and people. These might include barcoding, engineer data and quality costs.

Again, linked to time and cost, are the systems which facilitate *better decision making*. Service organisations may develop models to indicate locations for service points, capacity scheduling programs or systems for financial analysis. There is much to be said for giving employees at all levels business data rather than solely operational data to enable them to carry out their function. A view of the impact of what they do on the success of the business may promote more commitment to improvement.

It is worth separating out *market intelligence systems*. Feedback from customers on quality or changing needs is vital for product development. Tom Peters, in *Thriving on Chaos*, identifies one of the attributes of excellent companies as being 'obsessed with listening to customers'. Such listening may allow the organisation to identify further business opportunities. Rank Xerox created an early advantage by identifying when a customer's copier was overloaded and feeding this information through to the sales department, which was often able to sell a bigger copier at an attractive price. Rank Xerox was happy to do this because overloaded copiers mean higher service demands. Hewlett-Packard likewise has developed a combined sales-service database which facilitates the development of qualified sales leads.

Finally, it may be possible to give *enhanced customer service* through customer orientated systems. Jan Carlzon of the airline, SAS, recognised this when he stated that they were in the information business not the transport business. He recognised that the customer basically wants to find out quickly which is the best way to travel from A to B. The fact that it is by air may be incidental.

Examples of this approach are the garage that sends reminders to its customers that a regular service is falling due thus giving an impression of better customer care; or companies that provide support for complex products having the ability to produce equipment 'health checks' which allow the customer to manage the installation more effectively.

Customers expect contact staff to be fully informed about all areas of the business. It is important that managers consider what questions are likely to be asked of service providers and ensure that such information is given in the form of briefings, manuals, or training or at the very least, so that contact people know where to go to get the information with minimum delay.

Everything must be done to give a professional image to the customer. One of the high street banks gained a small competitive edge because the enquiry desks were equipped with on-line terminals which allowed the customer to see at a glance the state of the account with its debits, credits and standing orders. The competitor which still operated a microfiche system with information which was at least 24 hours old was at a serious disadvantage.

What Information can be provided?

In this section we will indicate the breadth of information used by organisations.

Financial systems

Many service and support organisations are run as a business or a profit centre and therefore require all the normal financial systems to indicate profitability, variance analysis, cash flow and so on. Also required will be asset management and capital budgeting.

Customer management systems

Under this heading come all the market intelligence systems. What is current and projected demand? What is our current market share? What trends can we identify? Can we identify any segments in the market which must be managed in different ways? Is there any reason why service demands are lower per installation in Region A?

We must also consider the way that individual customers are handled, so there should be information about maintenance contracts, sales order processing, invoice details, credit rating and so on.

Perhaps it should go without saying that there should be one integrated data base where possible. We visited one service centre where the staff couldn't tell whether the person ringing in was a bona fide customer or had rung the wrong organisation because there was no link between the service file and sales ordering process. In some cases the mistake was not discovered until the engineer arrived at site.

Quality systems

Data should be collected on product reliability (MTBF), faults, warranty claims, Dead On Arrivals (DOA), etc to allow trends to be identified as early as possible for product development. Information about service quality should also be logged, in particular the key dimensions of response time, time to first time fix and areas of customer perception.

Systems should be set up to monitor customer complaints. It is vital for the organisation to know how many complaints there are and to what they refer. Equally important is tracking the resolution of complaints. The best organisations have clear procedures as to how complaints should be handled, with standards such as phone back within four hours, letter within 24 hours, resolution within one week. There is no point in such standards if they are not monitored. The monitoring will emphasise the importance of the issue.

More positively, there should be information available to customers about product upgrades. In the case of computer software, it may be part of the service contract that upgrades are offered to existing customers. In other situations, there will be possible business in retro-fitting modifications.

Resource management

Included under this category will be information about resource utilisation. What equipment is overloaded and what is no longer required? The provision of inventory management systems is part of resource management. A key system will be scheduling of equipment and materials, as well as service personnel.

People management

In a sense, people are just another resource, but probably deserve their own category. The point has been made in other places that you get what you measure, so the design and emphasis of people measurement systems requires careful thought.

A system commonly used by customer support organisations is *call management*, giving the present status of all current requests for service and giving the organisation the capability to track and measure the effectiveness of its resource management and individual service personnel. Individuals may be monitored on a range of issues including repair times, call-backs, journey time and customer care.

The organisation should also have more general measures such as labour cost, absenteeism and turnover. If the second two are rising it is likely that excessive demands are being made on the staff and they are voting with their feet.

As the product range increases, it will become necessary to match skills and product knowledge to service demands. Hewlett-Packard has clear job specifications for its service and support staff itemising the product knowledge required and the training to be given to a new appointee.

Other companies have the ability to match service providers to specific customers taking into account both skill and personality. They have identified those engineers who deal most effectively with each customer.

The Trigger-Input-Process-Output model

Ives and Vitale have developed a useful way of analysing the service activity. In considering the elements of inputs, maintenance, triggers and outputs, in turn, a specification for an information system for day to day control of the service activity can be drawn up.

Ives and Vitale have gone on to develop this simple model to reflect different aspects of the service task. Triggers for service requests they say fall into three categories: repair because failure has occurred, actions to prevent failure, and enhancement to equipment as developments become available. Fig. 11.2 demonstrates the way that these triggers can be structured to indicate valuable information requirements.

Figure 11.2 also demonstrates a powerful way of dividing information requirements into customer concerns and repairer's concerns. The mere activity of thinking through each category may yield insight as to how customers could be served better.

Two organisations which have recognised the value of information

Otis Elevator

Otis provide low and high rise elevators in all parts of the world. They see themselves as manufacturers and *maintainers* of lifts. It is important to them to reduce the number of unscheduled call-backs to a minimum.

In 1981, North American Operations made the first step into investigating the use of information technology to accept customer requests for maintenance outside working hours. At this time they were using an independent answering service used by other maintainers to deal with this. By 1985 Otis had established a service centre to deal with all customer requests, 24 hours a day. This centre with its information systems is called OTISLINE.

Otis say that the system has dramatically improved the quality of products and service. Customers obviously prefer to be able to deal directly with Otis at all times rather than through an intermediary. The system provides good information to senior management on performance, particularly highlighting any installation that is generating a higher than average number of call-backs. This allows better customer service and, again, possible product improvement. The system was designed to cope with 100,000 calls per day, about a third of which would be customer requests for service, the others being communication to and from service personnel.

OTISLINE has been used to market the company to customers, giving them confidence that excellent service will be provided. OTISLINE has provided the basis for the company to make future developments in information systems, notably Remote Elevator Monitoring (REM), identifying problems before the lift breaks down, hopefully avoiding the

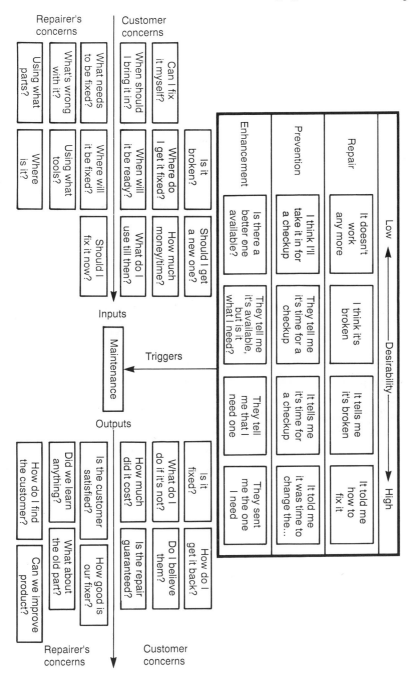

Figure 11.2 The TIPO model – developing information (Ives and Vitale)

worst situation with customers trapped until the service engineer arrives.

The system dramatically improved response times through better call management, improved diagnostic capability by building up repair histories, strengthened the service team by better communication and increased customer satisfaction levels.

Caterpillar

Perhaps the major component of Caterpillar's competitive strategy is the development of one of the most comprehensive information systems in the world. Part of this system is responsible for inventory and logistics to support the claim that Caterpillar can deliver any spare part needed anywhere in the world within 48 hours.

Apart from Logistics, though, there is a massive data base set up to monitor product performance in the field. Their marketing function have a department known as Service Engineering to deal with administering this set of systems.

Service Engineering operates a world-wide reporting system for dealers or the company's own service personnel to log failures by product area, part number and type of failure. On a weekly basis over 30,000 entries are processed. From this volume of data Caterpillar can identify when products are reaching an age where more defects will occur, and take action to reduce their use. Warranty information can be analysed to indicate design or manufacturing problems.

They have an ability to attach a signal to a potential failure code, so that at each new occurrence the designer responsible will be notified to analyse if some pattern is emerging. Over 6000 projects are 'live' at any one time. Once a problem has been identified as needing a solution, the progress of the remedial action is tracked, with full documentation once the design change is finalised, and tracking after to ensure that the solution is effective.

The information system is particularly important in maintaining communication with the dealer network. Once a dealer reports a potential problem, the progress of any investigation is reported back to him until such time as the solution is implemented. Information about failures is available to the dealer through the system, as are the full range of dealer performance statistics.

Caterpillar have devoted many man-years to their systems and are continually enhancing them to make them easier to use and to add new features.

Conclusion

Many organisations are discovering that there is considerable benefit in investing in information as a resource. A relatively small investment in information may increase the productivity of the service providers who may be a scarce resource apart from being the major element of service cost. Information can be used to deliver service more efficiently and to enhance customer care as well as creating confidence that the organisation is truly professional in its dealings.

Checklist

1   Are the information systems designed with the current business priorities in mind or were they more appropriate some years ago?

2   Are information systems designed for efficiency or customer service? What should they be?

3   What priorities are implied by the information systems that are currently in place?

4   Could competitive advantage be gained by better information? Are you losing position because of lack of information?

5   Are there any informal information systems that could give benefit to the whole organisation by the use of systems and information technology?

12 MANAGING THE MATERIALS

Introduction

Materials in the shape of inventories of spare parts or replacement products are the lifeblood of many service and support organisations. If the spares are not available, there is little point in the service engineer turning up to repair the equipment. All the customer care and smile campaigns will be to no avail if the basic product is not forthcoming.

For manufacturers of complex products there will probably be significant profits to be made from the supply of spares. Some have found to their cost that the spares business is sufficiently attractive to encourage 'pirate' manufacturers to enter the market, possibly with spares that do not meet the original specification. Managing inventories to provide good availability levels at a reasonable cost may be a defence against these competitors who may damage the safety reputation of the business as well as taking profits.

For the 'average' service and support organisation, inventory will be the largest element of operating cost after that of the cost of people employed. There are often opportunities to make savings in inventory cost which allow the organisation to make improvements elsewhere. Black and Decker financed part of its service enhancement programme through a review of its inventory policies.

This chapter is in three main sections:

1 *Why do we need inventory?* This section outlines the role of inventory for the service and support organisation in providing the appropriate level of customer service. In this section we will discuss the various reasons for holding inventory which will enable the customer service and support manager to formulate an inventory policy.

2 *How do we manage inventory?* What philosophies and techniques of inventory management are valuable for the customer service and support manager?

3 *Managing the Service Supply Chain.* Many companies are finding benefits in working in closer partnerships with other organisations involved in supporting the final customer. By working closely in this way it may be possible to reduce the inventory held by the chain as a whole, with benefits shared by all.

The cost of inventory

With the advent of the Just-in-Time (JIT) philosophy with its emphasis on elimination of waste, the pressure for inventory reduction has increased still further. The reasons for this are well known to service managers and broadly come under the following categories:

● The carrying cost of inventory is enormous, comprising cost of capital tied up, storage and system costs, 'shrinkage' and obsolescence costs. It is not uncommon for companies to fix the inventory holding charge at 40 per cent or more.
● Inventory represents waste; to a large extent it is held because processes, suppliers, or demand forecasts are unreliable. We hold stock because we expect things to go wrong.
● Inventory is present to act as a buffer. This may be necessary to some degree, but its very presence reduces the need to solve problems permanently. It may dampen motivation to improve products and processes to the extent that the inventory is no longer required or needed in much smaller amounts.

The JIT approach may help and we will return later to the place of JIT in service and support. In looking at the role of inventory we should always be questioning whether it is still required. One of the problems with inventory is that it tends to grow through many small routine decisions made by many people in quite separate functions. In this sense inventory is unlike a purchase of capital equipment or company vehicles. These capital decisions are large, visible, and non-routine, receiving a high degree of senior management attention. The aim of this first section is to describe the role of inventory so that managers will be able to develop a rationale to justify the level of investment in inventory, rather than merely saying 'we need an inventory of £10 million to manage effectively'.

Why do we need inventory?

In thinking about inventory it is useful to make the following distinctions:

(a) First, there is inventory which must be held given the current systems and processes employed, even if they work perfectly. So, if a service depot's stock is replenished once a week and the weekly demand is 50 units, the inventory holding will average 25 units if no safety stock is held and demand remains constant.

(b) The second portion of inventory is that which must be held because systems and processes do not work perfectly. Suppliers don't deliver on time, manufacturing processes may produce more scrap than anticipated and customers don't order to a predictable pattern. This inventory is a reflection of the variability in the system.

This broad distinction may already point up some areas for investigation and improvement. One of the traditional pleas for inventory has been that demand forecasts are always inaccurate. Though forecasts can often be improved, they will never be perfect, but the fact is that in our work with companies, we find that the majority of inventory is put into the system because of supply side problems, and demand side inventory is relatively small.

We can illustrate this in our example above. The weekly delivery cycle itself results in an inventory holding of 25 units whereas the extra inventory held because demand is variable is likely to be limited to one or two units. On the other hand, if the reliability of suppliers is such that only 90 per cent of what is ordered is received on the next shipment, a further five units may be held to ensure that availability levels are maintained.

This section describes four broad categories of inventory. The service and support manager should be able to identify how much stock is held for each of the categories; this will indicate priorities for improvement activity. The four headings are:

- Fluctuation Stocks. These are stocks held because a stated level of service or availability is to be maintained despite fluctuations in demand or supply
- Anticipation Stocks. This inventory is held because providing capacity to cover peak demand is believed to be too expensive. Spares are therefore manufactured ahead of the peak
- Lot Size Stocks. These are stocks held because there are discounts available for bulk purchase, or there are minimum economical batch sizes for manufacture

- Pipeline Stocks. These are materials that are in transit through the distribution network and may include both raw materials en route from suppliers, and finished goods in despatch to customers or service depots.

Fluctuation, safety or buffer stocks

These stocks are held because there is variability in the system but service levels to customers must be maintained. Typical reasons include:

- Suppliers do not deliver on time. Of course, internal suppliers such as the internal manufacturing function are included here and may be rather worse than external suppliers at meeting production schedules for service requirements
- The quantity of supplied items may not be to the required specification. It is not uncommon for orders to be received with quantities less than expected, often because of quality problems at an earlier stage but which have not been notified in sufficient time to take remedial action
- Inventory may be scrapped or damaged during the service or installation process itself. For example, carbon gland seals for pumps are extremely fragile and easily damaged during dismantling or reassembly
- The demand for items may vary considerably and be difficult to predict. Demand may vary between customers, for example a garage may have difficulty in predicting demand for brake pads as wear is a function of driving style.

Many supply issues can be addressed through supplier development or improved customer-supplier partnerships. This 'Supply Chain' approach is discussed in more detail later in this chapter.

How can we improve our inventory service level?

The demand side inventory level must be set in consideration with the required level of customer service. This relationship is illustrated in Fig. 12.1. The basic principle behind this curve is simple. If you want to increase customer service levels in terms of availability of inventory to meet a greater percentage of demand from stock there is an exponential increase in cost involved because the extra stock is effectively held longer than stock for lower availability levels.

The first question which arises from consideration of this relationship is 'What is meant by Service Level?'. Retail organisations, perhaps selling

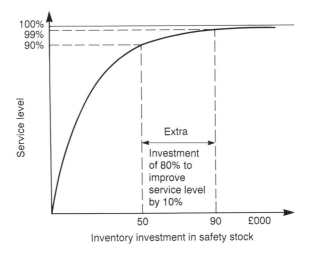

Figure 12.1   The service level problem

spares to the general public will measure *first pick availability*. Thus a 95 per cent first pick availability will mean that 95 customers out of 100 will be able to purchase and take away the required items in one visit. In fact, retail consumers will probably expect availability levels in excess of 99 per cent, particularly when equivalent products can be purchased from a variety of sources.

Service level may be defined in other ways. For example, a manufacturer supplying spares to a dealer network may measure the percentage of orders shipped to dealers within the agreed 48 hour turnround. A typical target would be between 90 and 95 per cent, with a complementary target of order completion within seven days.

It must be said that service levels are notorious for being 'adjusted' to look better than they are. It is possible to quote items or value shipped to meet a theoretical 95 per cent service level which hides the fact that a significant number of critical items have not been delivered, and customer satisfaction is falling rapidly.

Service levels must be managed alongside customer satisfaction monitoring. There are examples of companies which have consciously reduced their service level in order to contain cost. Unfortunately few of these also carefully monitor customer satisfaction at the same time to ensure that the savings in inventory cost are not overshadowed by potential loss of business.

There are a number of actions that an organisation can take in order to increase the overall service level without increasing cost. Better *fore-casting* will enable the inventory to be matched more effectively to demand. More *accurate stock control* will reduce the panic actions brought about by selling something which the system said was there but didn't exist in practice. These actions inevitably increase unit costs as premium charges are incurred in meeting impossible deadlines.

A useful approach for the customer service and support manager lies in reviewing the number of locations at which stock is held. There is a well-known relationship in inventory management which is: *Inventory is directly proportional to the square root of the number of locations.* There is a continuing trend towards *centralised stock holding* for this reason. Managers of field service departments will recognise the problem of controlling van stocks. Every service engineer likes to have a private store of 'goodies' just in case of emergency. The way to minimise this is not by sanction, but by ensuring that the service given by the central stores is excellent, perhaps tying part of the bonus scheme to overall inventory reduction. Information systems which are able to monitor these stocks to coordinate transfers where feasible will pay for themselves through inventory reduction.

Finally, service levels should be reviewed so that critical items have a higher availability than those which are relatively unimportant. We visited the central stores of a large company whose system made no discrimination between non-essential items such as pencil rubbers and forms which are essential for the company's business. The same service level and the same degree of inventory review were applied to both groups of items.

Two dimensions must be considered. The first dimension is criticality. The question is 'Which parts must I hold to ensure that key customers are not inconvenienced?'. We worked with a manufacturer of marine propulsion engines who decided that crankshafts of all units currently in service must be held as spares to ensure that bad publicity resulting from a ship laid up for months would be avoided. The direct cost of this decision could be justified for engines in current production, but not for 'semi-obsolete' models. It was, however, the right decision in overall quality cost terms.

The second dimension is cost, usually calculated by Annual Requirement Value (Unit Cost × Annual Demand). Here, the Pareto or 80–20 rule applies, with 80 per cent of the value represented by 20 + per cent of the parts. In ABC analysis, high value or A items receive more management attention to minimise the inventory investment.

Anticipation or seasonal stocks

This category applies largely to a manufacturing process and relates to the relationship between manufacturing capacity and peak demand. It is rarely economic for the organisation to provide capacity to meet peak demand and therefore will build up stocks prior to the peak so as to cope with it without increasing delivery times to customers.

The Service and Support Manager must be aware of this if the internal manufacturing unit allocates a fixed amount of capacity to production of spares. Within the service organisation this type of inventory may be built up in the form of service packs or assemblies which reduce the degree of work to be carried out on the customer's premises.

Lot size stocks

An organisation may hold this type of inventory for two reasons: firstly, because the process demands a certain batch size as, for example, in brewing a vat full of beer; or secondly, because the supplier offers discounts for larger order quantities.

Some organisations will be able to use the EOQ (Economic Order Quantity) and indeed in some cases the EOQ will give a useful guide to setting batch sizes. Fig. 12.2 shows the relationship between order costs and inventory carrying costs. The EOQ does not work well when demand fluctuates dramatically, and implicit in the calculation is the belief that it isn't possible to improve the processes involved so that they become flexible enough to allow smaller batch sizes at lower costs.

Increasing the frequency of deliveries to service depots may reduce the average inventory held throughout the system. A move from a monthly delivery to a weekly delivery will result in lower stock levels in the depots and also an increase in service level, it being easier to forecast one week ahead rather than four weeks ahead. There will of course be an increase in transportation and handling costs, but these may be minimised with the use of specialist carriers who have established complex networks to speed delivery and reduce costs.

Transportation or pipeline stocks

If the total network is geographically dispersed inevitably there will be inventory in transit. Japanese companies manufacturing in the UK initially found it difficult to source some items locally. For these materials there was therefore some six weeks of inventory on ships between Japan and the UK.

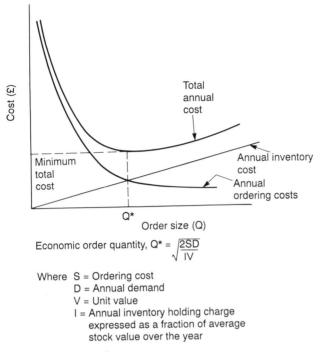

Figure 12.2 Economic order quantity

Does this matter to the customer? After all, surely the goods are not paid for until they arrive? The fact is, of course, that all costs are ultimately borne by the consumer. The cost of transportation and extra inventory owned by suppliers will eventually become part of the final product cost. This is why Marks and Spencer have worked so hard at developing suppliers in the UK who can then deliver rapidly direct to the store.

There is a second benefit arising from reducing pipeline stocks. If inventory is taking six weeks to travel from the Far East to the UK the feedback loop in the event of quality problems becomes rather lengthy. Reducing the time for feedback increases the possiblity of problems being traced to source and then solved.

How do we manage inventory?

There are numerous textbooks on inventory management which describe the various techniques in more detail than is feasible here. In this next section we will indicate the approaches which are most relevant to the service and support manager.

How much inventory have we got?

In a typical inventory profile, the organisation should be able to identify how much inventory is being held for each of the reasons described in the last section. This profile will be divided into two parts. There will be inventory which can be identified as that which was planned, perhaps to meet customer service level targets. There will also be unplanned inventory, arising because of failures in the materials system. The relative size of each component will indicate where attention must be directed.

Can the task be simplified?

It is an obvious statement to say that all management tasks are easier if levels of complexity can be removed. However, before embarking on massive investment in inventory and inventory control systems it is well worth reviewing product structures to see if some rationalisation can reduce the total need for inventory.

For example, the marine propulsion engine manufacturer, discussed earlier, discovered it was possible to hold one crankshaft forging that would cover several semi-obsolete engine types. Extra machining would be required in some cases as the forging would be bigger than necessary, but the saving that resulted from holding one forging rather than many far outweighed the extra unit costs involved. Of course, much of the responsibility for this activity lies with the product designers, but the business issues must be discussed by all, which must include the service and support function.

This move to simplification may be impeded by costing systems that apportion overheads to direct labour alone, taking no account of the extra costs that arise from low volumes or more complex products. If the designer is working on the basis of inaccurate unit costs there will be no motivation to simplify. Many organisations are now applying Activity Based Costing (ABC) and this approach is discussed in more detail in Chapter 10.

Managing the manufacturing-service interface

When inventory is within the control of the manager who needs it, problems may be manageable, but when stock must be ordered and therefore become part of another person's production plan, problems seem to multiply as differing priorities, second guessing and poor communication each contribute to complexity and confusion.

We conducted some inventory management workshops for a manufacturer of consumer goods. During a discussion about how good they were at meeting schedules, a materials manager said that they had recently met the full requirements of the service department only to find parts shipped back because they couldn't cope with the amount of inventory. This was the first time for many months that the service schedule had been met in full and in this situation 'second-guessing' and over-ordering becomes a way of life. Disciplines must be applied across the organisation for this practice to be eliminated and inventory managed more effectively.

All manufacturing units should have a formal master schedule detailing what must be produced and when it is needed. The master schedule must be based on what can be produced rather than being a wish list of what we would like. It should be put together with full knowledge of material and capacity availability.

Many companies employ a form of MRP II (Manufacturing Resource Planning) to facilitate both business planning and manufacturing scheduling. MRP II is driven by a master production schedule, put together on the basis that sufficient resource is available on the known capacity constraints. Businesses that succeed with this approach consider the Master Production Schedule (MPS) to be the company plan rather than merely a means of scheduling production. This means the composition of the MPS and any major changes to it must be subject to senior management review.

The service and support manager must be part of the master production schedule formulation and review process. The MPS is the manufacturing plan and therefore must reflect all demands for production. It must therefore contain all service requirements. The MPS review meeting has often proved to be a useful means of integrating all business functions and is one which can be used by the service and support manager to raise the visibility of the service function.

Some common sense must be applied here as to how the MPS is composed. A tractor company may operate its MPS at the level of major sub-assemblies, such as cabs, chassis and options. It would be unrealistic to create a new master schedule entry for nuts and bolts for service, but it may be possible to draw together 'Service kits' which could usefully be included in the MPS. An example of this approach would be to create a sub-assembly for a cylinder head overhaul including all the gaskets and fastenings required. Otherwise, such details would be included in a standard reorder point stock control system.

Good MPS management results in high strike rates (in excess of 95 per cent schedule adherence, period on period). Once this level of performance has been achieved it becomes relatively easy to maintain because the benefits of better control and lower inventory cost are then visible to all. Some actions that build successful MPS management are:

1   The MPS should be fully 'owned' by the business as a whole and should not be viewed merely as a manufacturing plan.
2   Senior management must be disciplined to work within the plan. This may cause frustration on some occasions but will yield benefits overall.
3   The business must be able to identify those areas or resources which constrain output. These constraints must be fully considered in the formulation of the plan.
4   Good MPS management depends on honesty from all concerned. Over-ordering or pretending that requirement dates are earlier than needed increase the probability that a realistic plan will not be formulated or achieved.

Maintaining a service focus in the manufacturing function

Complaints that service requirements receive too low a priority in the manufacturing schedule are common. Indeed, there may be a strong case for creating a separate spares manufacturing unit, particularly when there is need to make customised spares rapidly to respond to a breakdown situation.

There is likely to be a difference in the criteria by which original equipment manufacture and production of spares are judged. In manufacturing a component for original equipment build it is likely that the key task is to have it available for assembly in six months time whilst minimising unit cost. In the breakdown situation, speed is all, the inconvenience to the customer meaning that unit cost is comparatively unimportant. It is unlikely that the same operating systems will cope effectively with such opposing requirements. It is quite common to create a 'Plant within a Plant' for service needs.

Those spares which relate to current production can be scheduled into the main manufacturing plan, particularly if there are significant quantities involved. Once the product supported moves to 'semi-obsolete' status, however, this becomes increasingly difficult. It will be uneconomic to break down current production set-ups to make small quantities for spares, and original equipment build will probably take priority leading to lower availability levels for service.

Organisations deal with this by making a closing batch of components for service at the end of the main production run, estimating total needs for the next ten years, or by subcontracting these components to a supplier without the overheads of main production who will have the flexibility to provide the necessary items at reasonable cost.

Material requirements planning

In essence MRP II is directed at creating a master production schedule which can be achieved having considered all the capacity and material constraints in the system. Having formulated this top level schedule, MRP II then utilises Material Requirements Planning (MRP) to schedule all the detail activities of production and procurement which are required to meet the plan.

A form of Material Requirements Planning may be very useful for the service and support manager. It allows items to be tied together to ensure that imbalances in stock do not occur. Thus Fig. 12.3 shows a Bill of Material (BOM) for the parts required for a routine repair. By ordering at the top level, all the other parts are also ordered in the correct quantities.

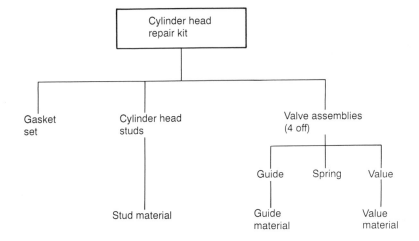

Fig. 12.3 Bill of material for cylinder head repair kit

There are many MRP and MRP II software packages available which range from the immensely powerful which run on main-frame computers and which are designed for complex manufacturing situations through to relatively cheap personal computer applications. Implementation of these systems will take some effort, but will reduce inventory cost and give better control in the long run.

The MRP approach is particularly valuable when kits of parts must be marshalled for specific jobs. The installation department, for example, may need to be sure that all necessary components will be available to meet a commissioning date. An MRP approach may prevent last minute 'borrowing' and provide much needed visibility to see when parts are currently promised.

Managing the bits and pieces

For many items, fasteners and other consumables, a major inventory control system will be overkill, or just impractical. Fig. 12.4 shows the two most common forms of simple inventory control, Reorder Point and Periodic Review.

The Reorder Point system can be operated using a simple card system, or frequently the two bin system will be used where the item is reordered when the first bin is empty, the second bin acting as the reserve which covers the order replenishment lead time. There are a number of simple computer packages available for this purpose.

The Periodic Review system is useful where a number of stock items are ordered on the same supplier. The system is set up to ensure that these items are reviewed at the same time, allowing one purchase order to be raised to cover a range of stock items, rather than raising many smaller ones at frequent intervals. Although the administration of the Periodic Review is simpler than Reorder Point, the safety stocks employed tend to be greater and the system is less responsive to sudden increases in demand. There is a higher probability of a stock-out in this case which may be counteracted by higher buffer stocks.

Safety stocks will be relatively high when:

- The pattern of demand is very variable and relatively unpredictable
- Large numbers of the stock item are used on each installation or service call
- There is a long lead time for replacement of the item. Long lead times tend also to mean that delivery reliability is reduced, increasing the pressure for high safety stocks.

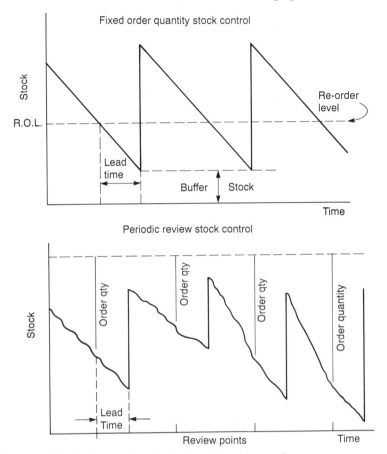

Figure 12.4 Fixed order quantity and periodic review stock control

Forecasting demand

Some stock control computer packages include a simple forecasting capability. We are surprised that so few companies use any forecasting techniques at all given that inventory is such a significant cost (and the cost of not having it when you need it may be even greater). Forecasting may be difficult for the service organisation where demand is 'lumpy' but some progress can usually be made with effort.

The service and support manager can employ some relatively simple methods of forecasting to take account of seasonal patterns and growth trends. The most simple form of forecasting is to use a simple *moving average*, perhaps weighted to take greater account of recent periods' results. With sufficient data, seasonal factors can be built in to give quite useful results for relatively little effort and would be suitable for use with many of the high usage stock items.

Exponential smoothing is perhaps the most popular forecasting method, and it is available with many stock control packages. The forecast for the current period, F_t, is calculated using the following formula:

$$F_t = a\,(D_t) + (1 - a)\,F_t - 1$$

The forecasting constant, a, reflects the weight which is given to the most recent actual demand figure, D_t. Previous demand data has been incorporated in the calculation of last period's forecast, $F_t - 1$. High values of 'a' will respond rapidly to most recent data and should be used if the situation is changing rapidly. It will be more common to use a smaller value of a, perhaps 0.1 or 0.2, to ensure that due account is taken of earlier demand. As with moving averages, exponential smoothing can also incorporate a seasonal adjustment.

The trick with forecasting is not so much in generating the forecast, but in recognising when the forecast is no longer accurate. To deal with this there are a number of error tracking techniques which indicate when the forecast accuracy has deteriorated. One of the most commonly used is Trigg's Tracking Signal, which may be incorporated in the forecast, giving an element of self-correction.

A useful technique for the service and support manager will be the linking of outside indicators to service demand. Thus, there should be some relationship between published figures of activity in the construction industry and the number of excavators used by contractors and therefore also the number of service calls generated. This relationship can be explored using *regression analysis*. Regression models can be simple, using one independent variable, or more complicated, known as *multiple regression*, where the relative value of each variable can be established.

A common application of regression analysis is to link the number of units operating in the field to service demand. This is particularly useful in comparing performance when the department is regionally organised. One might expect a region servicing 100 customers to generate more business than one serving 50. Care must always be exercised in ensuring that in making comparisons, similar conditions apply. A tractor company discovered that their European market which contained relatively new tractors generated a quite different service profile from its African market where the tractors were considerably older.

A final issue in forecasting relates to supporting the launch of new products. There will be no demand history to base usage on and stock levels can only be estimated on the basis of the demand profile of similar products, remembering that it will be very important for the product's reputation that spares are available when required. In this case higher safety stocks may be justified initially. Unfortunately it is often the case that manufacturing is struggling to meet the demands of original equipment programmes and spares inventory is slow in reaching target levels.

Commit the inventory as late as possible

Inventory savings can be made by holding the material in a state such that it can be made into several finished items. The example given earlier of the marine propulsion crankshaft forging which could be used for several applications illustrates this point. There may be a unit cost increase in the item held, but since the higher specification allows use on a wider range of applications, the total inventory cost will be reduced.

There are two approaches here. The first is to see whether a more expensive item can cover more applications, and the second is to improve manufacturing or assembly lead times to give greater flexibility to respond to the latest requirement.

Stock items should also be committed as late as possible in terms of their position. A spare part once delivered to a warehouse in Scotland is unlikely to be immediately available in France. Where possible, stock should be held centrally and this philosophy must be supported by an efficient distribution system.

Can the Just-In-Time philosophy be used?

Just-in-Time is aimed at reducing inventory in the total system by eliminating waste and involving people more effectively in the process. So, the straightforward answer is yes to some extent for any organisation. The heart of the JIT philosophy lies in providing a flexible and reliable system which provides the foundation for reducing inventory, cutting replacement lead times and giving impetus to improve the quality of products and processes still further.

Hewlett-Packard have made widespread use of this approach not only in manufacturing, but also in its repair facilities. Prior to JIT their repair workshops, in common with many others, were littered with returned units in various states of assembly. Ensuring that units were not allowed into the workshop area until all parts were available has brought the work in progress down dramatically, cutting lead times in some cases from months to days.

JIT brings visiblity to the process as Hewlett-Packard have discovered. As they pursued this policy, they realised that considerable disruption was being caused to the process by customers ringing in to discuss the state of their units with the engineer responsible. If the engineer was in mid-operation this lengthened the time spent by the unit in the repair area and increased the possibility of making errors as the number of interruptions increased. HP reviewed their customer handling policy, in this case restricting the access of customers to engineers to outside their core repair working hours. The improvement in repair turn-round far outweighs any relationship problems brought about by lack of access, and in many cases eliminates the need for the customer to ring up as the unit is returned faster.

Managing the service supply chain

There has been a shift in thinking over the last few years. Previously there was a desire to trade 'at arm's length', but today there are many examples of companies forging partnerships, believing that there is significant mutual advantage in working together closely. Effectively this is a return to vertical integration, with the advantage that one company isn't responsible for every activity; instead it can join forces with another and they can complement each other's strengths and weaknesses, not just those areas which it was good at but also those which it was not so good at.

Fig. 12.5 shows a supply chain for a manufacturer selling its product through a network of dealers who carry out service work for their customers. If the different parts of the chain work independently of each other, each will be working on less information than could be available and therefore will be less effective. In some cases there will be more inventory than is required, and in others insufficient inventory. This is known as the Forrester Effect, which observes that the swings in over and under supply become more dramatic the further you are from the point of initial demand (Fig. 12.6).

Supply Chain Management attempts to take out the 'unknowns' in the chain, tie the constituent parts closer together, and by removing excess

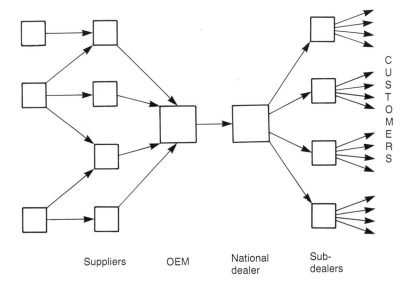

Figure 12.5 Service supply chain

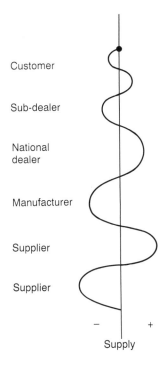

Figure 12.6 The Forrester effect

inventory, reduce the lead time from start to finish. As a result the total chain will be far more responsive to changes in customer demand. In fact the ideal is for the constituents of the chain to be 'making to order' rather than 'making to stock', thus removing inventory and excess cost from the system. These benefits must be shared across the chain.

What must the supply chain produce?

Customers are looking for ever-increasing levels of customer service. To some extent this reflects the impatience of modern life and can be summed up in the cry 'I want it now!'. In some markets, at least, immediate availability is becoming a 'given' or order qualifier and customers assume it. Thus the aims of the supply chain are as follows:

- At the very least, a significant improvement in response times. For example, Caterpillar spares can be sent anywhere in the world within 48 hours
- High availability levels. Inventory service levels of 95 per cent and above and increasing
- An increase in service level, but at reduced distribution cost and with reduced inventory levels
- High levels of management control and visibility of materials through the pipeline.

Clearly, the demands outlined above will not be met by traditional incremental improvement programmes. Service supply chain management requires a major change in attitude to dealing with both customers and suppliers.

What is needed to make the supply chain work?

At the risk of using too much jargon, an integrated approach is required to solve the problem of providing improved service at lower cost. All the components of the chain must be coordinated to remove the excess inventory and ineffective management effort from it.

Each stage must be as flexible as possible, able to respond to changes in demand rapidly. In order for members of the chain to invest in systems, people and processes to make this possible, there must be an apparent long-term benefit. Hence the move towards developing long-term partnerships with some confidence of sustained business, which should yield both improved flexibility and lower cost through time.

A key element in managing the chain is the development of schedules at each customer/supplier link that are realistic and give sufficient time to react. The ultimate aim is to move from suppliers *making to stock* to a situation where they can *make to order*. There is an element of continuous improvement here, a fixed schedule 12 weeks ahead being necessary today may be reduced to eight weeks after 12 months' cooperative action to develop more flexible and reliable processes.

Some key requirements for supply chain success are:

- Effort to generate realistic schedules and the discipline to keep them
- Investment in rapid information processing systems such as EDI links
- Action to build teamwork both internally and externally. Many organisations are forming product-based teams which cut across traditional functional barriers
- Joint projects to build channels which are more responsive to changes in demand. The emphasis is on creating planned flexibility, the ability to respond within defined limits.

Is supply chain management worth it?

Companies that have pursued this route have reported a number of benefits. A key measure is total supply chain inventory turns. If the inventory is merely shifted to a different place, typically back to a supplier, in the end no one wins. Companies that have developed partnerships are reporting a reduction in inventory across the chain, representing true cost savings.

Lower inventory levels mean faster throughput times, shorter lead times and therefore greater responsiveness. This in turn, means that schedules are achieved more often, with the positive benefit that much of the 'second guessing' disappears, reducing inventory still further. Schedules that are not continually changing are good news for manufacturing efficiency and also for quality, again yielding the possibility of improving still further.

What can the Service and Support Manager do?

There is much work to be done by all members of the chain to build relationships along the chain. For service and support, this means work with:

- Designers to improve the product

- All members of the chain to promote a customer focus, giving understanding of the customer's needs and problems
- All suppliers, whether internal or external, to give accurate timely information as to future requirements
- Working with customers to understand their requirements and to explain more fully how the support organisation works. This may promote joint improvement activities.

Conclusion

In recent years management has devoted effort to inventory reduction. In some cases this pressure has been misdirected, ignoring the fact that inventory has a role to play in the business. There are still significant cost benefits to be found in reviewing inventory policy but they will only be achieved as the organisation is clearer as to why the stock is required.

There are operating improvements to be gained through greater levels of integration both internally and externally. Incremental improvements may be achieved through internal changes but it is unlikely that these will be sufficient to meet the competitive demands of the future. These can only be met by gaining greater control of the total service supply chain from raw material suppliers through to final consumers.

Checklist

1 Have you carried out a full inventory review recently? Do you know how much inventory you should have to meet customer service level targets? How much do you have in reality?

2 Are inventory availability levels now competitive? What actions can be taken to increase availability but also to reduce cost?

3 Is it possible to reduce inventory by investing in a better information system? Are there elements of the MRP approach which could be utilised?

4 How is inventory for customer service and support managed by the manufacturing function? Do manufacturing functions reflect service priorities in the master schedule?

5 Are there any gains to be made in forming partnerships with key suppliers or major customers?

6 Is there general awareness as to which items of inventory are critical to maintain the effectiveness of customers' equipment and therefore merit greater attention?

7 Who holds the budget for inventory? Is this appropriate? What cross functional actions are being taken to manage inventory?

13 MANAGING THROUGH INTERMEDIARIES

Introduction

In Chapter 3 we discussed the structure of customer service and support and related it to the dimension of how much 'In-House Control' the original producer must retain of this activity. It might be said that it is always desirable to maintain control of the service activity for quality reasons and to build customer relationships, and of course there may be revenue to be earned from it.

However, for a number of reasons it may be deemed impractical, uneconomic or ineffective for an organisation to attempt to deliver service and support to all customers everywhere in the world. When this happens, there will be one and sometimes more organisations between us, as the Original Equipment Manufacturer (OEM), and the end consumer. We shall consider this issue primarily from the point of view of the OEM, with a final section from the viewpoint of a service provider who is not a manufacturer.

The decision to use an intermediary is not usually that of the customer service and support manager alone. Often, the marketing of the original product demands that there should be a local selling point, close to customers. If the primary motivation to appoint dealers is to increase sales turnover, the task of the Customer Service and Support Manager may become more difficult. In this case the intermediary may have been chosen for sales expertise, not for service proficiency, and will need considerable control and support.

Capital goods manufacturers do not face this issue to the same extent. Sales are often the responsibility of the OEM's own personnel and the decision to appoint an intermediary is likely to rest largely in the customer service and support function. A typical reason for appointing would be to ensure rapid response when there might be few installations in the geographical area. In this case the problem for the customer service and support manager would lie in imparting sufficient product knowledge to the agent.

In this chapter we will discuss the issues involved in operating a dealer or agent network and give some guidelines as to how they can be managed more effectively. The chapter concludes with a case study illustrating one company's approach to managing intermediaries.

Why use intermediaries?

Close to customer

The most common reason for choosing to use dealers or agents rather than an in-house organisation is that of geographical coverage. The ability to get close to customers both geographically and in terms of understanding their particular operating conditions may be critical both for original sale and for continuing support. Customers may feel more confident if there is a local presence. The organisation may desire to increase customer service and support coverage world-wide rapidly to meet higher sales targets and, as with franchising, building an independent dealer network may accomplish this using finance supplied by other people.

Local knowledge

The organisation may have insufficient knowledge of local trading conditions. This may be particularly pertinent for relatively small companies wanting to expand internationally but without knowledge of local conditions and culture. This option will be attractive if initial sales volumes are likely to be small making the commitment of opening a new sales and service branch economically unattractive.

Apart from the loss of control and the loss of potential revenue, a further drawback involved in using agents or dealers to expand internationally is that it reduces the opportunity for the organisation to move down the learning curve in working in that region and delays any proposed move to set up its own organisation.

Skill shortage

A third reason for using intermediaries is that of expertise. The manufacturer may feel that its strengths lie in design and production and doesn't want the organisational overhead of developing other skills. The intermediary may supply local selling skills as indicated above, or develop a specialist application of the equipment. For example, the vast majority of electronic products for security systems are installed and serviced by independent companies who combine products from various manufacturers to provide the most effective solution for the customer. The manufacturers at present have no expertise in designing, installing and maintaining the systems.

Another example is typified by the *total solution* approach much favoured by computer companies. A common scenario is for computer manufacturers to sell hardware and operations software directly to customers and also to Value Added Resellers (VARs) who have a particular expertise in applications software. The VARs are able to supply a solution rather than a toolkit to those customers who have no wish to become computer experts. In this case the OEM and the intermediary may be dealing with the same customer.

A service and support organisation may find that it is not able to support every technical aspect of its products. For example, many products which have traditionally required predominantly mechanical expertise are now incorporating an ever-increasing content of microprocessors. In the short-term, these skills may have to be supplied by subcontractors. The security systems company may have to subcontract the support of close circuit television equipment which requires specialist knowledge.

Low service income

Some manufacturers will use intermediaries because the service revenue is negligible. An example, again from the computer industry, would be that of peripherals which are likely to be replaced rather than repaired. In the event of failure the manufacturer must ensure that warranty claims are handled properly to minimise any irritation experienced by the customer. The customer must have ready access to operating advice either through the intermediary having sufficient resources or by provision of a help desk by the manufacturer.

Demand exceeds supply

The final reason for using intermediaries is lack of service capacity. A strategy employed for dealing with peak demand may be to use sub-contractors rather than have excess capacity under utilised. This approach requires much policing to ensure that the customer does not perceive any deterioration in quality of service. Some service organisations adopt a 'top and tail' approach, starting off the service activity by ensuring that the subcontractor has the right expertise and information, and inspecting the completed work before invoicing the customer. This may be possible where subcontractors are used sparingly, but it still does not control what happens between start and finish.

What approach should be adopted to controlling intermediaries?

This section outlines broad philosophies which may be used to manage the relationship between manufacturer and those organisations used to sell, service and support its products.

Economic rewards

Manufacturers of consumer products use distributor margins and allowances as an incentive to intermediaries to promote their product in preference to the competition. This approach may be particularly appropriate when the intermediary sells and services the products of more than one manufacturer. If the volume of business generated by any one product is relatively low a dealer may handle a range of products, and in some cases these may be competing offerings.

Manufacturers of more expensive products such as trucks or cars also employ financial incentives. It must be remembered that the intermediary exists to make profits for its owner rather than to service a particular product. Additional discounts for increased business, improved margin on spares or payments to improve equipment or facilities are all examples of this approach. This may ensure that adequate effort is applied to the product at the expense of the competing offerings.

A possible drawback of this approach is that it requires considerable administration, setting and reviewing targets and monitoring the total scheme to ensure that the returns are worthwhile, and to ensure that quality standards are maintained to levels that justify the bonus payment.

The car manufacturers make wide use of this tactic, though it can become devalued if the targets to qualify for payment are easily attained.

It is worth making a general point here. Managing a dealer network can be described as an art form. Dealers may be rather temperamental and therefore measures and rewards must be seen to be equitable if goodwill is not to be lost.

Strong arm tactics

Some organisations adopt the tactic of punishing poor dealers through reduction of rewards or in extreme cases total withdrawal of their franchise. This approach has not generally proved to be very effective in improving network performance in the long term. Organisations have found that frequent threats tend to lead to general discontent amongst dealers, even though those penalised were widely known to be below standard. Penalising one dealer sends ripples through the rest of the network with the others wondering if it will be their turn next. There may be a general loss of confidence in the parent organisation.

However, there may be a good argument for applying sanctions sparingly. Some automobile companies have taken franchises away for poor performance, and in the case of Nissan, the whole of the UK chain has been discarded. This tactic has its place 'to encourage the others', but it is not to be recommended as a general management style. Customers may be impressed that the parent has dealt decisively with poor perform- ance but, in general, more positive forms of motivation are more effective.

Providing expertise to support intermediaries

The intermediary chosen may not have the full range of management and technical skills available to the large organisation. The sales and service dealer has possibly been founded by a local entrepreneur who is excellent at building up businesses in the area, possibly an excellent salesperson, but is likely to be weak in sustaining the systems required to maintain business control as volume grows. The subcontractors used to cover gaps in technical expertise will be able to deal with the product but may be weak on customer management.

Identifying weaknesses is an opportunity to build the relationships in the network. Not only will the end customer see a better service if these weaknesses are addressed, but the intermediary should gain confidence in dealing with a professional organisation which is prepared to give support where needed. Caterpillar have succeeded in building a network of competent, committed dealers through good support in such areas as inventory management, marketing assistance and general management training.

The quality reputation – building a relationship

There is a general belief that some organisations are better to work with than the rest. They are perceived by customer and industry alike to 'have got it right'. Knowing that intermediaries have profited from the relationship consistently over the long term may motivate the intermediaries to provide high levels of service without the need for other inducements. This may result from fear of losing good business or may arise from knowing that the product which they support is genuinely the best in the market.

A white goods manufacturer dealt harshly with its agents in the days when demand far outstripped supply. When business conditions became more difficult and the manufacturer attempted to become more effective through developing more cooperative relationships, this was hindered because its earlier aggressive stance was remembered. As with any culture change, it may take several years for people to believe and accept a fundamentally different approach.

Most companies believe that good communication and open dealing are fundamental to effective network management. This applies at the level of the organisation as a whole as the intermediary deals with different business functions, but specifically with those individuals in the parent organisation who are appointed to control and liaise with the intermediary. Since relationships are a function of people, those employees who have specific responsibility for dealing with intermediaries must be chosen with care and once personal relationships are established they should not be changed without good cause. Managing these contact people effectively will mean that some specific issues such as career progression must be carefully addressed.

Manufacturer's rights to realistic controls

Some controls that the parent imposes on the intermediary may be seen as legitimate demands on the part of the manufacturer and therefore are not a matter for negotiation. For example, it may be a reasonable demand that the dealer employs staff who have received a given level of product training before they are allowed to service customers' equipment.

Standards and controls may be accepted as part of the requirements of the job or the conditions of being appointed as an approved agent of the company. Such standards should be regularly reviewed to ensure that they are giving the right result or are indeed reasonable.

An example of such a control might be some measure of stock cover. Current practice seems to vary tremendously from company to company with some imposing no requirement for stock cover to others insisting that at least one unit of each stock number must be held. This control could be put positively in terms of a recommendation, and then monitored by the nature of requests for replacement stock. If the dealer is always making emergency requests for stock, inventory levels are too low.

Quality of service from intermediaries is difficult to monitor. Some companies with relatively small service subcontractor networks are able to make sure that all service requests pass through the central service department so that completion and quality may be monitored. Larger service organisations must rely on customer surveys or incidence of customer complaints to monitor quality. Most dealers or agents would accept the right of the producer to impose some quality standards and to expect therefore to be audited regularly against them. This doesn't have to be in the nature of an 'end of term examination', but a more positive review of what works and what doesn't work with the aim of identifying joint action for improvement.

It is becoming common for the parent company to monitor overall customer satisfaction levels linking these with more specific quality standards. The parent company may publish league tables of customer satisfaction performance allowing the individual dealer to see his position in relation to the others. It may be wise to publish these figures anonymously so that the individual sees his score but is not able to identify other dealers. This allows the below standard dealer to generate self-motivation to improve rather than be ridiculed by those with better scores.

How can the network be improved?

A certain degree of conflict will occur in all relationships as goals differ or there are breakdowns in communication. The aim of the service and support manager is to ensure that these remain infrequent and minor, solved as they occur, rather than allowing them to escalate into long-term bitter disputes. Some actions can be taken to prevent disputes occurring and to raise the performance of the network.

Establish clear performance expectations

As has already been stated, setting up and managing a dealer network demands a great deal of administration. A key task in the early stages of relationships will be establishing appropriate goals for both parties. Inevitably, there will be continuing debates over margins and discounts which will be handled more effectively if the basis for negotiation is clear from the outset. The dealer will want to know how profitable the business will be in terms of volume and margin, whereas the manufacturer must be satisfied that service levels will be maintained. Key issues to be resolved, apart from the obvious financial targets, will include the number and competence of personnel employed, quality of service and facilities and range and level of inventory to be held.

Minimise network disputes by design

Those managing networks of intermediaries talk of two issues. The first issue is *channel density* which relates to the conflict which may arise because two dealers are trying to serve overlapping populations of customers. Giving exclusive rights to sell and service specific products in a geographical area will help to resolve this, providing the distribution of territories is seen to be equitable and sufficient to sustain profitability.

Computer companies have faced this problem where in one territory they may be competing with mini- and main-frame offerings against their independent dealer network who are largely selling and supporting personal computers. A major computer manufacturer belatedly imposed restrictions on the total number of dealers to be appointed after encountering severe problems of administration and overlaps which in turn led to a deterioration in service quality.

Car companies have faced problems of channel density as they have launched initiatives to increase market share. If the initiative works and the number of dealers has not increased, the new customers will be dissatisfied. On the other hand if new dealers are appointed in advance of the new demand, the existing dealers may find that their revenues are reduced in the short term at least as territories are reallocated.

The second major issue of network design is that of *channel length*. The greater the number of stages in delivering goods and services to the customer, the greater the opportunities for conflict. Some manufacturers appoint national dealers or distributors with regional dealers and even sub-dealers beyond them. The potential for financial disputes at each stage is multiplied as there are yet more relationships to be managed, and the performance of the chain in quality of service and level of inventory held is likely to deteriorate. Of course, it may seem attractive to deal solely with one national contact, but the loss of control may far outweigh the savings in administrative effort.

Select the right intermediaries

As with most management issues, time spent up-front in evaluation and planning will pay off many times over. It will be important to review the general health of the agent's business rather than concentrate on the specific requirements. So, an automobile dealer must have marketing and customer service skills as well as the ability to sell cars, and a sub-contractor installer must be financially sound as well as technically competent.

Some areas for review in selecting intermediaries include:

- Financial standing, credit rating, gearing
- Labour profile, skills, knowledge and industrial relations record
- Degree of market understanding
- Local market knowledge
- Whether competitors' products are sold or serviced
- Implementation of control systems: cost, quality, scheduling, inventory
- Percentage of total business that new contract would represent
- Assessment of overall desire to carry out the business to a satisfactory level.

Most manufacturers make progress carefully in appointing agents. Studies on the choice of dealers indicate that most organisations endeavour to draw up a reasonable shortlist of candidates to be visited by the management to audit the competence of the applicant before the final decision is made. This process is still adhered to even if an overseas dealer is to be appointed though government advice may also be sought in this case.

Positive motivation

As indicated earlier, management by threat is rarely an effective tactic. A study carried out by Shipley et al indicated that territory rights, keeping the dealer up to date with developments and plans, and regular contact were the actions felt to be the most effective in improving the performance of the network and the individual dealer.

Actions that were felt to be useful also included giving general appreciation when performance has been good, financial incentives, giving commitments to long term relationships and ensuring that the intermediaries are included in policy making. Some automobile companies retain a percentage of allowances against good performance. If the dealership meets its targets, this money can be used to upgrade its facilities.

Actions used less frequently were threats, sharing market research information and training of staff across all functions in the intermediary's organisation.

Train the people

Although the survey mentioned in the previous section indicated that relatively few manufacturers see training as a way of motivating their dealer network, our view is that it represents a good opportunity to build relationships and commitment on both parts. The survey indicated that 73 per cent of companies gave product training, whereas only 17 per cent gave any form of interpersonal skills training. Since the customer doesn't see that the dealer or subcontractor is an independent company, but rather thinks of them as the parent company, there is no doubt that poor customer service will not damage the intermediary's reputation alone but also that of the parent company.

The case study at the end of this chapter describes one company's belief that its intermediaries should be trained across a wide range of areas as a means of increasing commitment, and improving overall quality levels.

Regular evaluation

Many manufacturers review their dealers on a formal basis at least once a year, using the opportunity to discuss the business as a whole, consider future plans and set appropriate targets for the next period. The parent may also find it valuable to hold a dealers' conference, giving them the opportunity to meet others and to feel included in the service team. Some have shied away from this approach, perhaps fearing that the dealers may become too powerful if they take concerted action.

Regular evaluations of intermediaries will normally include:

- Volume of business
- New business generated
- Value of business
- Customer service performance
- Dealer administration costs.

This last item is worth considering. Some dealers will cost more than others to manage. For example, some will not carry as broad a range of spares, and will constantly request priority shipments over and above the normal service. Others will not have the same technical competence, needing the support and advice of the company's personnel. The review process should identify actions which will enable the intermediary to manage the business more effectively as this will represent cost savings to the network.

Many consumer goods manufacturers run continuous customer satis-faction assessments, asking their customers to rate the dealer service. Volvo, for example, was also able to relate high performance on the customer satisfaction index to dealer profitability.

Customer complaint management

Some customer complaints are not handled effectively by intermediaries because the parent company's policies on what is and what is not reimbursable are not clear. The procedures for dealing with customer problems and how the costs are to be apportioned should be developed with input from the dealers concerned. At least one car manufacturer operates a system of 'goodwill payments' to smooth over customer com-plaints. We feel that this approach skirts round the issue of improving service rather than managing in spite of poor service quality.

It is usually helpful to make it clear to the customer that there is recourse to the parent organisation if the customer is unhappy with the intermediary's performance and there appears to be no desire on the part of the dealer to resolve the issue. This is obviously a sensitive issue, but again it is better addressed head-on rather than avoided.

Meeting deliveries from parent to intermediary

One of the most common sources of dispute between parent and intermediary lies in the supply of spare parts. Of course the dealer must hold a reasonable level of stock, but must also have confidence that the stated replenishment lead times will be maintained. If the delivery schedules are not reliable, there is no basis for challenging the dealer's performance in inventory management.

This problem is obviously greater where there are cross-border deliveries to be made. It is unlikely that even after 1992, in the European Community, we will see the total dismantling of customs posts with their resultant delays.

The retailer's viewpoint – getting control

This chapter has been written from the viewpoint of the producer who uses intermediaries to provide sales and service. Most of the principles outlined apply in reverse to the service provider who needs to ensure that the supply of product, information and spare parts is maintained at a reasonable margin.

The secret of success lies in discovering and exploiting the mutual advantages of partnership. Some electrical retailers provide their own after sales service and whilst this may compete to a degree with the original manufacturer, it may be that the increase in sales volume arising from increased customer confidence may make it worthwhile supporting.

The retailer will be concerned to reduce the size of the service task. Each new product means an increase in inventory to be carried as well as new product knowledge to be gained. The way to contain this is to make sure that valuable feedback for quality improvement is given to the manufacturer so that both benefit from increased product reliability.

For this reason some sales and service providers may choose to limit the range of products dealt with to better manage those that remain. In order to do this, the service provider must have accurate information as to which products provide the majority of contribution to revenue.

The case of Earthmovers Ltd

The earthmoving equipment industry is extremely competitive. There are relatively few major competitors who each have world-wide sales coverage. The problem for service and support in this industry is that the equipment doesn't stay in the same place, being moved to wherever the latest construction project is taking place. Much of the equipment is sold to plant hire companies whose customers have a relatively low commitment to looking after it. On the other hand, the cost to the user of equipment failure may be catastrophic.

The task for Earthmovers Ltd is to ensure that its equipment is capable of the job demanded of it, that it is as reliable as is possible given the heavy nature of work carried out, and to ensure that should the equipment break down, the customer is inconvenienced as little as possible.

In order to ensure global coverage and to capitalise on construction industry contacts, Earthmovers Ltd chose to develop and support a network of dealers, some of whom would be owned by the company and others being independently owned. Many of these independent dealers were plant hire companies and were already customers of Earthmovers Ltd.

Because this was a major strand of the company's marketing policy as well as a means to deliver service and support, the needs of the dealership network were regularly communicated throughout the company, designers in particular being aware of the implications of engineering change for the intermediary. In order to justify higher product prices than its major competitors, Earthmovers Ltd emphasised the strength of its service back-up to its customers. To ensure that this was not seen as merely publicity Earthmovers set about training its dealers in the belief that this investment would result in improved dealer performance.

Technical training of mechanics was only one component of the programme. Earthmovers felt that it was equally important for the dealer to understand the needs of the customer and to be given general business awareness briefings. Earthmovers enabled their dealers to analyse local market conditions more effectively with the result that both businesses benefited. Marketing specialists spend time in each dealership every year.

Its strong dealer network has proved to be a major barrier to the competition, whose networks are relatively dispersed and less committed to the OEM. This aspect of local strength has increased sales turnover.

Apart from the training programme which dealers feel has contributed greatly to their own effectiveness in general management, sales and service, Earthmovers Ltd work hard at maintaining regular contact at all levels of the dealership with briefings, dealer conferences and engineer visits. Earthmovers' approach to managing its intermediaries is widely praised and the general approach has been copied by OEMs in other industries.

Conclusion

People do things for their own reasons, not for the reasons you would like to impose on them. Most of the strategies that work in improving service levels delivered through intermediaries stem from ensuring that the goals of the organisations involved coincide rather than conflict. The words may be slightly different, but the result must be the same. There is a lower probability of conflict if the organisations involved make it easy to do business by clear communication and by basically doing a good job. The service and support manager must act not just as a customer champion, but also as a dealer champion to ensure that the needs of the network are fully considered at every stage.

Checklist

1 Do you truly manage our intermediaries or are they allowed to develop their own targets and procedures?

2 Is it possible to involve the intermediaries more fully in policy development?

3 Are there any areas where you could use intermediaries more effectively than your own organisation?

4 How comprehensive is the training programme for the staff or intermediaries? What incentives are there for staff to attend? Is the training good but rather expensive?

5 What is the skill profile of the dealer network? Are there any major deficiencies?

6 Are there any sanctions that should be applied to poor performers?

7 How do you select your dealers? Does this take into account all the factors discussed in this chapter?

8 Have you established the cost balance between providing service and support through your own organisation versus intermediaries?

14 RECOVERY STRATEGIES: THE KEY TO CUSTOMER RETENTION

Introduction

In this chapter we will look at service recovery, and the reasons why it is important for service and support organisations. We will give some approaches for developing strategies for dealing with service recovery, including recovery procedures, empowerment and performance assessment related to recovery.

Why should we bother about service recovery?

Let us look at the experiences of two customer service and support organisations who supply domestic appliances, including washing machines and dishwashers. On different occasions we have had the following experiences with the two companies' service centres. In the case of the washing machine manufacturer we had a breakdown of our machine and called the service centre for an engineer to call. The engineer came at the arranged time and appeared to have repaired the fault. Unfortunately when the machine was next used there were still problems. On calling the service centre we were told the engineer would call again next day. Our experience with the dishwasher manufacturer was somewhat different. Again we needed to call out the service engineer to fix a fault. This was done but some problems still remained. Calling the service centre we were given an apology and reassured by the receptionist that the engineer would return later the same day. This happened with further apologies from the engineer for the inconvenience which his failure had caused.

It is clear that the second service experience was far better than the first. The dishwasher service organisation was willing to accept failure and to do something to recover from it. It is inevitable that to do so would involve extra cost of overtime or rescheduling of resources. Is it worth the cost? We would say from the market research which has been carried out for service companies in a number of sectors that it is. Why? Because it has been shown that good recovery from mistakes builds customer loyalty and increased profitability. Let us look at the evidence for this:

Customer satisfaction

Technical Assistance Research Programme Inc (TARP) is an American market research company that has worked with many of the leading service companies on customer satisfaction and customer loyalty. The focus of their work has been to examine how customer satisfaction is influenced by a company's approach to customer complaints and their performance in recovering from their mistakes. TARP also relates performance to loss of revenue.

TARP takes four service scenarios and examines the willingness on the part of the customer to use the service provider again. The four are:

1   The service is delivered to meet the customers' expectations and there is full satisfaction.
2   There are faults in the service delivery but the customer does not complain about them.
3   There are faults in the service delivery and the customer complains but feels he/she has been fobbed off or mollified. There is still no real satisfaction with the service provider.
4   There are faults in the service delivery and the customer complains and feels fully satisfied with the resulting actions taken by the service providers.

The reactions of customers to the four experiences is very different and greatly influences whether a customer will continue to purchase from the service providers. Fig. 14.1 shows some typical results from marketing research data of customers' intentions to continue to be customers of the service organisation. Clearly they show that dissatisfied customers who complain but are not happy with what happens feel worse about the service providers than if they had not bothered to complain at all. The result for the customer is to reinforce the impression of the service company being inadequate. On the other hand, good recovery from mistakes results in customers' loyalty being maintained at the level which would have been achieved from a first-time perfect delivery of the service. Obviously the precise values for intention to repurchase will vary according to the costs involved for the customers but the trends for the different scenarios are always the same. In addition TARP is able to relate the drop in customer satisfaction to losses in revenue and profits.

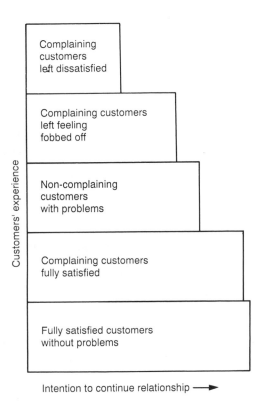

Figure 14.1 Customers' intentions from service experience

The other finding which has a bearing on this is associated with the effect of low customer satisfaction on word-of-mouth publicity about service experience. It has been found from marketing research that a customer who is satisfied with a service experience will typically tell five others whereas when they have not been satisfied they will tell ten people. When they have experienced good recovery they will tell three. Word-of-mouth advertising is important because if it is positive it can lead to referral of business.

Profitability

Studies by the American consultants Bain & Company have looked at the relationship between service, customer satisfaction and profitability. Their results show that the key to profitability is to be found in customer retention. Customer retention is defined as the number of customers present at both the beginning and the end of a period divided by the numbers of those present at the beginning. For instance, if we have 200 customers at the beginning of the year and 250 at the end of the year but only 100 of these were customers at the beginning, then our customer retention rate is 50 per cent.

The effect of high customer retention is to increase profitability. Why should this be so? Bain claim the following reasons from their work:

1   The cost of getting new customers is high. Retaining customers spreads these costs over a period of time. So the longer customers stay with us the higher the profits because there are not the costs associated with bringing in new customers.
2   Customers who stay are more willing to spend more. They will buy additional services and they may be more willing to pay a premium price for the service.
3   Regular customers cost less to serve particularly in administration costs.

The results of increased profitability from a 5 per cent increase in customer retention range from 25 to 125 per cent for a range of different types of service. These increases result from reductions in operating costs, extra profit from price premiums, profits from additional purchases, and profit from referrals because customers tell others of the good service we are providing.

What do these results tell us?

There are powerful messages coming from these studies. These are:

1   Doing everything we can to retain customers will increase profitability.
2   Getting a service delivery system which never fails to achieve customer satisfaction may be the ideal but may lead us to ignore the consequences of some inevitable failures. TQM programmes may concentrate on 'getting it right first time' and miss the consequences of failure.

3 Getting customers to report shortfalls in service gives an opportunity to redress our mistakes and maintain loyalty.

4 Recovery must be genuine and not lip service alone. Apologies may help, but real action is what counts in the end.

What's involved in developing recovery strategies?

Customer service and support organisations who are not good at delivering customer service will not be in a position to implement recovery strategies. Typically their customers will not complain but go elsewhere for their service. When complaints are made they are hidden and suppressed by the service managers for fear that it will affect their performance ratings. Good recovery is only possible once there is a service and support system in place which is in itself inherently capable of delivering good service quality and high customer satisfaction.

Avis, who have their mission statement in the three words 'We try harder', see the achievement of customer satisfaction being made up of the two components of 'Doing the job right first time' and 'Effective complaint management'. Therefore the starting point for recovery is in getting the system right to start with. We have talked about quality programmes and the techniques to identify failure points in service delivery and ways to rectify them in Chapter 9. We have to be careful that this approach is not so inflexible as to prevent us dealing with the unexpected and being able to act quickly.

Developing recovery strategies will involve us in a number of actions:

1 Getting better at the basics of service and support delivery.

2 Recognising when things are most likely to go wrong and developing coping strategies.

3 Getting the full potential from the network through escalation procedures.

4 Measuring what is happening with customer complaints and our ability to satisfy them.

5 Giving our service providers the means and power to act quickly to redress faults.

6 Recognising what customers value when things go wrong.

Getting better at the basics?

The first stage on the road to recovery is to make sure the basics of our customer service and support are working. This involves reviewing the whole of the service delivery. Is it capable of doing the task the service managers are asked to do? We can gain some idea if we are moving in the right direction by looking for answers to the following questions:

1   Do we have a clear idea of the nature of service and support we are trying to deliver?
2   Do we know who our customers are and what they value from our service and support?
3   Do we understand the patterns of demand and what they mean for managing our resources?
4   Do we know what unit costs have to be, so that we can meet profitability targets?
5   Do we understand the main constraints which might affect our service delivery?
6   Do we know how well we are performing against our competitors?
7   Do we have clear targets for performance for service quality and resource productivity?
8   Do we understand our delivery system in detail and are we aware of factors which limit the flexibility of our capacity?
9   Do we know the potential failure points in our service delivery system?
10   Do we consider that our resources are up to the challenge of meeting our performance targets?
11   Do we have a measurement system capable of giving information which enables us to meet our targets for service quality, customer satisfaction, and resource productivity?

If we can answer positively to all of these we are probably in a position to make real gains from concentrating on recovery strategies.

What are 'coping strategies'?

We have discussed capacity management and the effect on service quality and resource productivity from not getting a balance between effective capacity from the resources we have immediately available to us and the service intensity. The two capacity strategies of chase and level may enable us to manipulate both our level of resource and the demand creating service intensity. However there will be times when these capacity strategies fail us. It is inevitable for most service and support operations that at times they will run out of capacity, if only in the short-term; however, to prevent any shortages of capacity would be costly. We would have resources underutilised for much of the time in order to be able to cover the peak loads. So in most cases we are often in the position of running out of resource capacity when our chase strategy effectively becomes level and we are powerless to influence demand to bring it back to within our capacity limit.

The consequence is poor customer service either through the service being rushed or customers having to wait longer than they would expect to. Many service and support operations accept these times as a feature of the way in which they do business. They take the view that is hard luck on the customers who should realise the problems and accept them. We take a different view and suggest a solution: what is required is a *'coping strategy'* to deal with these 'busy' times.

We see the following as the stages in developing coping strategies for customer service and support:

1 *Understand what suffers for customers when things get busy.* Does it mean customers cannot make contact? Do they have to wait longer than contracted times for service or support? Do they incur costs from our failure in increased machine downtime or administrative costs? Do we find our front-line people become less attentive to the needs of customers? Do we find customers complain more about failures associated with our busy times? An understanding of what suffers will enable us to concentrate on the most important features of service and support delivery when we are coping.

2 *Recognise when the* limiting stage *for capacity is being reached.* In many cases this can be seen in response centres through the number of calls waiting or being lost from the telephone call management system. In a physical environment customers may be queueing in a service centre. Also we realise customers are not being visited within the target times by service staff.

3 *Decide on* policies *for limiting service provision.* These may include a prioritising system for responding to requests. Level of service contract is commonly used for this purpose. Different service contracts may promise alternative response times with the premium contract having the shortest times. These might be given the highest priority in the busy times. Alternatively the highest priority goes to the most important

customers who need to be retained at all cost.

4 *Develop* information systems. These give front-line people the opportunity to give customers an explanation of what is happening and what will happen. British Airways has improved the way in which it keeps passengers informed of reasons for unexpected waiting, for example extra security checks or air traffic congestion, and the length of time passengers can expect to be delayed.

5 *Encourage* customers *to tell us when service is poor*. This could be as a result of high demand. We should look to compensate them for the failure as quickly as possible.

The message from these stages is that the more we recognise that there will be times when we are under pressure and have developed ways of dealing with them the greater the probability of not losing customers. Moreover we are taking the positive step of trying to retain customers.

Using resources to best effect: escalation

Allied to coping strategies is the issue of how we can best use all our resources most effectively when things start to go wrong. We have been talking about the effects of not having resources to meet demand causing problems with customer satisfaction; however, there is another area which holds dangers. This is when one part of the delivery system runs out of resources through not having sufficient skills or knowledge to do the job.

The way to deal with this situation is to develop a clear *escalation* approach which is triggered either by individuals or through a service event tracking system. The use of escalation procedures is common in the computer services industry where inability to meet target times and close down one service or support job results in it being brought to the notice of the next level of management. If there is still no resolution within a set time the information is escalated to the next level of management and so on up to the CEO level. Needless to say in those customer service and support organisations which operate this type of escalation very few events reach the CEO! The pressure is on the service managers at the intervening levels to redeploy resources and to call on the skills and knowledge from the whole network.

Rather than the service management and staff activating an escalation procedure we might encourage customers to contact us as things start to go wrong. The use of special telephone hotlines gives an immediate signal to the service managers that something is wrong. Resources may be held in reserve to deal with these circumstances or other resources used as in the normal escalation process.

The use of escalation procedures is a way of flexing the capacity of the total service and support network in a way which makes sure that it is focussed on potential failure or responds to imminent customer complaint.

Measurement of customer satisfaction

Unless we are consistently measuring levels of customer satisfaction and their attitudes to service recovery we will not know what the cost is to us and whether we are doing the right things to recover from service failures. There are a number of ways in which this can be done:

1   Information gathered by the front-line people at the time of service either in a structured or unstructured way. The onus is on the service managers to encourage their staff to report failures. This method gives the best opportunity of responding quickly to failure and achieving customer satisfaction.

2   Getting customers to call when things go wrong can be encouraged through publicity, cards left with the users and the provision of a free phone to a hotline line.

3   Questionnaires left with the customers at the time of a service visit. The response rate from this technique may be low and it will fail to identify the really disgruntled customer whose only intention is to find another company to do future work.

4   Mailed questionnaires with some inducement to complete them, such as all responses being put into a draw for a prize. This will increase the response rate and also send the message that the service company is keen to get feedback on customer satisfaction.

5   Telephone calls to customers who have had contact with the service and support organisation in the recent past. This also gives the opportunity to pick up customers who might not have replied to a mailed questionnaire and yet are dissatisfied.

6   Telephone calls from managers to randomly selected customers. While the sample size may be low the impact on the service managers can be dramatic! It also gives customers a sense that the service and support management cares about what is happening to them. Organisations may carry out this work in-house or employ a specialised organisation like TARP to carry out the work.

The results from customer satisfaction surveys can be used most powerfully when they are translated into a cost of lost sales so that the impact on revenue and profits is clear to the service management team. The process may be refined to gather results in a way which allows the measurement of the performance of individual service branches. This can be used in the appraisal of service managers and incorporated into their reward package. Managers quickly realise that performance in recovering from service failures has a great influence on the satisfaction rating they receive from their customers.

Empowering the service providers

Much is talked about the empowerment of front-line service providers to recognise service failure, to take ownership of the problem and to resolve it. This can only work if the service providers:

- know what they can do
- know where they can call on help from other parts of the organisation
- are supported in their actions by front-line managers.

Knowing what to do
If our staff are to know what to do in cases of service failure they need to be trained. In some cases service failure will be associated with events which occur from time to time for which a distinct recovery procedure can be developed. For instance, a lack of spares could result in a courier service being used to deliver spares to a site. Special transport could be arranged to deliver equipment which had been repaired but was over the due time.

Where service failure is not clearly identifiable another form of training is required. This is to enable the service providers to recognise the reaction of customers and then be able to establish the causes of dissatisfaction at the point of contact. This means development of interactive skills for technical people.

Knowing who can help
Empowerment of service staff means they need to have a sense of what resources could be called on from their part of the organisation to help them out. This entails the service and support staff having a wide view of the service and support organisation and of the capabilities available, rather than a narrow specialist view.

Escalation procedures are one way of mobilising assistance as things get out of hand. The front-line people are guided in their actions through the service and support structure. However there are often cases of failure which do not warrant the use of escalation but which can be dealt with by the service team. Knowledge of the potential of the team becomes an important aspect of recovery. A team which is motivated to take responsibility for satisfying customers anticipating and recovering from service failures will be more successful.

Managerial support
Unless there is support from the service managers for initiative by staff to recover from service failures staff will not take on the responsibility. The role of the front-line manager is to build the service team to work to the quick resolution of problems as they occur. This process encourages customers to say when things are going wrong.

Reassuring the customers
There is one final reason why we should pay attention to recovery strategies. We have already talked about the importance to profitability of retention of customers over a length of time. In the area of customer service and support one of the prime features we are selling is 'peace of mind'. It is worth asking ourselves what we mean by this. Is it simply an aphorism or does it also have a real economic content?

Christian Gronroos has proposed a framework for looking at the costs of service from the viewpoint of the service provider and the customers. So for our customer service and support organisation the costs are:

- associated with the normal service delivery
- associated with maintaining the relationship with the customer. These include selling and other administration costs
- associated with putting right things which go wrong
- associated with the psychological wear and tear on staff from dealing with customers. These will include the costs of burn-out.

For the customers, the costs of the relationship with us as the customer service and support organisation are:

- costs which result from the price we charge
- costs associated with the administration of the normal relationship
- costs associated with getting mistakes put right
- psychological costs associated with the wear and tear on the customers from dealing with our organisation.

The normal production and administrative costs are widely recognised in most organisations, even if they are not measured and reported. However the cost of mistakes and the psychological costs are usually not acknowledged or measured. Those organisations who have instituted TQM programmes may be making measurements of the costs of poor quality, and so have some indication of the cost of mistakes. However these measurements are for the most part the customer service and support organisation's costs and not the customer costs. So overall there is little account taken of psychological costs on both sides and of the customers' costs associated with correcting mistakes.

The area of recovery is the one which has the greatest impact on the psychological costs and the customers' costs of dealing with mistakes. Quality programmes will help to reduce the number of error events. Recovery strategies will help to minimise the customers' costs of dealing with our mistakes and the psychological costs.

So if we have recovery strategies we have reduced the overall costs to customers, especially psychological costs, so that the customers feel reassured and have peace of mind.

Conclusion

In this chapter we have looked at the importance of customer retention and the part played by service recovery in making sure customers want to continue a relationship with a particular service and support provider. We have identified the costs of the relationship and have seen good recovery can increase customer reassurance and reduce psychological costs. Finally we have suggested approaches which customer service and support organisations can use to develop recovery strategies.

Checklist

1   What are the psychological costs to you and your staff from poor service and support?

2   What are the psychological costs to your customers of your poor performance?

3   If you considered your existing customers on a 5–10 year scale rather than the next year, would it change your assessment of their relative importance?

4   What steps do you take to make sure you retain existing customers?

5   When are things most likely to go wrong with your delivery of customer service and support?

6   What are your current recovery strategies?

7   Could you improve your escalation procedures?

8   Could you improve your recovery procedures?

15 INTERNATIONAL-ISATION: MANAGING THE NETWORK

Introduction

In this chapter we look at some of the aspects of customer service and support, including the issues for marketing and operations brought about by changes in the international regulations. We will examine the networks and their integration, and the management of the international supply chain.

What is changing in the international scene?

On the international scene there is the general increase in international trade by countries. This has brought with it opportunities for companies who manufacture products to sell into wider markets but it also increases competition from foreign manufacturers within home markets. Both of these factors have implications for customer service and support in the after sales area. We have seen this global spread from companies in sectors dealing with, for example, computers, automobiles, machine tools and domestic brown and white goods. Companies like IBM, Hewlett-Packard, Toyota and Caterpillar have established global networks for the sale of products and also for customer service and support. This situation will continue to intensify so long as world trading agreements like the General Agreement on Tariffs and Trade (GATT) continue in existence.

For European-based companies there is the added impetus of the single market in 1992 which will initially consolidate the present members of the EC into a single trading unit. However in the course of time the geographical area is likely to be extended to include the emerging economies of the old Eastern Bloc countries such as Hungary, Czechoslovakia and Poland, and possibly also the republics that made up the USSR.

These changes will have implications for companies in selling products and for customer service and support. Barriers in the physical, technical and monetary areas will disappear or be reduced. Work by the consultants Pittiglio, Rabin, Todd & McGrath (PRTM) has identified the following main effects in these areas:

Physical barriers:
The physical barriers to the movement of goods was made easier from January 1988 by the introduction of the Single Administrative Document (SAD) which replaced about 20 separate customer documents with one piece of paper. The effect has been to allow the movement of products and spares on a single document. Along with the SAD, customer tariffs have been equalised and there has been a move towards the relaxation of transport regulations in some if not all member states. Germany is a notable exception.

The result of the relentless removal of physical barriers is to make the movement of products and spares easier and quicker. There are implications for the logistic systems to support service activity. For instance, due to the changes it is no longer necessary to have supplies stock in each country. So companies can gain the benefits of centralisation which reduce inventory costs and raise service levels associated with the availability of spares. Reliable transport systems and structures are also needed to make centralisation attractive.

Technical barriers:
The ultimate goal for the EC is to have common technical standards. Industrial sectors like telecommunications and electrical products will ultimately have common standards. These changes will take time to implement and in the intervening time countries will have to recognise member countries' present standards in areas like electrical products. The immediate effect of this EC Directive will be the removing of trade barriers which excluded certain products because they did not meet the technical specification of a country. The process of harmonisation is likely to be seen most quickly in those sectors where there is rapid innovation with new technologies being introduced.

Allied to technical specification is the relaxation in the movement of specialists. Member countries will have to recognise the qualifications of technical specialists from all countries in the EC. Consequently service and support personnel will become more mobile and restricted in their use only by language.

Monetary barriers:
The removal of monetary barriers makes the movement of money between member EC states easier. The ERM is the first step in linking the different currencies together and any further steps towards a common currency will consolidate the process. The effect on companies is to reduce the risk from currency fluctuations.

While these changes will clearly affect manufacturers of products other sectors offering customer service and support will not be immune to changes. Any takeover of UK privatised utility companies such as gas, water and electricity can be expected to bring higher service standards as foreign companies introduce new approaches to delivering service. Retailers and agents may be expected to have to conform to higher standards driven both by their suppliers and the rising expectation of customers.

Pressure from global companies:
There is an additional influence on those suppliers to global companies. Increasingly firms in this category are looking to their suppliers to give customer service and support on a regional if not global scale. Rather than negotiating contracts country by country there is a trend for single contracts which cover a wider geographical area and with payment in a single currency. Failure to handle these needs at the selling level or in the delivery of a consistent service and support package will exclude some suppliers.

What will the changes mean for customer service and support?

The changes we have outlined will have implications for customer service and support for the structure of the network for service and support delivery, for the logistics supply chain system, and for the planning and control of consistency across the network. These issues, will have to be addressed at the strategic level and in the functional areas of marketing and operations, are:

1   *Strategic issues*: The strategic issues will mean a reassessment of the basic questions:
(a)   What is now the nature of the business?
(b)   What do the changes in the political, economic, social and technical environment now mean for us?

(c)   Who are now our main competitors and are there changes in the power of suppliers and customers? Do the changed circumstances mean there are greater threats of new entrants or substitutes for what we are selling?

(d)   What do we see as the basis of our competition in the new markets?

(e)   What do we see as being our main strengths and weaknesses to prosper in the new environment? Do we see new opportunities for business or threats to our existing activities?

Failure to address these issues and assume that the influences on our business will be exactly the same as in the past will undoubtedly mean that firms will miss opportunities and be unprepared for the threats to their business.

2   *Marketing issues*: Some of the main issues for marketing are:

(a)   Can we segment the markets in different ways for either the sale of products or selling and delivering customer service and support?

(b)   Where can we take advantage from standardisation of products which will reduce the variety of the service and support tasks?

(c)   How can we best build partnerships with major customers for the supply of products and customer service and support?

(d)   What channels should we use for the sale of products and customer service and support?

(e)   Can we harmonise contacts?

The role of marketing is to understand the new market structures and the needs of the customers so that competitive advantage can be gained by getting closer to major customers and segmenting the new market in ways which allow a focus on resources to the best effect.

3   *Service and support operational issues*: Some of the main service and support operational issues are:

(a)   What is the best network structure to deliver customer service and support?

(b)   To what extent can we integrate the network?

(c)   What is the best way to manage the logistics supply chain for spares?

(d)   What information systems do we need to support the network?

(e)   What are the implications for the recruitment, training and deployment of service and support staff?

(f)   How can we get the maximum capacity flexibility from the network?

(g)   Does a new network structure offer resource productivity gains leading to lower unit costs?

(h)   How should quality consistency across the network be measured?

(i)   How can we minimise risks of failure in achieving the goals of the new service operations task?

The role of the service and support operations managers is to create the new networks and to plan and control the service delivery to consistent standards of performance. The pressure for change will be greater on some providers of customer service and support than others. However it is fair to say that any organisation which does not review its activities in the light of the changes may be in danger. To take no action an organisation would have to be sure that its competitive position was protected by some long-term competitive distinctiveness or that it only wanted to operate in a niche market.

What are the options for service and support networks?

The new international environment means that the network for the delivery of customer service and support has to be reviewed. The options are going to be driven first at the strategic level because they mean a reassessment of the extent to which we want to maintain in-house control over the whole operation in the face of growing service intensity. The structures for customer service and support which we discussed in Chapter 3 still apply, although with more complexity.

When a decision is made to provide customer service and support through intermediaries as agents or dealers we will have to consider how they can be supported and controlled. The issues will centre on:

- The number and location of dealers
- The relationship of dealers, whether they are independent businesses or franchises. The extent to which they offer customer service and support on our products and our competitors'
- Training the dealers. There will be issues relating to the present skills of the dealers, their systems, and ways of delivering customer service and support
- Dealer training of customers means addressing the ways in which dealers are themselves trained, the expectations of the customers in the region for training as part of the customer service and support activity
- Supply of spares. We may wish dealers to hold their own stocks of spares or to manage the whole process ourselves
- Back-up support for dealers with information and specialists. This will

have a bearing on the location of back-up specialists and the information and communications systems which are used

- Tie in dealers with our information systems. We may chose to integrate
  dealers into our own information network or to leave them essentially
  independent.

Decisions in this area will depend on the nature of the service and support
and the extent of the penetration into new regions. If the decision is made
to maintain a high level of in-house control over the new network by the
use mainly of SAS and Regulars in the service structure model consideration has to be given to:

- The distribution of service intensity across the new geographic area to
  be covered
- The location of service and support centres
- The location of SAS specialists and Regulars
- Composition of the service and support teams and their skills and
  knowledge requirements
- The degree of integration of the service and support centres.

Service intensity

It is probable that in the early days of expansion into new markets that the
service intensity will vary considerably. This may frustrate the ability to
use an SAS/Regular structure because the service intensity in some areas
is too low to warrant the setting up of service centres. If field service staff
could be deployed from more remote locations within the response time
demanded then areas of low service intensity could be served from service
centres in adjacent territories. If this is not possible then in the early
stages of expansion resort would have to be made to the use of agents.
The issues which arise when intermediaries are used then apply.

Location of service and support resources

Where to position the mix of SAS specialists and Regulars is important in
the efficient use of resources. Under a structure which treated each
country as a separate and independent unit there would be a mix of each
in each country. If the whole of the new territory is seen as a single
network there are options for redistribution of the resources. Specialists
no longer need to be positioned in each country. One model is to set up a
number of centres of specialist support to cover the full product range

with one centre being responsible for each product group. Regulars no longer need to be positioned by country but rather according to the level of service intensity. Both of these changes lead to improvements in the level of service and customer satisfaction as well as resource efficiencies. Computer companies like Hewlett-Packard have started to organise their selling and customer service and support on product group lines rather than across products to build up distinct differentiating competences in each of the sectors serviced by the product groups.

It is the same for support activities and response centres. These no longer need to be positioned in each country but could be aggregated into a single centre or a reduced number of centres. The difficulties of language are very real and at least one computer company we know abandoned a single European response centre in favour of a small number of response centres each to serve a limited number of countries.

Composition of service and support teams

The possibilities of new locations and flexibility of the SAS/Regulars mix presents us with other possibilities for reviewing the composition of service teams. With a country structure the service teams may be organised in a way such that all teams give service and support to all products. Alternatively there may already be specialisation into teams giving service and support to specific product or customer groups. Multi-product teams require multi-skilling but give more resource flexibility while specialism in one product group gives increased learning and efficiencies from doing the job better. It is for each organisation to consider where the best trade-off for them lies. Extending the product group service and support model to the wider international scene would allow us to organise product service and support teams for the wider geographical area hoping for increases in effectiveness and efficiency.

The level of integration of the network

A fully integrated network is only feasible if there is the possibility of central control through fully compatible information systems and the supply chain. The stages to full integration are likely to be:

1   We have essentially separate operations, if not for countries then small regions.
2   We coordinate activities trying to have common standards and integrating the supply of spares.

3 We integrate information systems.
4 We consolidate centres of excellence and smaller numbers of response centres.
5 We move staff freely across the network.
6 All activities are controlled from one centre.

The move towards full integration will be tempered by consideration of customer needs in different geographic areas. While in some cases these national needs may be stronger than differences in types of customers the tendency across Europe is likely to be towards a greater homogeneity of social preferences and segmentation by type of customer rather than by nationality. If this is the case the pressure for integration to get the best from service teams dedicated to one product group or type of customer and serving the whole region becomes stronger.

How can we manage the supply chain?

It is in the area of managing the logistics supply chain that many customer service and support operations have done most. The influence of just-in-time thinking has made a great difference to the management of materials. The trends have been towards greater centralisation of the stocking of spares and a greater control of the levels of stocks held at points along the supply chain. The reduction or elimination of stocks at the service centre level and a greater control over van spares have given benefits in service levels and costs associated with holding stocks. The implementation of the changes has been made possible by a combination of improvements in information systems, EDI and transport.

Any customer service and support operations can learn much from the leaders in the field like Rank Xerox, Caterpillar and ICL. They have established specialist logistics operations to control the supply of spares to the service activity.

We can take the Rank Xerox experience as an example of supplying a customer service and support operation for Europe. Before 1980 each operating company in each country used to place orders for spares directly on the manufacturing units. The level of inventories was at least 15 months' supply and service levels for spares was not good. Over the last ten years they improved their systems and location of stocks to supply 'Field Business Units' (FBUs) of approximately the same service intensity. The result has been nine FBUs in the UK, four in Italy and three in Spain. The move has been towards centralisation of control with a single point for setting service levels, stock levels and van kits. This system gives control over stocks at both a country level and for the FBUs. While the system is not a fully integrated system it has gone a long way so far to deliver the benefits of high service levels and lower stocks.

Caterpillar, the manufacturers of earthmoving equipment, is a good example of a company who deliver their customer service and support through intermediaries, the Mercenary structure in our Military Model. They do not own any stocks within the dealer network but have concentrated their logistics efforts on improving the service levels to dealers from centralised sites throughout the world thereby allowing dealers to reduce their own stock levels. Service levels have been improved. Delivery times have come down from 17–19 days to 3–5 days and with 90 per cent of all items ordered being at the dealers in three days. Current performance is better with many items being with the dealers within a 48-hour period. This has been achieved by an increase in the order frequency from the dealers (from weekly to daily orders), improved systems, order processing and worldwide visibility of stocks. The whole logistics service is designed to give coverage.

A third example of supplying parts over a wider geographical area is the 'spares banks' operated by the express transport companies like Federal Express and DHL. These companies will hold stocks of spares for companies and distribute them as they are required by customer service centres. The operation is geared towards the supply of high value spares where the cost of rapid transport like aircraft can be offset against the savings in inventory levels.

Getting the level of improvement in the management of the logistics supply chain needs systems, good working relationship with suppliers and fast order taking and processing.

What upgrades in information systems are needed?

It is most clear from what we have said so far that any degree of integration of customer service and support across a network relies on the information and communication systems. These apply in the areas including:

- call handling from customers
- customer records

- remote monitoring of equipment
- supply of spares and integration of the supply chain from suppliers of materials
- escalation procedures utilising the full resources of the network
- measurement of performance
- transfer of advice.

One of the greatest problems faced by organisations in integrating systems is the incompatibility of software within existing systems at national locations. Unless this is overcome integration is impossible. Communications networks are especially important in the support activity. The use of data bases, giving information on products and their performance in operation and customer history, allows support activities to be delivered from anywhere in the network so long as there is no language barrier. This facilitates the centralisation of specialists associated with product groups which reduces costs and improves the turn round time of support problems because of the concentration of resources. It also has implications as we will see later for balancing the capacity across the network.

What is the affect on human resource policies?

The extent to which human resource policies are altered by a move to an international scale operation will depend largely on the nature of the network for customer service and support. There are two issues: whether we are using intermediaries as the main providers of customer service and support or if we have our own operation; or whether we still have an essentially discrete provision of customer service and support in individual countries or integration of the service centres into a coherent network.

When customer service and support is delivered by way of intermediaries the main issue is concerned with training and supporting the dealers. There is unlikely to be an involvement in the recruitment of staff although job specifications may be suggested especially for technical staff.

When we are delivering customer service and support ourselves the position is different. If we have discrete operations for service and support delivery in the different countries and regions the influence from the centre may be limited and personnel policies are more likely to be set by the separate units. The greater the integration of the network the more the policies will address issues which affect the network as a whole. For instance, the question of mobility of staff across the network and the training of staff on a network rather than a regional basis start to assume more importance. Such practices have implications for the spread of learning across the network and of the development of a culture for the whole business.

Our view of the present position is that the degree of international integration of networks is limited so far as the movement of people is concerned. Language problems often limit the possibilities and cultural considerations affecting the delivery of service and support can also make organisations reluctant to use front-line people who do not conform to the culture of suppliers. We can see at the present time the movement of personnel throughout the network is limited to managers and specialists mainly.

Can an international network help with capacity management?

Having a wide network does in concept allow us to think in terms of getting greater flexibility from the total resources. Let us take the common case of a customer service and support operation which has a number of response centres located in different countries. If we have the communication systems we are able to flow calls from one centre to another to balance the load. We gain from this in the quality of our initial response which becomes more reliable if not faster.

Clearly we can also get productivity gains from the use of network especially in the support activity where we do not need to visit the customer. If we need to maintain a 24-hour response on a global level we can use response centres located in Europe, the USA and the Far East, each operating a 12-hour day and transfer calls to one of the other centres out of hours. This eliminates the need to maintain staff in each centre for 24 hours a day.

We may gain further benefits from concentrating specialist resources in one centre either globally or within a region who are then available to the whole network. The international network is less likely to increase the capacity flexibility of the service activities. There may be some opportunity for transferring engineers on a temporary basis to give additional resources. Whether we can do this will depend on the costs of the transfer compared to the value and whether the timing is appropriate. This being the case it is more likely to occur for the service of capital equipment rather than low cost equipment.

Can we maintain quality?

Consistency of quality of delivery of customer service and support across an international network is of course important. When we have discrete operations in each region operated either by intermediaries or with our own resources the quality of service may be more geared to expectation of the customers in that area rather than wider standards, in which case we can perhaps leave the setting of standards to each regional area.

However, if our customer service and support is being judged by the consistency of delivery to common standards across the network, this fragmented approach to quality management will not be good enough. If we are providing service and support to another international company which does have an integrated network, there is the expectation that our service and support will meet the same standards wherever it is delivered. Providers of customer service and support as in other services have found that this requirement from their major customers has acted as a spur to their closer integration to improve consistency of service and support delivery.

What advice can we offer to service and support operations who find themselves in this position? Clearly there is a role for quality standards like ISO 9000 which can drive through common procedures for all areas of delivery and which take account of any local regulations. However, as with all quality programmes, this is only part of the story and we need to have in place other quality initiatives which drive quality improvement and motivate the front-line people. The use of competitions on an international scale can work in some cases to encourage a wider view of the network from staff at all levels within the organisation.

How can we minimise the risks from expansion?

Expansion of any business carries risks. When there is an increase in capacity there is a cost involved and this must be paid for with increased business. If we set up new service and support centres before there is the service intensity to pay for this capacity the operation will make a financial loss. We can minimise this expense by using intermediaries rather than establishing our own operations.

Alternatively we might take the view that we are willing to set up our own operation in order to learn, in which case we might discount some losses against the experience we gain delivering customer service and support in a new region. In the long run the extra experience may give us a competitive advantage.

So there is a trade-off between a cautious expansion through the use of intermediaries, which carries with it a limited amount of learning about the new markets, and the higher risk commitment of resources into the new area, which leads to rapid learning. Which route is taken will depend on an assessment of the potential of the market we are entering. We would need to assess whether the service intensity will rise quickly to make it worthwhile to commit resources.

Conclusion

In this chapter we have looked at the issues that arise when the network for the delivery of customer service and support is extended across international and cultural borders. There are decisions to be made on the structure of the delivery system. There are operational challenges over the nature and consistency of the service and support, and the efficiencies to be gained from a greater integration of the network.

Checklist

1   What are the pressures on your business which are forcing international expansion?
2   Which physical, technical and monetary barriers can you see coming down?
3   Which of these do you see as a threat and which as an opportunity?
4   Which regions do you see as offering the greatest potential for expansion?
5   Which structure for customer service and support delivery would you think would be the most appropriate initially for expansion in these regions?
6   What risks can you identify from the expansion?

7 How could you minimise the risks?

8 If you already have a network how could you improve your capacity management and quality management through greater integration?

Introduction

We started this book by outlining some of the ways that the service and support task has changed over the last few years. The pressure for change will not slacken over the next years. Some key factors are likely to be:

- Customer demand for ever more reliable products. Service in the sense of reacting to breakdowns will tend to disappear, with more emphasis on routine maintenance and ultimately no service at all
- As companies emphasise product image in marketing, service and support operations must be consistent to give the desired result. As service and support personnel may meet the customer more often than sales people they must be fully briefed as to what role they are to play
- There will be an increasing trend to identify yet more ways in which the customer needs support to ensure maximum use of the purchase. 'Total Solutions' and 'One Stop Shopping' are examples of this
- Product life cycles will continue to shorten, placing more pressure on the service and support organisation's ability to support more products
- The need to ensure that the customer is inconvenienced as little as possible will put yet more pressure on response times, in particular the rapid movement of materials through the network
- Customers continue to expect better levels of service in all senses of the word. They will expect to be dealt with courteously and promptly and will expect to be fully informed at all times.

Six steps for improving customer service and support

Step 1: Know and understand what must be done well

This statement reflects the fact that the world is changing, and customer service and support must change with it. Merely being good at yesterday's task is not sufficient. Changes in products, the competitive environment and customer expectations, all mean that success can only be achieved by recognising the implications for the organisation.

The measures used by customers to assess success will have changed. Having an excellent service organisation, able to respond to equipment failure in less than two hours, may have been the recipe for success yesterday, but today customers assume that you will perform to this level as a matter of course, and the winners are those organisations who are able to provide equipment that rarely fails, and have found new ways to create customer confidence.

The 'excellent' organisations are those that are constantly responding to the changing demands of the environment, understanding the implications of change for each detail of their operation.

Step 2: Build value in delivering service

In the course of this book we have discussed a number of aspects of service delivery. It is worth emphasising some key principles here:

- Pay attention to each detail of delivery, managing the processes, materials, people and information to give a consistent result
- Analyse the operation from the customers' viewpoint, understanding their needs and their perceptions of how well they are being served
- Work hard at forming strong links at each point of the chain of service delivery; front-line staff to customers, front-line staff to back room process personnel or support staff

The objective is that there should be a clear and consistent link between 'What needs to be done well' (Step 1) and how it is performed (Step 2).

Step 3: Balance resources

The best organisations manage to walk the tightrope of achieving consistently good service standards whilst at the same time keeping costs at such a level that good margins are preserved. This can only be achieved by a better understanding of how to match supply and demand by:

- Knowing the effective capacity of the service and support organisation, the rate at which demand can be consistently satisfied
- Forecasting future demand to ensure that appropriate resources are provided

- Knowing the point at which resources become profitable (Breakeven Point) and, the point at which extra demand results in a deterioration in customer perceived quality levels
- Building flexibility into systems and people to improve response to variability in demand
- Limiting the negative effect on customer satisfaction which occurs when demand outstrips supply by reducing the probability of it happening and preparing contingency plans for those increasingly rare occasions.

Step 4: Create a structure for quality

In recent years much has been written about the various aspects of quality, from Customer Care to Quality Assurance, from systems and procedures to Quality Circles and TQM. Whichever approach proves itself to be the most useful for your situation, the fact is that Quality must be managed, rather than allowed to find its own level.

Developing a structure for quality means developing a range of actions ranging through clear management commitment to quality, the dedication of resource to quality improvement, the use of measurement and data gathering, motivation and reward, involvement, creativity and quality assurance systems; there is no one right approach. In some cases, detailed systems and procedures must be put in place, which are then brought to life by employees who are motivated to deliver top quality service. In other situations, the route lies in recruiting and training the best people and underpinning their actions with broad systems to give coordination to their efforts.

Do not forget that Continuous Improvement is a vital element of quality management, and if encouraged may yield significant competitive advantage.

Step 5: Work on resouce productivity

As products, whether they be goods or services, mature, the opportunities for price increases diminish. Any differentiation through improved customer service must be paid for to some extent by increased efficiency or effectiveness.

As a first step, this will require a review of productivity measures currently in place, ensuring that they reflect the priorities of the business. The recent interest in Activity Based Costing is a recognition that simply spreading overheads over direct costs may give an inaccurate assessment of the contribution of each service product.

Identifying the major elements of resource cost may allow the organisation to compare itself against similar customer service and support departments – probably those who are not competitors – to question whether some areas might be more effective. This activity of benchmarking is becoming more common as customer service and support managers find that the issues and problems faced are very similar across most industry sectors.

Finally, the organisation must work hard at continuously improving the effectiveness of systems and people. Many organisations are discovering the value of looking at how the amount of time that work spends in the system can be reduced, on the principle that work expands to fill the time available. Others are finding that the value chain analysis described in Chapter 6 shows up areas where a marginal increase in one resource yields far greater savings in other resources.

Step 6: Manage change

This book is largely about the need to recognise change and to ensure that the customer service and support function moves with it. Recognising change, however, is only part of the task. People must be carried with you if change is to be implemented successfully. The next section indicates some areas to be considered if change is to be managed.

Where to start to manage change more effectively?

There has been a great deal written about the way to manage change, and all that we can do here is to try to distil out some of the factors which seem to us to be important for the customer service and support manager. First we should be aware of the effects of managing change badly. In a business environment this can often be seen in the way in which organisations implement strategy; what happens in many instances is that the actions pursued by organisations bear little resemblance to the strategy as written in any corporate document. This may be caused by not communicating the intended strategy clearly through the organisation, or by the strategy being not easily understood as presented, by the planning being too inflexible to take account of changes in circumstances.

More often than not the failure to realise a planned strategy has an organisational context.

Are we caught in a cultural web?

Professor Gerry Johnston at the Cranfield School of Management has identified many failures of managing change and attributes these to the nature of the *cultural web* of the organisation. If the cultural identity of the organisation is at odds with the intended strategy, it is doomed to failure. For example, a customer service support operation in which the engineers believe they are concerned with repairing equipment at times set by themselves, will not align easily to a new strategy that calls for greater customer choice in appointment times and more attention given to supporting the customers.

At the heart of the cultural web are the common assumptions held by people in the organisation, often unspoken but taken for granted. In one National Health Service Hospital, the assumption was that the medical staff knew best and that the hospital was run for the convenience of the medics and the nurses. When the strategy became one of treating patients as people who have a say in their own treatment, this conflicted with the set of beliefs held by the medics, administrators and nurses. There is little chance of change for the organisation until these values change.

While we may all recognise the central theme of a cultural web from our own experiences, what lies behind it and supports it may not always be apparent. There are six factors that seem to contribute, which relate to power, the nature of the organisation, control systems, the routines and rituals, symbols, and the stories and myths.

Power

Where does the power rest within an organisation? It might be in one function, or with 'the old guard', a mafia, head office rather than within branches, or with regional heads.

Organisation

The organisation may be run along hierarchical lines, with many layers of management, and decisions made by passing up and down the organisation. It may be very centralised or the converse. The organisation may have very strong functional divisions.

Control systems

The control systems refer to the formal control systems within the organisation, for example the planning systems, budgetary systems, and the formal communication systems.

Routines

The routines and rituals are associated with the informal control systems and reflect the way that things actually get done. They may reinforce the formal systems or they may disregard them, so communication may always be by telephone or face to face, with little use of memos, or the converse may be true. Promotion may be on the basis of the fittest and ablest, or of age and seniority.

Symbols

Symbols are often the outward demonstration of status in the organisation, for example office size and furnishing, special lunch or coffee arrangements, cars, and credit cards. They are the visible signs of the cohesiveness of front-line staff and their managers and supervisors. Changing the symbols can often reinforce the verbal message about change, for example taking managers and supervisors out of closed offices, providing common areas for rest and refreshment, having open car parks, and managers serving in the front-line are all illustrations of the power of symbols.

Stories and myths

The stories and myths are often the glue of the cultural web. They are the campaign and horror stories which are told to newcomers and repeated often within the organisation. In some cases they might lose something of the truth in their telling and some may be apocryphal. There is the story of Fred Smith, who, in the early days of starting Federal Express in the States, found that he did not have the funds one week to pay his staff. He was unable to raise money from any of the normal sources and was on the point of despair when, on flying out of Dallas airport, he caught sight of a flight to Las Vegas. On impulse he caught the flight and went to a casino where he won sufficient money to meet the wage bill.

When trying to manage change to implement a new strategy, all aspects of the cultural web need to be considered. While it may be relatively easy to create a statement of intent through the use of mission statements, they will only be taken on board by the majority of staff if there is a demonstration of the change from senior managers and a will to accept change on the part of the majority. A crisis in the business caused by a drastic downturn in business fortunes or a takeover or merger may act as a catalyst for change. However, the opportunity for driving through change may be lost if there is a series of these events leading to little alteration in the way in which the front-line service people are treated or treat their customers. In this case, staff are more likely to incorporate into the stories and myths part of the cultural web tales of senior managers who attempted change but failed and left the organisation. The message becomes one of 'Keep your head down and sooner or later things will go back to *normal*'.

Where to start?

1   Keep people informed and involved.
2   Build some teams (internal and external).
3   Review use of technology.
4   Ask the customer.

The Black and Decker service division

Black and Decker UK is unusual in the industry in that it has always maintained its own network of service points, though also supported by numbers of agents often acting as 'drop-off' points for equipment to be repaired at a central location.

In the 1970s there were 15 service points in industrial locations in the UK. The approach to service at this time was said to be functional, the service points being workshops rather than consumer orientated, often located on industrial estates. By the mid 1980s the network had grown to 25, but Black and Decker recognised that this was not sufficient to meet the needs of the professional users in geographically remote areas. Agents were appointed to deal with the needs of the professionals with collection points in retail outlets arranged for the domestic user.

Company senior management were concerned that whereas a reasonable service was being given when necessary, the company possibly was not receiving some more positive benefits to be derived through better customer contact. A full review of the current service operation was carried out by managers drawn from all functions within the business, not just service management, to ensure that the review was as objective as possible.

A Mission Statement was evolved on two levels:

1 *Primary*: 'To administer the warranty policy and satisfy the product related needs of all our customers.'

2 *Secondary*: 'To provide any other related service requirement, conveniently and efficiently, in line with corporate policies and marketing objectives.'

This mission statement was translated into a set of objectives for the next three years which were both general and specific. General objectives included the aim to administer the warranty policy in such a way as to be seen to be equitable to the customer and to enhance the company image by making sure that customer contact was both friendly and efficient, while a specific objective was to provide access to a company-owned service point within 30 minutes' travel to 90 per cent of the population.

Active participation from all service division personnel was encouraged through formal presentations and 'Total Customer Service' seminars. Senior management visited every service point to discuss proposed plans and to review 'mini-business plans' developed by the local staff. This element was felt to be the most significant in managing the transition in the service division.

Over a period of three years some significant improvements were carried through. These were:

1 The number of locations where 'on the spot' repairs can be made have been increased, with a reduction in time and cost. This has resulted in increased demand.

2 The support for professional users has been improved, with a four-hour 'urgent' service and also a loan service.

3 Information from the repair centres and through warranty claims has been fed back to product development for improved reliability.

4 Retail design consultants were used to develop a new concept for service centres to be incorporated in new locations, increasingly sited in the high street rather than industrial estates.

5 The quality programme 'Total Customer Service' has improved customer service. This is monitored by a continuous programme of customer questionnaires and response to complaints.

6   Staff flexibility has resulted in productivity gains in excess of 20 per cent.

7   A new information system was designed with full input from all service personnel which has improved the speed and quality of decision making.

The service division recognised the need for change and took positive steps to manage it, setting clear objectives across the business. The key to the results has been the involvement of management from across the Black and Decker business and active participation of all service division personnel.

A workshop approach to change in service and support

We have found it useful to adopt a workshop for groups of managers and front-line staff, in order to build up an understanding of the business, identify the implications of change, and consequently to move to an action plan that is the result of the combined efforts of those involved.

The aim is to address the three main factors in the customer service triangle, namely strategy, systems, and the sparkle provided by the people. Each topic is introduced, briefly explaining the area to be addressed, but much of the value we have found comes from the participants working together to answer questions specifically related to their organisation. This takes place in syndicate groups with feedback, questioning and a summary of issues.

The process consists of seeking answers to some basic questions:

What business are we in?

1   What are our customers really buying from us? What value are we giving them?

2   What makes us different from our competitors?

3   How do we want to compete in the future?

4   How do we build *value* in our service delivery and where are the cost drivers?

5   What tends to go wrong with our delivery of customer service and support, and how serious is it?

6   How can we maintain the best balance of service intensity and the capacity to satisfy this demand?

7 How can we build a structure for quality in our customer service and support?

8 How can we best measure and improve resource productivity?

9 Is our culture consistent with the way in which we want to do business in the future?

In seeking answers to these question we use the techniques and more detailed questioning contained in the earlier chapters. Within the lifetime of one workshop a resolution of all the questions will not be reached; we find that organisations often do not have the information to hand to be able to answer all the questions, and this can lead to actions to redress the gap. The asking of the question may reveal that areas of service delivery which had previously been considered to be all right are inadequate for the changing circumstances. The end of the process centres around action plans, which include the search for new data and information and changes to the service delivery and the operational control of quality, capacity, and resource productivity.

Postscript

We believe that delivering excellent customer service and support will be a key task for all organisations in the next few years. This will not be achieved by customer service and support managers alone. Organisations must become more and more integrated, ensuring that the efforts of product designers, manufacturing people, sales and marketing, and customer service and support combine to deliver what the customer wants.

We hope that this book will assist in this process of integration by explaining the challenges and problems of customer service and support.

BIBLIOGRAPHY

Chapter 1

Albrecht, K. and Zemke, R., *Service America, Doing Business in the New Economy*. Dow Jones-Irwin 1985.

Carlzon, J., *Moments of Truth*. Ballinger 1987.

Levitt, T., *After the Sale is over*. Harvard Business Review. September–October 1983.

Harvey-Jones, Sir J., *Getting it Together*.

Peters, T. and Waterman, R., *In Search of Excellence*. Harper & Row 1982.

Lele, M. M. and Sheth, J. N., *The Customer is Key*. John Wiley 1987.

Drucker, P., e.g. *The Practice of Management*. Heineman 1955.

Normann, R., *Service Management*. John Wiley 1984.

Chapter 2

Bowman, C., *Perceptions of Competitive Strategy, Realised Strategy, Concensus and Performance*, PhD. Thesis, Cranfield Institute of Technology, 1991.

Heskett, J. L., Sasser, W. E., Hart, C. W. L., *Service Breakthroughs: Changing the Rules of the Game*, Free Press, New York, 1990.

Johnson, G., Scholes, K., *Exploring Corporate Strategy*, Prentice Hall, 1988.

Porter M. E., *Competitive Strategy: Techniques for Analysing Industries and Competition*, Free Press, New York, 1980.

Porter, M. E., *Competitive Advantage*, Free Press, New York, 1985.

Peters, T. J., Waterman H. R., *In Search of Excellence*, Harper and Row, 1982.

Peters, T. J., Austin, N., *A Passion for Excellence*, William Collins, 1985.

Mathur, S. S., *How Firms Compete: A New Classification of Generic Strategies* Journal of General Management, Volume 14, Number 1, 1988.

Waterman, H. R., Peters, T. J., Phillips, J. R., *Structure is not Organisation*, Business Horizons, June 1980.

Chapter 5

Lovelock, C. H., *Services Marketing* 2nd Edition, Prentice Hall, 1991.

Christopher, M., Payne, A., Ballantyne, D., *Relationship Marketing*, Heinemann, London, 1991.

Kotler, P., *Marketing Management* 6th Edition, Prentice Hall, 1967.

McDonald, M. H. B., Morris, P., *The Marketing Plan – A Pictorial Guide for Managers*, Heinemann, London, 1989.

Chapter 6

Carlzon, J., *Moments of Truth*, Ballinger, Cambridge, Mass., 1987.

Clark, G. R. and Armistead C. G., *Improving Service Delivery. Managing Service Quality* IFS, July 1991.

Shostack, L., *Designing Services that Deliver*, Harvard Business Review, 1984.

Porter, M. E., *Competitive Advantage*, Free Press, New York 1985.

Naisbitt, J., *Megatrends*, Macdonald, London, 1984.

Normann, R., *Service Management*, John Wiley, 1984.

Johnston, R., '*The Customer as Employee*', Proceedings of the Operations Management Association (UK) Conference, January 1989.

Chapter 7

Handy, C. B., *Understanding Organisations* 3rd Edition, Penguin Books, 1985.

Kakabadse, A., Ludlow, R., Vinnicome, S., *Working in Organisations*, Penguin Books, 1988.

Peters, T., Austin, N., *A Passion for Excellence*, Collins, 1985.

Lele, M. M., Sheth, J. N., *The Customer is king*, Wiley, 1988.

Chapter 8

Lovelock, C. H., *Services Marketing*, 2nd Edition, Prentice Hall, 1991.

Richardson C., *Staffing the Front Office*, Operational Research Insight, Volume 4, Number 2, 1991.

Sasser, W. E., *Matching Supply and Demand in Service Industries*, Harvard Business Review, November–December, 1976.

Chapter 9

Clark, G., *Managing Service Quality*, IFS Publications, 1990.

Crosby, P., *Quality is Free*, McGraw Hill 1979.

Gronroos, C., *Facing the challenge of Service Competition: costs of Bad Service*. Proceedings of the 'Workshop on Quality Management in Service'. SQM Brussels, May 1991.

Garvin, D., *Managing Quality: The Strategic and Competitive Edge*, The Free Press, New York, 1990.

Schonberger, R., *Building a Chain of Customers*, Hutchinson 1990.

Berry, L. L., Parasuraman, A., and Zeithaml, V. A. *Quality Counts in Services, too*. Business Horizons, Vol 28, May–June 1985.

Oakland, J. S., *Statistical Process Control*. Heinemann, 1986.

Oakland, J. S., *Total Quality Management*. Heinemann 1989.

Black, S.,*Creating the Competitive Advantage*. The TQM Magazine Volume 1, No. 1, November 1988.

Deming, W. E., *Out of the Crisis*, MIT Centre for Advanced Engineering Study, Cambridge, Mass., 1986.

Chapter 10

Innes, J., Mitchell, F., *Activity Based Costing*, The Chartered Institute of Management Accountants, London, 1990.

McLaughlin, C. P., Coffey, S., *Measuring service productivity*, International Journal of Service Industries Management, Volume 1, No. 1, 1990.

Norman, M., Stoker, B., *Data Envelopment Analysis*, John Wiley, 1991.

Potts, G. W., *Raising productivity in customer services*, Long Range Planning, Volume, 21, No. 2, 1988.

Chapter 11

Edwards, C., Ward, J. and Bytheway, A., *The Essence of Information Systems*, Prentice Hall International, UK 1991.

Porter, M. E. *Competitive Advantage*, Free Press, 1984.

Ives, B., and Vitale, M. R., *After the Sale: Leveraging Maintenance with information technology*. MIS Quarterly March 1988.

Chapter 12

Vollman, T. E., Berry, W. L., and Whybark, D. C. *Manufacturing Planning and Control Systems*. Irwin 1984.

Saunders, J. A., Sharp, J. A., and Witt, S. F., *Practical Business Forecasting*.
    Gower 1987.
Christopher, M., *The Strategy of Distribution Management*. Gower 1987.

Chapter 13

MacGrath, A. J., and Hardy, K. G., 'Gearing Manufacturer Support Programs to
    Distributors', *Industrial Marketing Management*, Vol. 18, pp. 239–244, 1989.
Cavusgil, S. T., 'The importance of Distributor Training at Caterpillar',
    Industrial Marketing Management, Vol. 19, pp. 1–9, 1990.
Anderson, J. C., and Narus, J. A., 'A model of Distributor Firm and
    Manufacturer Firm Working Partnerships', *Journal of Marketing*, January,
    1990.
Frazier, G. L., and Rody, R. C., *The use of Influence Strategies in Interfirm
    Relationships in Industrial Product Channels*.
Moore, R. A., 'The Conflict Gap in International Channel Relationships',
    Journal of Marketing Management, Vol. 6 No. 3, pp. 225–237, 1990.

Chapter 14

Gronroos, C., *Facing the Challenge of Service Competition: Cost of Bad Service*,
    Proceedings of a Workshop on Quality Management in Service, Ed Wiele &
    Timmers, Strategic Quality Management Institute, Rotterdam, 1991.
Heskett, J. L., Sasser, W. E., Hart, C. W. L., *Service Breakthroughs*, The Free
    Press, New York, 1990.
Lash, M. L., *The Complete Guide to Customer Service*, John Wiley, 1989.

Chapter 15

Christopher, M., 'Customer Service Strategies for International Markets',
    International Journal of Logistics?
Loeb, J., 'Europe 1992: The Implications for Field Service', *PTRM Insight*,
    Volume 2, No. 4, 1990.
Livingston, I., '*Design for Service*', Proceedings of the 1st International
    Conference on After Sales Support, IFS, 1988.

Chapter 16

Johnson, G., and Scholes, K., *Exploring Corporate Strategy*, Prentice Hall, 1988.

INDEX

Activity Based Costing (ABC) 185–7, 213, 216, 272–3

advantage, competitive *see* competitive advantage

agents 229–42, 260–1, 264, 268, 276 *see also* 'Mercenaries'

Albrecht, K., 12

Annual Requirement Value 213

Avis car rental 86, 247

Back Room 99–100, 131–2, 144, 187, 271
  process flow, customer 113
  remote diagnostics 100
  standards 158
  systems design 121

Bain & Co. 246

barriers
  to market entry 23, 198
  removal of, in EC 257–8
  to resource productivity 192–4

'benchmarking' programmes 165–6, 273

Berry, L. L. 162, 164

Bill of Material (BOM) 219

Black & Decker Ltd 104, 109, 208, 276–8

'boundary spanners' 106, 121

Bradford University 166

branding 86

British Airways 86, 119, 165, 250

British Gas 109

British Standards
  (4778) 158
  (5750) 175, 176

British Telecom 109

'burn out' 101, 117, 122, 130–1, 134, 143

call management 203

capacity
  chase strategy 142–5, 147, 248–9
  coping strategy 147–8, 177, 249–50

definition 137–8

effective 139, 147, 148, 181, 248

level strategy 145–7, 248–9

levels 138–40

service 153

Carlzon, Jan 7, 97, 201

Caterpillar Tractor Co.
  competitive strategy 206
  dealer network 47, 234, 256
  design philosophy 8, 66–7
  quality program 168
  supply control 263–4

centralisation 67–8, 105, 257, 263

characteristics, customer 83

charts, control 168, 170, 171

chase strategy 142–5, 147, 248–9

Citroen 68

Comet 8–9, 47

communications mix 91–2

compass, strategy 26, 32–3, 88

competences
  managerial 117, 123–5, 132–4
  staff 38, 162

competitive advantage 56, 65, 259, 268
  Customer Service Triangle 12–13
  differentiation matrix 29–32
  Five Competitive Forces, Porter 25, 197
  relative 33–5

competitive strategy 6, 26, 36–40, 54, 79, 206

complaints, customer
  Avis response 247
  Black & Decker Ltd response 277
  busy periods 249
  escalation procedures 250–1, 253
  ineffective handling 239
  monitoring system 2, 202
  quality indicator 235
  TARP findings 244

warranty claims 62, 63
confidence, customer 5, 63, 100, 156, 198, 200, 240
  accessibility of service 68, 104–5
  guarantees provided 62, 115
  image of company 109
  OTISLINE 204
  personal contact 110
  quality of service 73, 158, 159, 271
  quality of staff 162
  telephone contact 61–2
contact, customer
  face to face 101, 103, 110, 275
  paper 103–4
  telephone 5, 61, 102–3, 200, 250–1, 275
coping strategy 147–8, 177, 249–50
corporate business plan 37
cost drivers 26, 28, 186–7
Covedale training 132
Cranfield School of Management 123, 274
Currys Ltd 47
Customer Service Triangle 12–13, 117, 119, 278

Data Envelopment Analysis (DEA) 188–9
Dead On Arrivals (DOA) 202
dealers 229–42, 260, 264, 268 see also 'Mercenaries'
Delivery Triangle, Service 98
demand
  altering 145–7
  elements 140–1
  forecasting 141–2, 145, 150, 209, 210, 221–3, 271
  service, managing 153
  variation in 191
Deming, W. Edwards 97
design
  Front Office involvement 99
  product 9, 11, 66, 76, 161, 163, 172–3
  service delivery 61, 115
DHL International Ltd 264
differentiation matrix 26, 29–32, 35–6, 37, 38, 40
directors, service 11
Disney World 121
distribution 7, 88, 223 see also logistics
Dixons Ltd 47
DOA 202
downtime, customer 11, 28, 70–1
drivers
  cost 26, 28, 186–7

uniqueness 26

80–20 rule 66, 213
Earthmovers Ltd 240–2
EC single market 256–8
economic cycles see PEST effects
Economic Order Quantity (EOQ) 214
Eight Dimensions of Strategic Quality, Garvin's 159–61, 162, 163
Elecspeed 86
Electronic Point of Sale (EPOS) 109
empowerment for staff 129–30, 252
'Enemies' 47–8, 49, 53, 57
environment, business 19–21, 25, 39, 40, 123, 258
EOQ 214
EPOS 109
ERM 258
escalation procedure 250–1, 253, 265
European Commission 20
Exchange Rate Mechanism (ERM) 258
expansion of business 267–8
expectancy theory 129

face to face customer contact 101, 103, 110, 275
Failure Mode and Effect Analysis (FMEA) 172–3
Federal Express Ltd 264, 275
Field Business Units (FBUs) 263–4
fishbone diagram 173
Five Competitive Forces, Porter 21–5, 197
FMEA 172–3
Force Field Analysis 173–4
Ford Motor Co. Ltd 175
front-line managers 122, 127, 134 see also management: service and support
Front Office 99–100, 113, 144

Garvin, David 159, 161, 163
General Agreement on Tariffs and Trade (GATT) 20, 256
Georgia Light and Power 62–3
Goffin, Keith 66
goodwill 101, 233
Granada Services 47
Gronroos, Christian 156, 253

Hartford boiler inspection service 74
Harvard Business School 156, 159
Harvey-Jones, Sir John 4
help-line, customer 61–2

Herzberg, 129
Hewlett-Packard Ltd 201, 203, 224, 256, 262
Hierarchy of Needs, Maslow's 128
hygiene factors 33, 35, 60, 81, 129
IBM 256
ICL 263
image 5, 6, 201, 270
    Black & Decker Ltd 104, 109, 277
    brand 31
    creation 91–2
    enhancement 95
    quality 156, 158, 161
in-house control 49, 54–6, 58, 88, 229, 260
incentives theory 129
industry sector 19, 23, 199
information systems 99, 105, 196–207
    Black & Decker Ltd 278
    confidence factor 109
    integrated 260–1, 262–3, 264–5
    value chain 28, 111
intensity, service see service intensity
interviews 94
inventory 110, 208–27, 263
Ishikawa diagram 173
Ives, B. 203

JCB 47
Johnston, Gerry 106, 274
Just-in-Time (JIT) philosophy 209, 223–4, 263
Knowledge, Skills and Abilities (KSA) mix 126–7, 131, 134
Komatsu 47

level strategy 145–7, 248–9
Levitt, Ted 7
life cycle, product 49, 196, 270
location, service 28, 104, 276
logistics 7, 166, 188, 206, 258, 259, 264 see also distribution
London Transport 46
Lovelock, Christopher 125
loyalty, customer 2, 7, 80, 108, 244, 247

management
    of customers 106–8
    education 6, 72, 74
    quality 97, 115, 136, 153–8, 167–8, 175, 267, 272
    service and support 117–34
    style 38 see also organisations: culture

supply chain 110–11, 209, 224–8
supply chain (international) 256, 258, 259, 262, 263
Manufacturing Resource Planning (MRP II) 217, 220
marketing
    customer focus 79–82, 101
    intelligence systems 200, 202
    mix 79, 80, 86–93
    oriented organisations 77–8
    positioning 82, 85, 86
    relationship 79, 95
    research 94
    segmentation 36, 82–5, 259
Marks & Spencer Plc 74, 119, 157, 215
Maslow, 128
Master Production Schedule (MPS) 217–18
Material Requirements Planning (MRP) 219, 220
Mathur, Shiv 29, 30, 31, 32, 38
McClelland, 128
McKinsey & Co. Inc. 37
Mean Time Between Failure (MTBF) see also reliability
    electronics sector 8
    product design 60, 163
    productivity measure 188
    reliability measure 68, 81, 160, 202
Mean Time To Repair (MTTR) 66, 188
Megatrends (Naisbitt) 110
'Mercenaries' 47, 49, 53, 55, 56, 57, 58, 66, 264 see also agents; dealers
    merchandise, definition and differentiation 29, 30, 31
'Military Model' 28, 38, 44–9, 53, 58, 60, 88 see also 'SAS'; 'Regulars'; 'Territorials'; 'Mercenaries'; 'Enemies'
Mintzberg, Henry 120
mission statement 37, 39, 86, 247, 275, 277
'Moments of Truth' 7, 97, 103, 109
motivation 108, 117
    dealer performance 238
    empowerment 252–3
    management role 134
    quality, effect on 166, 174, 267, 272
    theories 128–31
MPS 217–18
MRP 219–220
MRP II 217–220
MTBF see Mean Time Between Failure
MTTR 66, 188
Naisbitt, John 110

National Health hospital 274
needs theory 128
networks
    Black & Decker Ltd 276
    capacity management 151, 152
    Caterpillar Tractor Co. 47, 234, 256
    dealer 230, 233, 234, 236–7, 241
    international 256–68
    resource productivity 184
Nissan 233
Normann, Richard 97
Norris, Peter 123

Oakland, Professor John 166
objectives 37, 277
organisations
    activities, scope 19
    aim 1
    culture 129, 167, 274–6
    marketing orientated 77–8
    power within 274
    '7 S Framework' 37–9, 40
    structure 38, 42, 44–58
Original Equipment Manufacturer (OEM)
    229, 231, 242
Otis Elevator Plc 204, 206

paper customer contact 103–4
Parasuraman, 162, 164
Pareto effect 66, 213
perceived added value (PAV) 32, 33, 35, 37,
    40, 88
Periodic Review system 220
PEST effects 19–21, 25
Peters, Tom 4, 37, 132, 200
Phillips, J. R. 37
PIMS 156
Pittiglio, Rabin, Todd & McGrath (PRTM)
    257
policy see strategy
political scene see PEST effects
Porter, Michael 21, 25, 35
Porter Five Competitive Forces 21–5, 197
positioning maps 86
Post Office, UK 46
'post-purchase dissonance' 5
power 22–3, 199, 259, 274
priorities, customer support 61, 75–6
process flow, customer 111, 113–16
productivity
    Activity Based Costing 185–7, 213, 216,
        272–3

branch performance 188–9
definition 180
improvement 190–3
managing 180
measurement 180–5, 188, 193–4
trade offs see trade offs
profiles, customer 33–5, 60, 76, 84
Profit Impact Market Share (PIMS) 156
PRTM 257
quality see also total quality management
    customer support 2, 85
    definition 158
    dimensions 159–64
    equipment 110, 115
    intermediaries 234–5
    management 97, 115, 136, 153–8, 167–8,
        175, 267, 272
    product 5, 8
    standards 164–6, 181, 235, 267
    systems 174, 202
    techniques 168, 170–4
    triangle 166, 175–6
Quality Function Deployment (QFD) 172
questionnaires 94, 251, 277
queueing theory 149

Rank Xerox Ltd 8, 166, 167, 201, 263
Ratner, Gerald 157
recovery strategy 243–54
'Regulars' 57, 66, 131, 261–2
    control 53, 54, 55
    definition 45
    product: early stages 49
reliability 9, 11, 162 see also Mean Time
        Between Failure
remote diagnosis 51, 70–1, 101, 147, 194,
    204, 206
Remote Elevator Monitoring (REM) 204,
    206
Reorder Point system 220
resources 105–11
    arrangement 26
    capability 19
    control of level 136–7
    customers as 143–4
    information as 207
    network flexibility 266
    planning and control 148–51
    productivity 111, 151, 179–95
    quality 153
    transferring 144, 150, 151
responses by customers 83

responses to customers
  centres 149, 262, 266
  cost 90
  initial 61–4
  times 65, 137, 162, 176, 229, 270
retention, customer 246, 253, 254

'7 S Framework' 37–40
SAD 257
SAS (airline) 7, 97, 201
'SAS' (support structure) 57, 58, 131, 142,
    143, 261, 262
  control 53, 55
  definition 44–5
  product: early stages 49
satisfaction, customer 73–4, 244–52, 272
  index 35, 93–5, 164, 239
  quality standards 155, 174, 235
  remote diagnostics 194
  response time 176
  service levels 212
  service location 262
Schonberger, R. 162
Service Delivery Triangle 98
service intensity 137, 181, 185, 268
  and capacity 145, 179, 248, 249
  demand patterns 140, 141, 142
  forecasting 150
  in-house control 54, 55, 58, 88, 260
  influenced by 50–3
  meaning 49
  reducing 147
service strategy 13, 14, 79, 82
  compass, strategy 26, 32–3, 88
  competitive position 25–6
  differentiation matrix 26, 29–32, 35–6,
    37, 38, 40
  meaning 15–16
  mission statement 37, 39, 86, 247, 275,
    277
  objectives 37, 277
  PEST effects 19–21, 25
  Porter Five Competitive Forces 21–5, 197
  '7 S Framework' 37–40
  stages in process 19
  tactics 16–18, 196
  value chain 26, 28, 36, 105, 111, 186, 273
'Service Trinity' 125
Shipley, 238
Single Administrative Document (SAD)
    257
skills 38, 117

'smile' campaigns 97, 208
Smith, Fred 275
social changes see PEST effects
standards
  agents 234–5
  BS (4778) 158
  BS (5750) 175, 176
  EC common 257
  EN (29000) 175
  ISO (9000) 175, 267
  quality 164, 181, 267
  service 145, 166, 271
Statistical Process Control (SPC) 168, 175–6
strategy
  chase see chase strategy
  competitive see competitive strategy
  coping see coping strategy
  level see level strategy
  recovery see recovery strategy
  service see service strategy
Strengths, Weaknesses, Opportunities and
    Threats (SWOT) analysis 85, 173, 259
stress see 'burn out'
structure of organisations 38, 42, 44–58
subcontractors 144–5, 231, 232, 233, 235,
    237
substitution threat 23, 198–9, 259
Sun Tzu (quoted) 17
supply chain 211, 265
  design 121
  international, management 256, 258, 259,
    262, 263
  management 110–11, 209, 224–8
  standards 164
support, definition and differentiation 29,
    30
surveys of service 66, 68, 165
SWOT analysis 85, 173, 259
systems
  control 13, 275
  information see information systems
  '7 S Framework' 37–40
  service delivery 121
  stock monitoring 213, 216

tactics 16–18, 196
Technical Assistance Research Programme
    Inc. (TARP) 244–5, 251
technology 36, 110, 182, 194, 204 see also
    PEST effects; remote diagnosis
telephone customer contact 5, 61, 102–3,
    200, 250–1, 275

'Territorials' 46, 49, 54, 55, 107
Thriving on Chaos (Peters) 200
time, dimensions of 61–4, 200
total quality management 117, 121, 159,
    179, 246, 254, 272
Toyota 70, 256
trade offs
    cost/confidence factors 68
    cost/excess resources 150
    expansion 268
    productivity 179, 194
    service level 64–6
    team composition 262
training, customer 51, 72–3, 107–8
Trigg's Tracking Signal 222
uniqueness 19, 26, 28, 35, 36
Uplifts plc 136–7
uptime, customer 65, 66, 68–71

Value Added Resellers (VARs) 231
value chain 26, 28, 36, 105, 111, 186, 273
value for money, 5, 7, 89, 115, 159, 162
Vitale, M. R. 203
Volvo 239

warranties 63, 157, 171, 194, 202, 231
    Black & Decker Ltd 277
    comprehensive, effect of 51
    customer training 73
    in-house control 54
    misuses of product 160–1
    'money back' guarantees 62
Waterman, H. R. 37

Zeithaml, 162, 164
Zemke, R. 12
'zero defects' goal 167